# Cultural Diversity

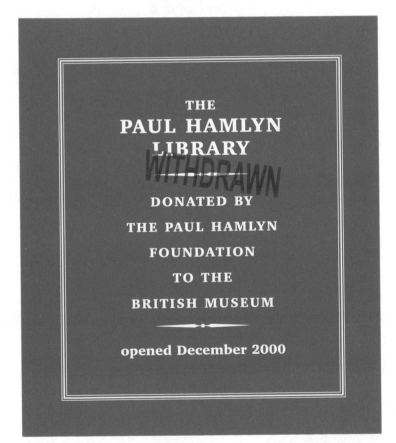

**Contemporary Issues in Museum Culture**
Series Editors: Susan M. Pearce and Elaine Heumann Gurian

Other volumes in the series:

*The American Art Museum: Elitism and Democracy*
Nancy Einreinhofer

*Experiencing Material Culture in the Western World*
Edited by Susan M. Pearce

*Material Obsessions: Postmodernity and the New Collecting*
Steve Chibnall

*Museums and Popular Culture*
Kevin Moore

# Cultural Diversity
## Developing Museum Audiences in Britain

Edited by
EILEAN HOOPER-GREENHILL

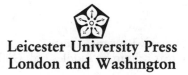

Leicester University Press
London and Washington

Leicester University Press
*A Cassell imprint*
Wellington House, 125 Strand, London WC2R 0BB
PO Box 605, Herndon, VA 22070

First published in 1997

**British Library Cataloguing in Publication Data**
A catalogue record for this book is available from the British Library.
ISBN 0 7185 2411 X

**Library of Congress Cataloging in Publication Data**
Cultural diversity: developing museum audiences in Britain / edited
  by Eilean Hooper-Greenhill.
       p.    cm.—(Contemporary issues in museum culture)
    Includes bibliographical references and index.
    ISBN 0 7185 2411 X
    1. Museums—Great Britain. 2. Museum attendance—Great Britain.
  3. Museums—Social aspects—Great Britain. 4. Multiculturalism.
  I. Hooper-Greenhill, Eilean, 1945 II. Series.
  AM41.C85 1996
  069'.0941–dc20                                                        96-7177
                                                                          CIP

Typeset by BookEns Limited, Royston, Herts.
Printed and bound in Great Britain by Biddles Ltd, Guildford and King's Lynn

# Contents

List of illustrations                                           vii
List of contributors                                            ix
Acknowledgements                                                 x

Towards plural perspectives                                      1
*Eilean Hooper-Greenhill*

**PART 1: Museums as cultural institutions: issues and
    perspectives**

1   Making other people                                         15
    *Susan Pearce*

2   Black cultural museums in Britain: what questions do
    they answer?                                                32
    *Sam Walker*

3   Contextualizing the black presence in British museums:
    representations, resources and response                     50
    *Stephen Small*

4   Background notes: Ajay Khandewal in conversation with
    artist Shaheen Merali                                       67
    *Edited by Pamela Merali*

5   Analysing macro- and microenvironments from a
    multicultural perspective                                   81
    *Julian Agyeman and Phil Kinsman*

6   Speaking other voices                                       99
    *Helen Coxall*

PART 2: Inclusive strategies: exhibitions and educational
         programmes

7    The *Peopling of London* project                          119
     *Nick Merriman*

8    Academic and public domains: when is a dagger a sword?    149
     *Nima Poovaya Smith*

9    Walsall Museum and Art Gallery and the Sikh community:
     a case study                                              159
     *Alison Cox with Amarjit Singh*

10   Audience participation: working with local people at the
     Geffrye Museum, London                                    168
     *Steve Hemming*

11   Developing new audiences at the National Portrait
     Gallery, London                                           183
     *Roger Hargreaves*

12   Meaning and truth in multicultural museum education       203
     *Vivien Golding*

Index                                                          226

# List of illustrations

Figure 1.1   Mental structuring of the 'Other' from a traditional
European and museum perspective.                    16

Figure 1.2   Mental structuring of division within Europe from
a North-west (or British) perspective.              24

Figure 4.1   Shaheen Merali, 1987; 'The Unilever strike', batik
on cotton, 6 × 5 ft.                                74

Figure 4.2   Shaheen Merali, 1990–1991; 'It pays to buy good
tea', sculpture, sound and slide projectors, variable
size.                                               75

Figure 4.3   Shaheen Merali, 1993–1994; 'Channels, echoes and
empty chairs', duratran prints, lightboxes, sound-
beam, astrological charts and texts, size variable.  79

Figure 7.1   The ayahs' home, Hackney, 1900. The presence of
ayahs (Indian nannies) who had travelled to London
with British families returning from India, was one
of the neglected aspects of London's history that
the *Peopling of London* project wished to highlight.  126

Figure 7.2   Outreach work for the *Peopling of London* project
with the 'Museum on the Move'.                       133

Figure 10.1  Period room interior decorated by the Chinese
community in Hackney for the Geffrye Museum's
exhibition *Chinese Homes: Chinese Traditions in
English Homes*. The room shows Chinese New
Year being celebrated by a family recently arrived
in East London. Photo Steve Hemming.                174

Figure 10.2  Ranjan Dasani, a participant in the Geffrye
Museum's course 'Historic Crafts for Women',
cuts a stencil for use in fabric printing. Photo
Julian Anderson.                                    179

Figure 11.1  Photography workshop for deaf children at the
National Portrait Gallery, London, June 1994.       189

Figure 11.2   Sculpture workshop for blind and partially-sighted
              people at the National Portrait Gallery, London,
              March 1995.                                              190
Figures       Photographs made by participants at the
11.3–11.5     Richard Avedon Workshops, National Portrait
              Gallery, London, summer 1995.                          197–9
Figure 12.1   Nana Appiah and Kwame Addo work with
              children from Stockwell Infants School at the
              Horniman Museum.                                         211
Figure 12.2   Children from Stockwell Infants School handle
              Squirrel and Hedgehog as part of a storytelling
              workshop at the Horniman Museum.                        216
Figure 12.3   After listening to the West African dilemma tale
              about Squirrel and Hedgehog, children are
              encouraged to draw and discuss possible endings
              for the story.                                          220

# List of contributors

**Julian Agyeman** is co-director of the Centre for Local Environmental Policies at South Bank University and co-editor of the forthcoming journal, *Local Environment*.

**Alison Cox** is Education Officer (Community) at the Tate Gallery, London.

**Helen Coxall** works as a freelance language consultant in museums and art galleries throughout Britain, and teaches English and cultural studies at the University of Westminster, Oxford Brookes University and Central St Martins School of Art.

**Vivien Golding** is Assistant Keeper of Education Services at the Horniman Museum, London.

**Roger Hargreaves** is an education officer at the National Portrait Gallery.

**Steve Hemming** is Community Education Co-ordinator at the Geffrye Museum, London.

**Eilean Hooper-Greenhill** is Senior Lecturer and Director of the Department of Museum Studies, University of Leicester.

**Phil Kinsman** is a research officer in the Department of Geography, University of Nottingham.

**Shaheen Merali** works as an artist and curator and teaches at Central St Martins College of Art, Dartington College of Performing Arts and Chelsea College of Art and Design.

**Nick Merriman** is Head of the Department of Early London History and Collections, Museum of London.

**Susan Pearce** is Professor of Museum Studies, University of Leicester.

**Nima Poovaya Smith** is Keeper of Arts at Bradford Art Galleries and Museums.

**Amarjit Singh** teaches part time at Walsall College of Arts and Technology in the Learning Support Department, as well as pursuing freelance community arts work.

**Stephen Small** teaches in the Department of African American Studies, University of California, Berkeley.

**Sam Walker** is the Director of The Black Cultural Archives/Museum in Brixton, London, and a founder member and Secretary of the African Reparations Movement.

# *Acknowledgements*

I am grateful to the following for permission to reproduce photographs: Shaheen Merali, Museum of London, Geffrye Museum, Channel 4 Television, Horniman Museum, National Portrait Gallery and Stockwell Infants School.

# Towards plural perspectives

## EILEAN HOOPER-GREENHILL

## Museum audiences

During the last decade museums and galleries have undergone a sea-change. More democratic philosophies, greater public scrutiny and accountability, heightened marketing awareness combined with changes in structures of museum governance have led to the development of new visions of what museums might become. These visions frequently focus on the nature of the experience that museum and gallery visitors might have, and many new developments are justified through a call to broader access and more effective educational opportunities. As part of this movement, many museums are searching for methods to develop their communicative competence, and part of this may involve broadening the audience base.

Until recently, few museums or galleries had researched their patterns of visitation – it was enough to collect visitor numbers (rather inaccurately in many cases). However, since the arrival of marketing officers and the demand from local and central government and other funders for detailed and accurate audience profiles, much greater knowledge has been built up about the nature of visitors at individual institutions.

Visitor profiles vary enormously from one museum or gallery to another, depending on the location, type of collections and exhibitions, and strength of commitment to the audience. The Design Museum in London, for example, has an unusually high proportion (34 per cent) of people aged 16–25 (Design Museum, 1995). At the National Museums on Merseyside the figure for 18–24-year-olds is 12 per cent. The National Museums on Merseyside attract a large percentage (33 per cent) of visitors in social classes C2, D and E; the British Museum, in comparison, attracts between 12 and 8 per cent from this group, varying slightly across the year (National Museums on Merseyside, 1995; Caygill and House, 1986). Within one museum service visitor profiles are likely to vary between different museums. On Merseyside, for example, the gender of visitors is variable – at the Liverpool Museum, which is the area's free general museum, male visitors make up 63 per cent and female visitors 37 per cent of the total, while at the Maritime Museum, a new charging museum with maritime collections, male visitors make up 48 per cent and female visitors 52 per cent of the total (National Museums on Merseyside, 1995). On Merseyside the vast majority of visitors are from the UK, with only 4 per cent of visitors from outside the UK, while at the British Museum, during the summer months, overseas tourists make up 50–60 per cent of the visitors (Caygill and House, 1986; Dove, 1995; National Museums on Merseyside, 1995).

This diversity of audience is lost when a broad picture of museum visiting is drawn across the population as a whole. Large-scale participation studies consistently discover that 'museum visiting in the UK remains primarily a white upper/upper-middle class pastime' (Eckstein and Fiest, 1992, p. 77). A highly generalized statement such as this fails to acknowledge the range of visiting patterns at individual institutions and equally is unable to indicate how the picture might be changing.

However, the large-scale surveys are not entirely wrong. It is true that people who are more highly educated, wealthy and white are more likely to be museum and gallery visitors; education is the most important variable in influencing the decision to visit a museum, but social class is also important. Although there are substantial numbers of visits made by people who are not in the highest social classes, and museums, although not galleries, are much more democratic in their audience profiles than opera, ballet and the theatre (RSGB, 1991), there are still gaps in the audience profile. Black and Asian people are frequently conspicuously absent, but other less visible minorities are also unlikely to find museums relevant to their own cultures and therefore do not visit them.

Many people working in museums and galleries in Britain are unhappy about this largely monocultural visitor profile. They are aware that the museum or gallery is not fulfilling its role in relation to the needs of a more culturally diverse audience, but they do not know how to change this. It is sometimes difficult even to know where to begin, and lack of time and resources means that it is all too easy to push the 'problem' into the background and to concentrate on matters that are more easily implemented.

However, this is not a position that can be held for much longer. Many groups and communities who have felt excluded from museums and galleries are beginning to demand their rights as citizens – their rights to have their contribution to society recognized, and their children's rights to see their cultures represented in a serious and respectful manner.

The first objective of this book is to raise awareness in the museum and gallery community of the moral, ethical and philosophical issues that underpin the day-to-day decisions that museum professionals make when deciding which objects to collect and which exhibitions or educational programmes to support. If black and Asian people and those from many different ethnic groups feel excluded from museums, think that museums are irrelevant or, worse, consider that museums are representing their cultures falsely, then many of the working practices we in museums take for granted must be re-examined. The first part of the book examines some of these matters.

The second objective of the book is to bring into public view some of the initiatives that have enabled the building of successful relationships between museums and galleries and some of their previously excluded publics. The strategies used in the development of these initiatives have a broader application, both in Britain and elsewhere. As we move into the twenty-first century, it is incumbent on all museums to review their social functions in relation to the kind of society we would like to see emerging.

## Museums as cultural institutions: issues and perspectives

The first part of the book consists of six papers that examine the ways in which museums, galleries and other heritage environments operate in relation to issues of cultural diversity. Four of the papers are written from a range of black perspectives and, as such, present views that challenge the comfortable consensus that is enjoyed by museums and galleries in Britain. All six papers are concerned to analyse conventional ways of making museum culture and, in doing so, to expose the attitudes, values and practices that act to exclude significant parts of the potential audience for museums.

Deep-seated cultural reasons underlie the exclusion felt by black, Asian, Chinese and other ethnic groups in Britain, and indeed also by women and the white working class. Susan Pearce shows how the ideas which structured Modernity still cast their shadow over ways of thought, the constitution of meaning and the operation of social institutions, including museums. A fundamental characteristic of Modernism was the binary division of meaning, including the opposition between 'Us' and 'Other', where 'Us' meant the male middle-class European mind-set, and 'Other' meant the rest of the world. Pearce discusses the mental structuring of geographical and historical relationships between Britain and the rest of the world that underlay collecting and other museological practices during the Modernist period of museum establishment. This mental structuring devalued and frequently vilified that very large part of human culture that fell outside the white European (British) male experience, and these attitudes, Pearce argues, shaped and still shape our approach to collections and to the people associated with those objects in their contexts outside museums.

This fundamental refusal to acknowledge diverse cultural value, which manifestly still underlies British society today, is challenged by Sam Walker and Stephen Small. Walker argues the case for a black museum, which will work against the general ignorance of black contributions to society, and which will promulgate positive instead of negative images of black people. Walker looks at black histories and ancestries in Africa and discusses some of the ways in which the relations between Britain and Africa have been distorted, especially through the mobilization of past and present stereotypes.

Stephen Small describes the contexts from which black people come to view museums and galleries. He points out that the facts and legacy of slavery, the British Empire, colonial history and black immigration to Britain since World War II are part of the consciousness of black people in a way that it is perhaps difficult for non-blacks to grasp. These histories are generally seen from a negative viewpoint and as playing a significant role in shaping the prejudice and hostility experienced by black people in Britain today. He stresses that, while museums and galleries cannot be held responsible for all pejorative images of black people, or for all the problems continually encountered, museums have played a role in these matters and, equally, can now play a role in trying to find solutions.

In a very personal statement, Shaheen Merali discusses the background to his artistic and curatorial work with Ajay Khandelwal. Merali came to Britain from Tanzania in 1970, at the age of 11, finding himself in a very difficult personal and social situation. His descriptions of racist attitudes, bullying at school and feelings of extreme isolation poignantly reveal the challenges routinely faced by some in Britain today. Artworks and gallery installations, as well as teaching, have provided a way for Merali to explore some of the painful contradictions of which many museum and gallery professionals are unaware.

The next paper takes a rather different approach, examining macro- and microenvironments in relation to notions of multiculturalism. Julian Agyeman and Phil Kinsman examine popular conceptions and writings about the natural and rural environments. From the turn of the century they identify aesthetic and spiritual conservationist sentiments that involve frictions between rural (native) and urban (alien) elements. These frictions are still articulated today, frequently through overt reference to plants, but with underlying covert reference to people. Comparisons have often been made between people and natural phenomena – in nineteenth-century America, for example, the Irish were nick-named 'sparrows' because they were numerous and prolific. Both sparrows and immigrants had 'low morals' unlike the clean hard-working American birds (and people). Deeply racist ideas, which are otherwise generally controlled in everyday speech, are clearly expressed when discussing the environment. Agyeman and Kinsman go on to examine black experiences in a range of environments, including the countryside and museums.

Finally, in the first section of the book, Helen Coxall discusses the use of language in relation to the construction of meaning. Her basic thesis is that language has evolved in part to serve ideological ends, and that therefore embedded in common sense uses of language are attitudes, perceptions and points of view that privilege existing power structures in society. Equally, words do not mean the same thing to all people – meanings are made by the reader at the moment of reading, and there is no guarantee that what was meant by the writer will be what is construed by the reader. In writing exhibition or other texts in museums, it is important to acknowledge both these points. A knowledge of the audience is crucial when beginning to write, and assessing the texts with representatives of the target audiences will also help to produce writing that does not undervalue or demean specific cultural experiences. These issues are further examined in an exhibition case-study, *Transatlantic Slavery: Beyond Human Dignity*, at the Maritime Museum on Merseyside.

The first part of the book opens up some difficult areas. Some readers may find some of the issues and feelings that are discussed here difficult to accept. Some may dispute the views of history and of the black and Asian experience that are offered. However, whether or not you agree with the ideas discussed, these are the perceptions that many members of black and Asian and other communities have towards monolithic white histories and towards museums that construct and continue to communicate an unmediated white culture. These histories and cultures construct exclusions, demoralize children from many cultures and communities and make adults feel that museums are irrelevant. Whether this matters is, of course, for individuals to decide.

## Inclusive strategies: exhibitions and educational programmes

Some museums in Britain have begun to address issues of cultural diversity, although it must be admitted that the numbers doing so seem to be disappointingly small. There is very little research in this area, and there are few documented case studies. The preliminary findings of one of the most recent pieces of research, the National Report on Museum Education, suggests that only 9 per cent of museums specifically target events and teaching programmes for minority communities (Anderson, 1995). This figure must be treated with some caution, and seen in the context of the pattern of museum provision in Britain. *Cultural Trends* points out that 83 per cent of museums attract annual attendances of less than 50,000 and only 2 per cent achieve audiences of more than 500,000 (Eckstein and Feist, 1992). What this means is that the vast majority of museums and galleries are very small, and indeed many of them are run by volunteers or have only two or three professional members of staff. The evidence suggests that it is the larger and better resourced museums and galleries that are prepared to expand their approaches and that many of the very small museums remain resistant to change. It is thus the larger institutions that lead the way in museum practice.

It is debatable as to how significant the targeting of events and educational programmes for minority communities might be. Although in terms of exhibitions and adult education such targeting is a useful and effective strategy, and is discussed by several of the writers in this section of the book, much museum education work focuses on provision for schools, where targeting minority groups is inappropriate. Many museums and galleries are located in town centres, and are likely to be close to ethnically diverse communities. Any work with local schools is very likely, therefore, to mean working with ethnically mixed groups, including many minority cultures. Of course this does not necessarily mean that cultural difference is recognized or acknowledged in the educational work carried out by the museum. The paper from Vivien Golding at the Horniman Museum describes multicultural museum education approaches that are overtly anti-racist, and that are able to accommodate very young children who may be recently arrived in Britain, perhaps as refugees. Roger Hargreaves at the National Portrait Gallery, working with older students, has found ways of working through photography to enable workshop participants to express and develop their identities, both individual and social. Although targeting remains a useful strategy for some situations, it is perhaps not appropriate for all audiences. It is not always easy to identify specific groups with which to collaborate. Much outreach work involves identifying particular community groups and then contacting their leaders or meeting places and working through these, as is described here by Hemming in relation to the Chinese community in Hackney, East London. Some people do fall into clearly identifiable groups with defined locations and cultural or religious characteristics. The Sikh community is a case in point, where religious leaders and locations offer access to much of the community. For other groups, and perhaps especially black people, who may belong to a number of different religions and who may fall into a number of diverse communities, cultural divisions are not so clear cut. As Alison Cox and Amarjit Singh point out, this makes things more difficult. Communities cannot be invented to suit museums. However, a complex and highly effective approach was developed to reach a range of communities for the *Peopling of London* project at the Museum of London (Merriman). Strategic planning of educational programmes, events and written materials around a temporary exhibition enabled a great deal of participation from a large number of different minority cultures.

It is clear from the repeated references to a few exhibitions which have attained an almost iconic status (*Warm and Rich and Fearless, Peopling of London* and *Transatlantic Slavery*) that, although there seems to be a great deal of interest in developing culturally inclusive approaches, there are few large-scale exhibition projects. It is one of the characteristics of exhibitions that they are time-consuming and expensive to carry out, and at the same time may not always last for longer than a few months. Although it is often the case that new approaches are easier to try out in temporary exhibitions, it is important to change the more permanent displays as well. In many institutions this distinction between permanent and temporary exhibitions is breaking down as ways are found to renew small sections of displays, to replace selected objects, or to incorporate short-term displays within longer-term exhibitions.

In analysing the case studies of exhibitions and educational programmes that make up the second part of the book, a number of themes emerge. Perhaps one of the most vital is that of institutional commitment. At the Museum of London (Merriman) and the National Portrait Gallery (Hargreaves), decisions were taken to broaden and diversify the audience following statistical surveys of the existing museum audiences which pointed clearly to a lack of certain groups, including black and Asian people and other minority groups. In both cases a commitment to audience development and appropriate policy decisions on behalf of the museum management has enabled a planned, carefully controlled and monitored approach to new ventures.

It is vital that the working environment of the museum or gallery is sympathetic towards change, and prepared to allow development time for tentative beginnings and evolution. At both the Geffrye Museum (Hemming) and Walsall Museum and Art Gallery (Cox and Singh), it was necessary to proceed slowly and to allow the appropriate ways forward to emerge from the situation. Consultation, listening and sympathetic negotiation of possibly differing agendas is necessary, all of which take time and need skill. The papers discussing the exhibition *Warm and Rich and Fearless*, which was initiated by Bradford Museums (Poovaya Smith) and travelled to Walsall Museum and Art Gallery (Cox and Singh), demonstrate the value of consultation and negotiation with the exhibition's target audiences during the stage of exhibition planning and later during the use of the exhibition.

Museums and galleries are not always seen as appropriate partners by non-traditional audiences. Museums stand as representatives of authority, within either local or central power structures. As such, those who see themselves as being disadvantaged by 'authorities' and who feel that no one in a position of power will be speaking for them may tend to be suspicious of museum representatives in the first instance. The identification of benefits for all participants, the establishment of mutual trust, and the comfort of friendly familiarity in the context of sincere and respectful acknowledgement of cultural expertise and cultural difference will in time break down barriers.

Staffing is a critical issue. If people from differing backgrounds perceive things in different ways, as they do, then the backgrounds of the museum project team will be important. Where museums seek to work with a range of culturally diverse groups, it is useful to work jointly with someone who understands the cultural perspectives concerned. At the Geffrye Museum, the outreach officer, Steve Hemming, worked closely with Hackney Chinese Liaison Officer, Gillian Tan, in the design and development of a community education project that led to the exhibition *Chinese Homes*; Walsall Museum and Art Gallery employed a member of the Sikh community, Amarjit Singh, for their presentation of the exhibition *Warm and Rich and Fearless*. An ongoing commitment to education or outreach work requires a permanent staff member with experience of educational or community work who is able to instigate and sustain community relationships and networks.

Larger museums and galleries will be able to employ people with experience of a range of cultures on a permanent basis. Poovaya Smith, in this volume, speaks with direct experience to the Asian communities in Bradford, and at the Victoria & Albert Museum, for example, two members of the Education Department are the Chinese Arts Education Officer and the South Asian Arts Education Officer (Akbar, 1994). Much of the funding for these appointments has in the first instance been additional to the main museum budget, with some national and independent museums and galleries being successful in obtaining sponsorship, and with 'Section 11' funding (Local Government Act 1966), which focuses on 'linguistic and cultural disadvantage', being used in local authority museums (Hooper-Greenhill, 1991, pp. 146–147).

Traditionally, museums and galleries have chosen their staff on the grounds of their subject and collection knowledge, defining this very narrowly within Modernist canons from a European perspective. It is becoming more imperative to employ people because of their knowledge and experience of audiences, and who from their cultural backgrounds will also be able to offer more diverse approaches to the interpretation of the collections. While it is important to broaden the cultural mix of museum staff, it is equally important to pay attention to the composition of governing bodies.

Cultural diversity means moving beyond the narrow confines of Modernist interpretations of collections. Traditionally, artefacts in museums have illustrated or been used in the constitution of white histories. Golding shows ways in which she uses natural history specimens (a squirrel and a hedgehog) in conjunction with a West African dilemma tale with very young children at the Horniman Museum. Merriman points out that for the *Peopling of London* exhibition at the Museum of London a more complex view of the histories of objects was taken than was usual in order to find the relationships to specific cultural groups. This involved researching connections to communities, and also identifying more generic relationships which were perhaps undocumented. This approach had not been previously necessary, as the objects had not been specifically related to people, but once this approach was adopted, it became clear that the museum's collections did reflect the diversity of London's population in a fruitful way. In developing ways of making collections relevant to black, Asian and Chinese people, more imaginative and more focused ways of presenting objects will become necessary. Objects will need to move out of their traditional museum-store related classifications and be placed within cross-cultural and cross-disciplinary perspectives.

Consultation with some communities has shown that some cultural groups wish museums to adopt a celebratory approach to their culture. This may conflict with the museum's wish for a more 'objective' standpoint. There may be times when careful positioning of the approach to representation will have to be negotiated, although as Poovaya Smith points out, unrealistic glorifications of histories are likely to be controlled through internal community checks and balances.

The strategies and approaches discussed through the case studies have emerged through thoughtful, carefully planned projects that have been seen as central to the health and future identity of the museum or gallery concerned. Some of the projects have incorporated internal or external evaluations, so that a constant watch is kept on the project in relation to previously defined objectives. The projects have all been managed from within a supportive institutional culture, and have been developed within an open-minded approach to the final outcome. Changes have been facilitated as the projects have progressed. Accommodations have been made to encompass a range of perspectives. This is not the way that all museum projects proceed, some of which are carried out too quickly, with inadequate planning and inadequate external consultation. The future for museums will consist more of projects using the methods outlined here, than of projects which are internally self-referential. Museum and gallery professionals will become more self-analytical, more self-aware and readier to incorporate the ideas and needs of others.

British society is becoming more rather than less ethnically and culturally diverse. The London Research Centre has shown recently that the ethnic population of London, which currently makes up 20 per cent of the population of London overall, will expand to 28 per cent during the next 15 years (Timmins, 1995). It is likely that similar shifts will take place in other parts of the country. It is also true, as the *Peopling of London* project conclusively demonstrated, that London has been a city of migrants, immigrants and refugees for the 15,000 years of its existence (Merriman, 1993). Again, this is true for Britain as a whole. It will become increasingly untenable for museums and galleries to offer monocultural approaches. Modernist meta-narratives are universalizing and totalizing, and we recognize the museological application of this from museums like the British Museum, which claim to be universal, representing the whole of culture (Wilson, 1989, p. 13). In Modernist museums, whatever the rhetoric, the collections are mobilized in the interests of the European mind-set, which gathers the huge diversity of the world into a single world view, a single perspective that fails to recognize itself as a framing which is limited to the standpoint of the white middle-class European (British) male. Post-modern culture recognizes that there is no single valid view of the world, but that many perspectives exist, and that reality is correspondingly partial and fragmentary. The claims of museums to represent universal truths are manifestly unsustainable – all representations are selections from material and mental worlds. Post-colonialism insists that cultural analysis recognizes the effects of colonialism and Empire, effects which polarize relations of advantage and disadvantage (Williams and Chrisman, 1993). In post-colonial Britain, as the second section of the book demonstrates, museums and galleries have the potential to use their collections and their educational spaces to develop ways of developing, presenting and celebrating culturally plural perspectives.

## References

Akbar, S. (1994) Social change and museum education, *Journal of Museum Education*, **19** (1), 6–10.

Anderson, D. (1995) National report on museum education, *GEM News*, 58, 4–10.

Caygill, M. and House, G. (1986) *A Survey of Visitors to the British Museum*

*(1982–1983), by Peter Mann*, British Museum, London.

Design Museum (1995) Visitor profile, supplied by the Press Office.

Dove, P. (1995) Personal communication (telephone call), 19 December.

Eckstein, J. and Feist, A. (1992) Attendance at museums and galleries, in *Cultural Trends 12, 1991*, pp. 70–79, Policy Studies Institute.

Hooper-Greenhill, E. (1991) *Museum and Gallery Education*, Leicester University Press, Leicester.

Merriman, N. (ed.) (1993) *The Peopling of London: Fifteen Thousand Years of Settlement from Overseas*, Museum of London, London.

National Museums on Merseyside (1995) Visitor profiles, supplied by Anne Pennington.

RSGB (1991) *RSGB Omnibus Arts Survey: Report on a Survey on Arts and Cultural Activity in G.B.*, Research Surveys of Great Britain, London.

Timmins, N. (1995) London: Europe's new ethnic melting pot, *The Independent*, 13 December, p. 15.

Williams, P. and Chrisman, L. (eds.) (1993) Colonial discourse and post-colonial theory: an introduction, in *Colonial Discourse and Post-colonial Theory*, pp. 1–26, Harvester Wheatsheaf, New York.

Wilson, D. (1989) *The British Museum: Purpose and Politics*, British Museum Publications, London.

# PART 1

---

# *Museums as cultural institutions: issues and perspectives*

# 1

# *Making other people*

SUSAN PEARCE

## Introduction: brothers and others

We live in the Third Age, the much-heralded dawn of the global village, of accepted cultural diversity, and of relative values. The Third Age of the Post-modern has succeeded that of Modernity which ran onwards from around AD 1500, and of Pre-modernity which came before, but only just: the notions which structured modernity, and which are rejected by the Post-modern world, still cast their shadow over ways of thought, the making of meaning and the operation of institutions, museums among them. Central to the mind-set of Modernity was the notion that meaning is binary, and one of its fundamental paradigms is the opposition between 'Us' and 'the Other', in which 'Us' means those of the Modernist European mind-set, and 'the Other' was everybody else.

It is probably true that European culture in the long term of Pre-modernity possessed a number of features which made it likely that what is conveniently called Modernism would develop. These include a view of the material world as separate from humankind, a kinship system which tends to stimulate individual competition for this world's goods, the long-running social practice of hoarding to create relations between men and gods and men and men (of which museums are the Modernist version), and a liking for distinctions which lead to classification. With this is closely linked a disposition to think in what anthropologists call 'oath and ordeal' terms, contrasting with the more usual 'totem and taboo' paradigm which eschews distinctions in favour of an holistic world view. This is accompanied in European culture by a view of time which sees forward movement, rather than the more common cyclical time mode, and therefore stimulates ideas like the ability of 'history' to explain events, and a notion of progress. Scientific, technological and industrial development, which in the period of high Modernism made Europeans the rulers of the world, belong within the same cluster of cultural traits. All these are difficult

issues (discussed in greater detail in Pearce, 1995). What matters here is
how the mentality of Us:Other was structured by nineteenth- and early
twentieth-century Europeans, especially Imperial Britons, and how
museum collections and displays have reinforced and encouraged this
construction.

Europeans have been accustomed to construct themselves and the
Other into a single system of understanding which brings together the
human diversities of the present and the past, and the natural world of
the Other outside our own species, into a coherent pattern: we can
sketch it out along the lines shown in Figure 1.1. This shows the two
life axes of time and space combining to give a cosmological view of
how human experience was regarded by a modern Western European.
It should be stressed that the order of cultures from the crossing point
outwards represents the ordering of the mind, rather than any actual
geographical or historical order, although, in fact, the two orders

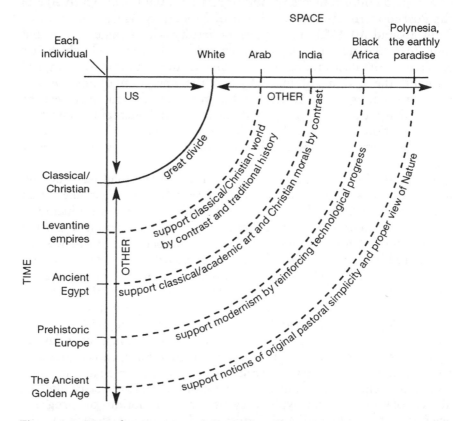

Figure 1.1 *Mental structuring of the 'Other' from a traditional European and
museum perspective.*

match each other fairly well. It is also evident that Britain sits comfortably at the crossing of the axes, representing the apex of Europe (rather than its off-shore north-western extremity), and that the first curve represents the land boundary of Europe as seen from Britain, with the remaining curves spreading away.

Each of us, lonely and fearful individuals, needs to feel that there is an 'us', a broader grouping of like souls with shared culture, which can, of course, be defined only in relation to something which is seen as 'different'. For Europeans generally, the great divide is seen to fall when 'white' gives way to 'non-white' in geographical terms, and the classical Christian tradition, our preferred ancestors, gives way to non-classical and 'pagan'. This gives us a 'Europe' crudely defined as including geographically everything north of the Mediterranean except Turkey, with the arc of inclusion swinging through the Hellespont and the Dardenelles to cross the Black Sea and make its (rather fuzzy) way across the Russian Steppe to the Arctic Sea. Historically, Europe runs back to the beginnings of Classical Greece, perhaps with Homer in the seventh century BC. We should add that 'Europe' of course includes those of European descent in other parts of the world.

Beyond this, contemporary Arab and Moslem Middle Eastern cultures are linked with the Levantine empires of Babylon and Assyria, both of which flourished in the same closely adjacent Middle Eastern area and both of which are the traditional 'baddies', first of the Old Testament and then of the Crusades and of later history. Beyond again, Eastern cultures like India and China are the geographically distant equivalent of Ancient Egypt, both seen as gorgeous in their cultural opulence, but essentially un-European in their attitudes. The primitiveness and illiteracy of black tribal Africa is equated with prehistoric Europe, dark continents both. Finally the 'earthly paradise', as many have called it, located variously in the New World or the coral islands of Polynesia, is linked with haunting ideas of the ancient Golden Age, the Garden of Eden, in which men and animals lived together in true and peaceful harmony, the State of Nature. Such nostalgia for a Golden Age that never was is an important strand in the way in which we have created our understanding of the natural world. Each of these distinctions within the Other, and also the notion of 'us', claims further discussion. We will consider the Others first.

## Others, beyond and before

Three key traits were seen as characterizing those immediately beyond the great divide. They were not Christian; they were not 'white', although manifestly 'non-whiteness' included a range of skin tones running from Middle Eastern pallid to Southern Indian dark, a point to which we shall return; and they were possessed of Oriental luxury, something un-Christian, un-Greek and un-European. The immorality of the Levantine world and its hostility to true religion had Old Testament backing in the stories of Assyria and Babylon, and the Moslem Arabs inherited this character, adding to it the very real threat which they have posed to Christendom from the seventh century AD to the present day. When the technically competent but often very brutal sculptures from the Assyrian palaces began to appear in European museums, as they did about 1850 when Layard and Rassam, whose finds are in the British Museum, excavated the palace sites of Assyria and Babylon, worst fears were satisfactorily realized in material and visual form.

The Middle Eastern world had always been familiar to Europeans, and had been accommodated within their scheme of things, but the appearance in the West of substantial quantities of Indian and Chinese, and of ancient Egyptian material posed a serious challenge. The quality and quantity of the material bore eloquent witness to the reach of the cultures that had produced it: manifestly, these were the products of high civilization. Far Eastern material had, of course, been known in Europe since at least late Classical times, as had some knowledge of Indian religious philosophy, but its appearance in quantity was part and parcel of the late fifteenth/sixteenth century, early phase of Modernism, one aspect of which was a desire to accumulate wealth by exploiting the seaways.

The applied arts of the Far East, particularly Indian textiles and Chinese ceramics, and the design themes of both, were painlessly absorbed because they added considerably to the pleasures of European life without posing any fundamental philosophical or spiritual problems (see, for example Mukerji, 1983). Indian sculpture was another matter. It had important periods and schools of its own, it was naturalistic and 'artistic' in accordance with received classical canons, but also took liberties with the human figure by showing beings with more than the usual number of arms, by confusing human and animal bodies, and, above all, by being deeply erotic. The first collection of Indian sculpture to arrive seems to have been that brought to London by Charles Stuart, known as 'Hindoo' Stuart, who served as a general in the East India Company Army from 1777 to his death in 1828. He took an enthusiastic interest in Indian temple sculpture and simply appropriated fragments from ruined temples, much as his compatriots were doing throughout Greece and Asia Minor. Stuart came to acquire a fine collection, particularly of the Pala period, which eventually found its way into the collections of the British Museum in 1872. Stuart himself and a number of fellow officers in the Indian service, like Sir William Jones, founder of the Asiatic Society of Bengal in 1784, and Sir

Charles Wilkins, who in 1798 offered to curate the collection accumulated by the Asiatic Society and was eventually appointed its librarian, took an enlightened interest in Indian culture.

However, this cultural openness did not last. Nicholson quotes from *The Times* of 9 January 1823 an account of Indian material in the collection of the London Missionary Society, which showed 'idols given up by their former worshippers for the folly and sin of idolatry' (Nicholson, 1983, p. 26). This line sets the tone, glossed in a number of ways with the ideology of the day. Writing at about the same time, Hegel classified the incomprehensible 'horrible, repulsive, loathsome distortions' that he saw in Indian plastic art as representative of the earliest primitive 'symbolic' plane in the one universal evolutionary development of art forms (Mitler, 1927, pp. 189–220). Moreover, because in Hegel's view art expressed the innermost soul of a people, and therefore a specific kind of art could only spring from a particular kind of people, the ideological ring is closed.

In 1879 the South Kensington Museum (eventually to become the Victoria & Albert) accepted most of the old East India Company collection, and Sir George Birdwood was appointed Art Referee for the new Indian Section of the Museum. He wrote, 'The monstrous shapes of the Puranic deities are unsuitable for the higher forms of artistic representation; and this is possibly why sculptures and painting are unknown, as fine arts, in India' (1880, p. 125). As late as 1910 he could describe a Javanese figure of Buddha displayed at the Royal Society of Arts as: 'The senseless similitude, by its immemorial fixed pose, is nothing more than an uninspired brazen image, vacuously squinting down its nose to its thumbs, knees and toes. A boiled suet pudding would serve equally well as a symbol of passionate purity and serenity of soul' (Smith, 1991, p. 21). These remarks produced a response in the form of a letter to *The Times* of 28 February 1910 signed by a roll-call of young artists:

> we the undersigned artists, critics and students of art ... find in the best art of India a lofty and adequate expression of the religious emotion of the people and of their deepest thoughts on the subject of the divine. We recognise in the Buddha type of sacred figure one of the great artistic inspirations of the world.

The place accorded to Indian sculpture mirrors the progress of European Modernist art by acting as its other self. By being cast as indecent it enabled the viewer to recognize decency in the classical, Renaissance and academic tradition of the 'nude', and as the power of this tradition began to crumble in the late twentieth century, so Indian art became more interesting. The difficulties that the class of traditions can cause, however, are still not yet dead. A few years ago, a major

South-east Asia museum chose one of its most important artworks as the subject of its greetings card. The picture, in full colour, showed the loves of Krishna; underneath it said 'Happy Christmas'.

European collectors seem to have been acquiring Egyptian antiquities from the sixteenth century; certainly by the seventeenth century the trade was sufficiently well established for fakes to be on the market (Whitehouse, 1989). However, it was not until the organized looting of the nineteenth century that Egyptian material began to appear *en masse* in the collections and exhibitions of the West. Those which the British Museum had on exhibition by the end of the nineteenth century were reflected on a smaller scale in many of the regional city museums of Britain, including Liverpool, Bolton, Manchester, Bristol and Exeter. Interest concentrated upon mummies, not only of humans but also of cats, birds and crocodiles, on grave goods, and on the effigies of animal-headed gods. The hugeness of Egyptian projects was engraved upon the visitor's mind by the gigantic head and arm of Amenophis IV, displayed in the British Museum's Lower Gallery. Ancient Egypt was cast as a gloomy culture in love with death, with the massive products which only slave labour made possible, and with what Milton, as early as 1645, described as 'the brutish gods of Nile'.

Interestingly, Bernal (albeit not a 'respectable' author) has set out for us the evidence which suggests that Greek culture did not gain its pedestal without some trouble (Bernal, 1987, pp. 121–215). The Greeks themselves seem to have believed that they had learnt much from the 'ancient wisdom' of the Egyptian priests, some of whom carried the unbroken and accumulating traditions of more than 2000 years by the sixth century BC. Under various arcane guises, the notion of Egyptian wisdom was a serious focus of Renaissance enquiry and remained so well into the seventeenth century. Its devotees included the Roman Jesuit Athanasius Kircher, who made one of the most significant collections of his day. Hellenism, in the usual sense, did not begin to develop until the earlier eighteenth century, and did not reach its full form until the work of Johann Winckelmann in mid-century. When Egyptian material arrived in Europe from the time of Napoleon's Egyptian campaign onwards (1798), it was able to resurrect some old enthusiasm among collectors as well as establishing itself as a new fashion.

## Seeing ourselves in a state of nature

Prehistoric European and black African materials began to arrive in cultivated Europe at about the same time. A small trickle appeared in the late sixteenth- and seventeenth-century cabinets of curiosity (Impey and MacGregor, 1985) and, continuing through the eighteenth century, grew to a flood in the nineteenth, as colonial administrations and missionaries gathered and brought home material from Africa, and their professional equivalents in Britain (and France) excavated and accumulated pottery, metalwork and stone implements (see Pearce, 1990, pp. 7–30).

There were obvious similarities between the two sets of material: both were clearly the product of technologically primitive, non-literate people whose social organization and personal characteristics were presumed to be on the same child-like level. This offered a double-pronged support to Modernism. On the one hand, the technological contrast between the primitive and the modern showed how far the most successful humans had progressed, and therefore underpinned the notion of progress itself. On the other hand, European prehistoric people had (ultimately) become European moderns, and Africans showed a similar, if much more limited, capacity to absorb progress once it was offered to them, which reinforced Modernist notions about an innate human capacity for development and goodness.

Central to this in Africa was the Christian missionary activity. The African collections were able to contain a broader range of material than the prehistoric ones, and included not only many small personal pieces but also much organic material, especially wooden religious carvings, 'fetish' figures from the Congo region studded with crude iron nails and pieces of mirror, and 'witchdoctors' bundles' from across the continent (see Cannizzo, 1989, for discussion of a typical ensemble). The acquisition of these pieces, their voluntary cession into missionary hands by their newly converted former owners, could easily be constructed into a story of Christianity triumphant. Moreover, the same zeal required Africans to wear clothes which approximated to European coverings (the operative word), and to use cheap substitutes for European knives and forks, tables and chairs, and so on. The material culture of European daily life, like its religion, was sustained as somehow especially proper and correct, which underlined how right Europeans were to behave as they did. Naturally this required some double thinking. African dwellings were described as 'mud huts with grass roofs', while in Devon the same were called 'cob cottages with thatch'. But the collections on display made the points so clearly that minor discrepancies could be ignored in the grand design.

If black Africa and prehistory were child-like, the earthly paradises of Polynesia and the ancient Golden Age showed nature and humanity before children were conceived in sin. Europeans, principally English and French, first confronted the Polynesian islands of the Pacific at a significant moment in the history of European development, when the tide of enlightened rationalism was rising to its flood. Bougainville's voyage to the Central Pacific took place in 1766–1769. Cook's three voyages, in the course of which he visited most of the principal island groups, took place in 1768–1771, 1772–1775 and 1776–1779. The quantity of ethnographic material which duly arrived back in England was considerable. Some went into the London curio market more or less immediately, and went through a number of public collections and sales, including that of Sir Ashton Lever (disposed by lottery in 1786 and sold on in 1806) and that of William Bullock (sold up in 1819). Some remained in private hands and does to this day. Other pieces have found their way into a wide variety of museums (Kaeppler, 1979). The collections of flora and fauna have similar histories. Neither as ethnographic nor as exotic natural history specimens were the Cook collections the first to come to Europe, but they stand in a particular position to the development of Modernist thinking. The islands had seemed to those who had experienced them to embody all the delightful characteristics of the exotic Other, to be an earthly paradise of sun and sea. In this timeless Eden, both nature and human society seemed to be in a state of nature from which universal inferences might be drawn, and a kind of rational, enlightened benchmark established to act as the positive measure against which other natural and human history might be set. Clearly, such a mark was crucial: rational positivism works by measurement and comparison, no matter how sophisticated this might become, and for this to operate there must be a point of department and a recognized standard.

From notions of the equation between physical evidence and positivist understanding comes the academic paradise of stability, predictability and the capacity to form explanatory theories, which have been characteristic of social anthropology since its tentative beginnings in the later eighteenth century and its subsequent developments. We are offered the idea of an 'essential culture', much like that of an 'essential individual', which can be documented, recorded and analysed. Broadly the same has been true of the natural sciences. All these, in their naive Modernist forms, can be perceived as romantic, pastoral ideas, academic fantasies as irresistibly seductive as the islands whose collected materials did much to establish them.

Neither then nor now, needless to say, were the Polynesian islands the natural paradise of European imagination. Most of the island groups were possessed of particularly hierarchic societies in which position was determined by birth, chiefdoms of classic form. Cook himself was killed on an Hawaiian beach in 1778 either as a ritual sacrifice to the fertility gods, as some modern anthropologists have thought, or, as Obeyesekere has recently argued (1992), as a result of his own increasingly erratic behaviour. Now, as David Lodge has put it, Hawaii has an interest of quite a different kind:

'Really?' said Bernard. 'I'd no idea that tourism came into anthropology.'

'Oh yes, it's a growth subject. We get lots of fee-paying students from overseas – that makes us popular with the admin. boys. And there's bags of money available for research. Impact studies ... Attractivity studies ... Trad anthropologists look down their noses at us, of course, but they're just envious.' (1991, p. 60)

In other words, the meanings to be attached to all this material are as 'poly' as the islands from which it comes. Polynesian material is not the fundamental collecting statement which underpins the 'natural order' and the transparent 'rightness' of European thought, because such positivist ideas cannot exist in such an essential way. What the Polynesian collections did, and to a certain extent still do, was to occupy a vacant space in the Modernist mind-set, a vacancy which had to be filled if the Modernist narrative was to proceed.

## The others within

Thus far, I have treated 'Europe' as if it were a single monolith in which the unflawed here-and-now represents an unchanging and unchallenged moment of correct knowledge, aesthetics, social morality and ways of understanding. But the alert reader will have noticed a confusion of terms between 'West' and 'Europe', and will remember that, in geographical terms, Britain sits at the cross-roads of the axes. In other words, although Europe, both east and west, does share some very significant cultural characteristics – language systems with a common ancestor, an oath/ordeal mentality, an absence of proscriptive cross-cousin marriage, and Christianity – it also has its own structure of otherness. Some are inherent and some have arrived from the 'outside'.

The period of Modernism coincided, for reasons which have been much discussed (Tawney, 1938) with the steady swing of cultural and other power away from Southern Europe and towards its North-west, particularly Britain and France, and to the German-speaking states, especially Prussia. The mind-set which this division created matched well with the criteria of otherness (Figure 1.2) to produce an inner 'Us' and an outer arc. Southern Europeans are not so 'white' as those of the north; indeed many of them are the same Mediterranean shade as those to the immediate east and south. They were also Catholic or Orthodox rather than Protestant. Eastern Europeans were Slavs, the traditional view of whom is well demonstrated by the fact that this name is the same word as 'slave'. These, although usually very 'white', were again Catholic or Orthodox. Moreover, they lived largely within regimes notorious for tyranny and oppression, whether of the earlier monarchist states or the later communist ones. In historical terms,

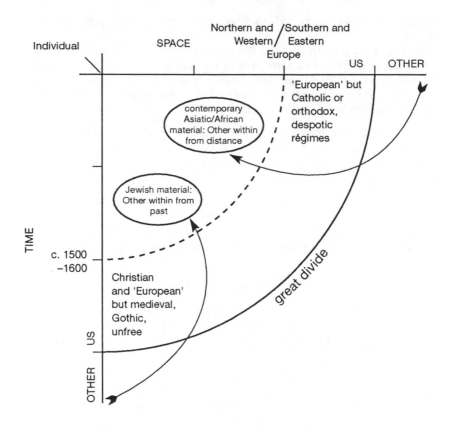

Figure 1.2 *Mental structuring of division within Europe from a North-west (or British) perspective.*

these characteristics could be happily equated with the Medieval period, recognized by its priest-ridden cruelties and suppressions.

Naturally, even those facts of geography and history which had to be recognized did not entirely fit this comfortable framework. France was Catholic, although indeed politically in a detached way, and Ireland was a small piece of Southern Europe which had floated north. More to the point, both glorious Greece and the Italy of the Renaissance lay on the wrong side of the track, but this was managed by counting the great periods of Greece and Italy as somehow 'with Us', while discounting their clearly degenerate successors. Viewed from this perspective, the wars between France, Britain and Prussia/Germany, which, in various combinations, dominated the eighteenth, nineteenth and twentieth centuries, take on the character of civil conflicts, which is why the two great wars of this century have sometimes been described as the First and Second European Civil Wars.

Within the European heartland also there were, and are, Others from beyond the great divide. From the historical perspective these are the Jewish communities, who seem to have existed north of the Mediterranean since the Roman Empire. Anti-Semitism has been a cultural thread of the long term throughout European history, because Jews were recognized by their non-Christianity, their non-European customs, especially circumcision, and the language in which their cultural traditions were clothed, which was unintelligible, which looked 'Oriental' when written, and which was read 'backwards' (see Felsenstein, 1985). From the geographical Other there are those who have come in from beyond the divide: Indians, Pakistanis and Bangladeshis in Britain, those of black African descent in Britain and France, Southern Mediterraneans in France and Italy, Turkish 'guest-workers' in Germany and East Europe, and many others.

The uneasy relationship between North-western Europeans and the rest of those living within what had to be recognized as Europe's cultural boundaries goes a long way towards explaining why these communities are so very obviously absent from the collected material record. European material in British museums from beyond the magic circle of Britain–France–Germany–Renaissance Italy–Classical Greece and Rome is very rare, and much of the material from France and Germany is connected with conflict.

## A bit of the Other

One kind of Otherness is missing from the explicit text, because, of course, it is implicit in the system as a whole, and this is the Otherness of the female. The traditional white, Christian view of woman, having succumbed to the snake and eaten the apple of knowledge, as essentially sinful, needs no urging, and it has been conveniently matched by the corresponding Classical perception of woman as raging maenad whose social control is a prime condition for civilized life. The theme is encapsulated down the Classical and Christian centuries in the artistic treatment of the female nude. As Nead (1992, p. 11) eloquently shows, 'The formless matter of the female body has to be contained within boundaries, conventions and poses'. The notion of woman as at once sexual temptress, amoral evil and desirable territory awaiting invasion modulates across the ribs of the system, as once she did across Adam's. As Said (1978) has shown, an alluring sexuality clad in diaphanous garments and a dark beauty is the abiding image through which Europe has constructed its idea of the Arab world and the Middle East; and probably of the further Orient also. The political metaphor is of veiled mystery, seduction and a possession which turns out to be enthralling in more ways than one. The European male, from his colder and purer clime, is possessed by his possession and, like Alexander before him, becomes the victor vanquished.

Frequently, the love is that which cannot tell its name. Many homosexual writers of the nineteenth and earlier twentieth centuries, particularly English and French, dallied with Oriental themes, just as many of the great travellers in the Arab world were generally believed (at the very least) to have been drawn thither largely by the prospect of boys. The ancient Levant was similarly heliotrope-scented, and the Cities of the Plain, where in the final degradation men treated other men like women, was a correspondingly all-embracing image (although the Greeks, of course, were different). When late-Enlightenment Europeans looked backwards, to the empires of the Mediterranean and Levantine world, they saw the figure of Salome, with her hypnotic mixture of sexuality and sadism, of flesh glimpsed through silk and bloody severed heads, a potent mixture for pleasurable shudders.

Prehistoric European women made little mark on the communal imagination, probably because the known actual remains offered the imagination few hints, but much of the popular imagery of black Africa focuses upon the female equivalent of the noble savage: women washing at the river or carrying water pots on their heads, strong of limb, proud of carriage, open and free. This slips into the notion of the distant earthly paradise, and of its past equivalent, the ancient Golden Age before the fall. In both, men are living in a state of nature, in which the earth gives forth good without effort, the women are beautiful and willing, and sexuality is unashamed. The sexual aspect of this is characteristically repeated again and again by the first European explorers of Tahiti. The naturalist on Bougainville's Pacific voyage said that the Tahitians were 'without vice, prejudice, needs or discretion and knew no god but Love', while Joseph Banks, who accompanied Captain Cook, observed, 'the scene that we saw was the truest picture of Arcadia, of which we were going to be kings, that the imagination can form'. As Beaglehole, Cook's biographer remarks, 'they were standing on the beach of the dream-world, they walked straight into the Golden Age and embraced their nymphs' (all quoted in Moorhead, 1987, pp. 51, 38, 66). The same fantasies are on display today at the travel agents.

As we have seen, the 'naturalness' of the Pacific and of the Americas was seen as legitimizing and so encouraging the enlightened analysis of nature which proceeded in the Modernist world from the forerunners of Linnaeus to the followers of Darwin, but it is now becoming clearer that this view of nature is itself cast in terms of sexuality and sexual opposition. In the winter of 1993–1994 Nancy Shoemaker visited the Smithsonian Institution's National Museum of Natural History, The National Museum of Man in Washington, DC, and the Field Museum of Natural History in Chicago to examine representations of gender and its relationship to nature and culture (Shoemaker, 1994). She found that 'gender became crucial in this comparison between animals and humans' for 'gender is the device that enables natural history museums to show how humans simultaneously belong to nature and transcend nature' (p. 321). As Shoemaker rightly points out, because of the resources that new natural history exhibitions consume, natural history museums are today showing exhibits which draw upon a legacy of several hundred years of scientific thought, although 'even the newest exhibits, though overflowing with good intentions, present women and men in traditional ways' (p. 322).

Shoemaker points out that she knew which figures in the natural history and early human history displays were women, because they were the ones with the breasts. As she says, 'breasts have a special significance in natural history museums, where quasi-nudity adds to the exotica of the "Other" because it challenges our own cultural taboos and because the West has traditionally determined nudity to be both savage and natural' (1994, p. 324). The same, of course, might be said of the prevailing image of the female nude or semi-nude representing women *within* the European tradition, a tradition as we have noted designed to control both savagery and naturalness within acceptable limits.

The American museum exhibitions make it clear that it is the family, mammary glands well to the fore, which 'ties humans to brutes', and the 'tool' (*sic*) that 'makes our separateness' (Shoemaker, 1994, p. 324). The invention of the tool separates humans from animals and men from women. Characteristically, 'the family' is used as a device to show that humans and animals are alike, as at the Smithsonian where the adjacent 'Great Mammals of North America' and 'Hall of Native Americans' exhibits both slow nuclear families of females and young over which a male stands guard. Equally, as in the Neanderthal daily life displays at the Field Museum, men are shown using implements to hunt and kill in the outdoor, public space, while women tend infants in the privacy of the cave.

In fact, the gendering of the natural world runs further and deeper than this. In two interesting articles Schiebinger has shown that Linnaeus's (probably semi-conscious) approach to classification is fundamentally gendered (1991, 1993). The shift to the new scientific study of botany in the early eighteenth century coincided with the realization that plants, like the animal world, are possessed of gender, even though their sexual organs take the form of flower parts, which are so much prettier than those of most animals. It was these flower parts that Linnaeus used as the key forms in his new classification system, and the fundamental divisions he devised as the basis of his taxonomy recapitulated the traditional European sexual hierarchy. His system used the number of stamens (male parts) of the plant to determine the superior group, the *class*, to which it belonged, and the number of pistils (female parts) to determine its *order*, next below *class* in the taxonomy (Linnaeus, 1735). This has no scientific basis, which is why it has now been abandoned, although Linnaeus's binomial system of nomenclature remains. Linnaeus's writings abound in sexual terminology like 'husbands' (Greek *andria*), wives (Greek *gynia*), lawful marriages and others: plant husbands of his 'Class xxiii' – *polygamia* – live with their wives and harlots in distinct marriage beds (i.e. arrangement of stamens, pistils and petals, thought of as 'beds').

Equally pertinently in the 1758 tenth edition of his *Systemma Naturae* Linnaeus introduced the term *mammalia* into zoological taxonomy. This newly devised word, meaning 'of the breast', was used to distinguish the class of mammals embracing those animals with intermittently active milk glands in the females, and hair, three ear bones and a four-chambered heart in both sexes. Of all his animal classes, *mammalia* was the only one to focus on reproductive-related organs, and the only one to highlight a primarily female characteristic. The traditional term for most of the animals which came within this class was *Quadrupedia* (four-legged), but this raised the problem of where humans fitted in, because in other biological respects their affinities were clearly with the four-legged beasts. Faced with this difficulty, Linnaeus devised his new term with the words 'mammalia; these and no other animals have mammae – all females have lactiferous mammae of determinate number, as do all males (except the horse)' (1758, pp. 14–16). The term met with instant success, and remains with us. In his 1758 edition, Linnaeus also introduced two other key terms, *Primates*, which included apes, monkeys and humans, and *Homo sapiens* ('man of wisdom') to distinguish humans from the other primates: both of these, of course, also continue as normal usage.

The notions informing all this are obvious enough. A long European tradition, stretching back in literature to Plato, saw women, with their menstruation, childbirth and milk, and their lack of reason, as beast-like, while men were possessed of wisdom, regarded as the essential hallmark of non-animal humanity. The double notation enabled (and enables) the world of biology to link humans with the animal world through the female breasts, but to preserve an essential difference through the recognition of male mental and spiritual qualities. As the system of botanical taxonomy had described the correct hierarchy for men and women, so its biological counterpart provided a solution to the difficult question of the place of humankind within nature, and of womankind within culture, which both drew on what had gone before and encouraged the future to do likewise.

## Conclusion: the West and the rest

This has necessarily been a brief treatment of a range of immensely complex issues. Nevertheless it does suggest that underlying the complexities is a single, and relatively simple, structure through which Western Europeans during the heyday of Modernism were able to construct a cosmological system which supported their own view of themselves. Because the culture of Europe is essentially material, this expressed itself primarily through the view taken of material things as they were collected and displayed in museums. The cultural world of the Levant, past and present, contributed a dark Other of irreligion, brutality and sensuality against which the virtues of the European showed clear. The gorgeous 'high civilizations' of India and Ancient Egypt, with their life-denying imaginations and their grotesque art supported, by comparison, the proper and artistic (i.e. Greek) view of humanity. Black African and prehistoric European confirmed the achievements of true religion, progress and the moral excellence of domestic European family life. The state of nature, beyond and before, provided pastoral affirmation of European philosophy, particularly that natural philosophy we now call 'science'. And, shot through all this, was that view of the female which justifies the masculine case in the heading of the Introduction.

These simplicities are not without their internal contradictions, some of which are set out in Figure 1.2, but in their broad outlines they operated as shown in Figure 1.1. The same pattern can be expressed in a set of binary oppositions, that understanding-by-distinction which is characteristic of the European mind-set:

| Us | Other |
|----|-------|
| Christian | heathen |
| Classical | barbarian |
| men | women/animals |
| white | black |
| reason | magic |
| knowledge | ignorance |
| morality | amorality |
| progress | stasis |
| culture | nature |

We should not forget that, just as this sketches the mind-set of Modernist society, and of its institutions – museums particularly as the institutions charged to demonstrate visual culture – so it sketches that of individual collectors, for whom the lure of the exotic has always been powerful, just as it has always been socially prestigious. Indeed, home:exotic, might be added to the list of structuring paradigms, under the rubric of 'find it and bring it back' and 'see how well it fits what we thought'. If European Modernist enterprise operated under one banner, it was that whereon was embroidered 'Seek, and ye shall find.'

# References

Bernal, M. (1987) *Black Athene: the Afroasiatic Roots of Classical Civilization*, Free Association Books, London.

Birdwood, G. (1880) *The Industrial Arts of India*, Black, London.

Cannizzo, I. (1989) *Into the Heart of Africa*, Royal Ontario Museum, Toronto.

Felsenstein, F. (1985), *Anti-Semitic Stereotypes: a Paradigm of Otherness in English Popular Culture 1660–1830*, John Hopkins University Press, Baltimore.

Impey, O. and MacGregor, A. (eds) (1985) *The Origins of Museums*, Oxford University Press, Oxford.

Kaeppler, A. (1979) 'Tracing the history of the Hawaiian Cook Voyage, Artefacts in the Museum of Mankind', *British Museums Yearbook*, Vol. 3, pp. 168–186.

Linnaeus, C. (1735) *Systemma Naturae*, Uppsala.

Lodge, D. (1991) *Paradise News*, Secker and Warburg, London.

Mitler, P. (1927) *Much Maligned Monsters: History of European Reactions to Indian Art*, Oxford University Press, Oxford.

Moorhead, A. (1987) *The Fatal Impact: an Account of the Invasion of the South Pacific 1867–1940*, Harmondsworth, Penguin.

Mukerji, C. (1983) *From Graven Images: Patterns of Modern Materialism*, Columbia University Press, New York.

Nead, L. (1992) *The Female Nude: Art, Obscenity and Sexuality*, Routledge, London.

Nicholson, J. (1983) Tinsel, terracotta or tantric: repressing Indian reality in museums in Caruthers, A. (ed.), *Bias in Museums. Museums Professionals Group Transactions* 22, pp. 26–31.

Obeyesekere, G. (1992) *The Apotheosis of Captain Cook: European Myth-Making in the Pacific*, Princeton University Press, New Jersey.

Pearce, S. (1990) *Archaeological Curatorship*, Leicester University Press, Leicester.

Pearce, S. (1995) *On Collecting: an Investigation into Collecting in the European Tradition*, Routledge, London.

Said, E. (1978) *Orientalism: Western Concepts of the Orient*, Oengiub Books, London.

Schiebinger, L. (1991) The private life of plants: sexual politics in Carl Linnaeus and Erasmus Darwin, in Marina, B. (ed.), *Science and Sensibility: Gender and Scientific Enquiry 1780–1945*, pp. 121–143, Blackwell, Oxford.

Schiebinger, L. (1993) Why mammals are called mammals: gender politics in eighteenth century natural history, *American Historical Review*, 98, 382–411.

Shoemaker, N. (1994) The natural history of gender, *Gender and History*, 6(3), 320–333.

Smith, V. (1991) *A History of Fine Art in India and Ceylon*, Dent, London.
Tawney, R.H. (1938) *Religion and the Rise of Capitalism*, Pelican Books, London.
Whitehouse, H. (1989) Egyptology in the seventeenth century. The case of the Bodleian Shabti, *Journal of History of Collections*, 1(2), 187–196.

# 2

## Black cultural museums in Britain: what questions do they answer?

SAM WALKER

### Introduction

When I was approached to write this chapter, my first reaction was to refuse. It took me some time to convince myself that this chapter may reach a certain audience which is sympathetic to the cause of disseminating the history of black people in the UK and the contributions of African people to the development of Western civilizations.

I have given many talks and lectures on the necessity for a museum and archive of black African and Caribbean history in Britain, and it would have been simple for me to put these speeches together, but I wanted to go into more depth and explore the historical and socio-economic dimension of the problem of ignorance, racism and discrimination that has permeated our society because of the absence of, among other things, a national museum of African people's history, and the self-deprecatory attitude of some black people who remain ignorant of their own history.

I hope that this chapter will generate a swell of support and stimulate more debate, but above all I hope that there will be a concerted action which transcends racial or class barriers for support of a black cultural museum in Britain.

### Definition of terms

I have used the terms African and black to refer to Africans, African/Caribbeans, British/Africans and those with African/European or African/Asian parentage.

## Overview

The passing of the Race Relations Act of 1965 and further amendment to the act in 1968 and 1976 was to make discrimination unlawful on the grounds of race, and to make it possible to achieve equality of opportunity for all irrespective of race, colour and origin. The passing of the Act was an acknowledgement of the fact that Britain is a multicultural society. However, since the Act was passed the representation of black people in the socio-economic organs of the state, or in the law enforcement or reforming institutions such as the judiciary, the police or prison does not reflect proportionately the size of the black population. They are visibly absent from these power structures of state, but they are well represented within the reforming institutions such as prisons, where they constitute over 20 per cent of the prison population. In fact, the situation which existed before the Act was passed has remained in place. Overt discrimination may have disappeared, but covert or subtle discrimination is common and widespread.

What are the underlying causes for discrimination and racism? In all Western multiracial countries, black people are at the lowest level of the achievement pyramid. Is it that black people are universally incompetent or could this be a biological phenomenon? Are white people endowed with extra powers, intelligence and knowledge to have been able to suppress black people for so long? Or is it that white people are bad people? I believe that the reason lies in the shared social/historical experiences of Western countries.

Black people have been resilient in resisting discrimination and racism for a very long time, but their efforts have largely failed because of the system of institutionalized racism and discrimination, and the excluded absence of the black perspective of history.

One of the institutions which have been used to promote and maintain this power differential between white and black people is museums. There are more than 2,000 museums in Britain. Most of these are government supported or privately run. They are largely white institutions, collectively interpreting and displaying artefacts which reflect white society, thought and history. There has been no mainstream institution in Britain which has been given the responsibility to collect and document, interpret and display African artefacts which reflect black African thought and history. This will help to explain one of the reasons for the ignorance of the majority of both black and white people of the history and contributions of black people to the development of society.

Museums and archives are the main institutions which serve as repositories for the collection and study of documents and objects of social, artistic, scientific and educational interest. Objects in museums help us to understand ourselves as humans and our development. There are, however, some who do not like any new archaeological discovery or new historical thought which changes or challenges the status quo. Therefore any new discovery which shows that life started in Africa, or that the rise in human civilization, science, art, industry, law, medicine and architecture all started in Africa is vehemently challenged, because these discoveries confront the accepted norms and simply put people out of business. This attitude is not new; for example, Galileo was called a heretic for saying that the Earth revolved around the sun. The church forced him to deny his discovery. Some other pioneers lost their lives for challenging current thought and practice, but truth ultimately prevails.

The growth of nationalism around the world after the end of the Cold War should serve as a warning to European governments, and particular the British government, of the importance and urgency of educating the masses in the contribution each section of society has made to the development of the whole country, and that each section forms an integral part of society. In Britain, as in some states in America, there should be a museum solely responsible for the collection, preservation, study and interpretation of African artefacts. A museum of this kind is absolutely necessary and urgent for use as one of the weapons against racism, bigotry and ignorance.

## Representation of black history

Britain needs a black cultural museum/archive for the following reasons:

- to serve as a resource centre;
- to educate the wider public about the contributions of Africans in the development of society;
- to dispel the ideology of racism;
- to disseminate contemporary research into the black presence in Britain;
- to provide materials for a multicultural education.

A vast number of people are not aware of the contributions black people have made in the past to the sciences, art, religion and education. Their present contribution is equally unknown. The fallacy has persisted that black people are not achievers. Black people are not given merit for having achieved, created or participated in anything worthwhile. The abolition of slavery is presented as the success of a few white people who were stricken by their consciences and moral conviction to campaign against this inhuman trade. Black people such as Olaudah Equiano, Ottabah Coguano, Harriet Tubman, Toussaint L'Overture and many others, including the many slave uprisings, do not get a mention; whenever they do they are not presented as wars of attrition, but treated as mindless violence from ungrateful savages rebelling against those who are trying to bring them into a civilized world.

Indeed a large part of the problem we face today in Britain between black and white people in our local communities, at work, in church, etc. is due to the ignorance and devaluing of the contributions of black people to British society and the world.

There is a persistent focus on Africa as the dark continent, a continent bedevilled with primitive ways, with images of Tarzan fighting constant battles against black savages to protect white people from African cannibals. However, there is ample evidence that Africa played a crucially important role in world development, and the evidence continues to accumulate. The earliest transformation of hominids walking erect on two legs to *Homo habilis* with more control over his tools, to *Homo sapiens* with intelligence and power of thought may have taken place in many other regions of the world, but to date the overwhelming evidence points to Africa as the one place where these stages occurred within the same region, that is from the savannah regions of East and Central Africa, Northern Kenya and Ethiopia. Furthermore, there is evidence that species of man-like apes that did not evolve into man have a higher survival rate in Africa than anywhere else in the world (Ajayi, 1993). So much for the evolutionary school of thought. If we put aside anthropological discoveries, the biblical story of creation also points to the origins of man in Africa. This is the reason for the claim that Africa is the cradle of humanity from where *Homo sapiens* spread to other parts of the world.

The physical transformation to *Homo sapiens* was matched by social and technical changes such as the development of agriculture in the Ethiopian Highlands and the Nile Valley, in North Africa as part of the Mediterranean zones and in the Niger delta. The people here were also the first to use tools, paint pictures and worship God. They founded great empires like Ghana, Mali and Songhay (Barley, 1990).

In the light of this evidence it is incomprehensible that black people continue to be so negatively stereotyped. Indeed it is a perversion of the truth to depict Europeans taking the benefits of civilization to naked savages. According to Dr Nigel Barley, there were established communities in Africa in 500 BC around the Niger Valley. Before European intrusion, these Africans had developed techniques to smelt iron to make weapons and tools. By the turn of the Middle Ages there were powerful African kingdoms. As early as 1000 AD the people of Songhay, Bornu and Benin were able to build stone walls around their cities. In the fourteenth century the Shona Kingdom of Great Zimbabwe built palaces solely from granite. This evidence of black advancement has been trivialized in order to credit and justify European oppressive action against black people. Africa's nemesis gave rise to European expansion and advancement, and consequently black people in Europe and Britain became invisible, not because of their absence, but because of a myth that required their absence. This myth operates, not only by misrepresentation, but by silence, omission and exclusion (Hall, 1985). By simply not mentioning certain facts, by excluding black people from scenes where they have played crucially important roles, those who manipulate these myths have changed the reality of the past in order to control perceptions and actions of the present. It is therefore no accident that many people will support the view of Arnold Toynbee, writing in 1934 and quoted in *Nile Valley Contributions to Civilisation* (Browder, 1992, p. 17), when he said: 'It will be seen that when we classify mankind by colour, the only primary race that has not made a creative contribution to any civilisation is the Black race.'

We therefore find in Britain and in European countries that the dominant popular imagery of black people is that of either the lazy, impudent and carefree individual, intellectually inferior, the mugger and drug smuggler from a broken family, or at best a good sportsperson or dancer. As for black women, well, nothing better could be expected from them. This is all a fallacy which a black cultural museum will help to disprove and, in the process, perhaps help to reverse the damaging process and thus help to eradicate racism, discrimination and ignorance.

## Pervading perceptions of Africa and black people

A story is told of an English minister who was talking to some children at a family service in 1994. The minister was demonstrating to the children how some Africans draw water from a well, using a bucket tied to a rope which is then lowered into the well. These children immediately reminded the minister that there are no buckets in Africa. The minister calmly disagreed. These children had a perception of Africa as being so poor and undeveloped that people could not afford buckets, and this in 1994. The misrepresentation of Africa and Africans has continued throughout the ages. Sixteenth-century English people were poorly informed about Africa. English travellers made the situation worse by confusing the reality of African life with myths. At the same time as they wrote about African civilization, African family life and wealth, they were also absorbed with fables about Africa. In much of their writing about Africa it was hard to distinguish between fact and fiction. There were composite views held about Africa, such as that in the Old Testament where the kingdom of Kush, a strong and powerful country, was an ally of King Solomon. The other Africa, according to these writers, was that of the legendary King of Ethiopia, Prester John, who it was said lived to the age of 562 years in the late twelfth century. Another view of Africa is that described in the folklore of Pliny the Elder in AD 77. These tales were translated into English in 1566 and published under the title 'A summary of the Antiquities and Wonders of the World'. This popular book contained references to Africans without noses, tongues and some with one eye and others with heads like dogs (Pieterse, 1992). These myths entered English literature and were taken as truths. Similarly, a common misrepresentation of African people originates from Edward Long, a slave owner in the Caribbean who wrote his books, *Candid Reflections* (1772) and *History of Jamaica* (1774), in equally grotesque language, supporting the outrageous view that Africans were not fully humans and were inherently lazy, carefree and lustful. Such images are still alive today, but these are expressed in more subtle and covert ways. TV news is a good example where news on Africa is mainly about wars, famine, economic aid, *coups d'état*, HIV/AIDS and corruption. News reportage on Africa does not include success stories. Reports of the Third World and Environment Broadcasting Project (September 1991– August 1992) shows that over two-thirds of the coverage of TV news items on developing countries is on conflicts and disasters (Iziren, 1994). It is important that news coverage of wars and disasters in Africa is balanced with documentaries and educational programmes showing African art and culture and what Africans and black people in the diaspora are doing to tackle their own environment and development problems.

Coverage of disasters is usually accompanied by comments from white British or other European aid workers. There are many African aid workers who remain invisible and unheard. The impression is always that nothing gets done in Africa unless it is done by a white man/woman. Negative images about Africa may reflect some aspects of the truth, but these represent only a small fraction of the reality. Charitable organizations have been accused of distorting and misrepresenting situations in Africa, and though these agencies have denied any attempt at misrepresentation in order to get funds, they will undoubtedly agree that the message received by the public and commercial donors is not altogether free from distortion. Nearly all advertisements from charities contain the following messages – 'the Third World is in chaos and poverty because of ignorance and bad weather. People who live there are desperate, sick, unskilled, often dirty, grateful for a little help *and black [implied]*. Westerners can solve their problems for them by supplying aid, technology and more experts through charitable organizations. Westerners are skilled, generous, wealthy *and white [implied]*. The advertisements contain a range of glowing suggestions about Westerners and an unsavoury and pitiable view of the Third World. Besides this two-way distortion, there is a chronic lack of sensible explanation for the causes of poverty in the first place and instead merely an examination of its symptoms' (Multi Ethnic Education Review, 1985).

The media does not help because they take what is fed to them without any attempt to offer a balanced perspective. Over 80 per cent of British people get their information from television, and so it is not surprising that when children were asked to draw up a list of images they associate with Africa, they came up with famine, war, huts, corruption and AIDS. The origins of the images were attributed to television news and children's programmes (Iziren, 1994). These distortions could be corrected quite easily if there were programmes to show the achievement of Africans in the continent and the diaspora. This a black cultural museum education programme will be able to do with its educational support.

## Black British heritage and stereotypes

Many black people cannot claim to have a British heritage. The difficulty for them is one of interpretation and meaning. For British, read white; for black, read African. Black British is therefore a contradiction. This is one of the urgent reasons for a black cultural museum to educate the confused and promote better understanding between black and white people. Although the growth in black settlement in Britain is predominantly a post-war experience, black people have been in this country for many centuries and have contributed to the development of Britain. In his book *Staying Power*, Peter Fryer states:

> There were Africans in Britain before the English came here. They were soldiers in the Roman imperial army that occupied the southern part of our island for three and a half centuries. (Fryer, 1984, p. 1))

In his poem, 'The True Born Englishman', written in 1701, Daniel Defoe had this to say:

> The Romans first with Julius Caesar came,
> Including all the Nations of that Name,
> Gauls, Greeks, and Lombards; and by Computation
> Auxiliaries or slaves of ev'ry Nation.
> With Hengist, Saxons; Danes with Sueno came

In search of Plunder, not in search of Fame.
Scots, Picts, and Irish from the Hibernian shore:
And Conquering William brought the Normans O're
All these their Barb'rous offspring left behind,
The dregs of Armies, they of all Mankind;
Blended with Britains, who before were here,
Of whom the Welsh ha'blest the Character.
From the Amphibious Ill-born Mob began
That vain ill-natured thing, an Englishman.

(Quoted by Sherwood, 1992)

This poem illustrates that Britain has never been a homogenous society. There have been Vikings, Normans, Anglo-Saxons, Hugenots, Jews. There were also the black Celts (Ali and Ali, 1992). There were African people in Britain about 2,000 years ago. They were part of the Roman army consisting of North African soldiers which was stationed in the South of England and led by Septimus Severus, a black Roman emperor. Septimus Severus was born in Leptis Magna, now known as Libya. He defended Hadrian's wall against the Caledonians, and spent his last three years in this country.

Records also show that there was at least one black musician employed in the courts of Henry VII and VIII. This black trumpeter is depicted in the painted Roll of the Westminster Tournament in 1511, which was held to celebrate the birth of a son to Catherine of Aragon. In 1515 a group of five Africans came to England. This was before Britain had potatoes, tobacco or tea and before the birth of William Shakespeare. These five were to learn English and return to West Africa to serve as interpreters for English merchants who were interested in African gold, ivory and pepper.

In Scotland, early records attest to the presence of Africans in the Court of King James IV, who was imitating other kings in Europe by introducing African retainers to his court. By 1510 there was an established black community in Edinburgh.

The occurrence of the Atlantic slave trade and its aftermath brought many more black people to England. It became the norm for wealthy people to have among their servants a couple of slaves. It showed privilege and power – it was the exotic thing to do (Fryer, 1984, p. 4).

However, in 1596 Queen Elizabeth sent an open letter to the Lord Mayor of London authorizing all black people to be transferred to Spain and Portugal. In 1601 she issued a proclamation for all 'negroes and blackamoores to be transported to the place where they have come from'. She felt the country was being swamped by foreigners (Acts of the Privy Council, 1596–1597).

Lady Thatcher made a similar statement 380 years later. She voiced the opinion that 'people are rather afraid that this country might be swamped with people of a different culture', and that 'the British character has done so much for democracy, for law, and done so much throughout the world, that if there is a fear that it might be swamped, people are going to react and be rather hostile to those coming in' (*Daily Mail*, 31 January 1978). Her statement implied that British society has always been homogeneous, and that foreigners will dilute that homogeneity and thus the purity of the white race.

The experience of black people in Britain is not a separate experience or history. It is a part of the mainstream of British history in its totality. The elements of the black experience in that history are these:

- the antislavery *v*. the pro-slavery movement;
- radical, democratic and working-class movements which included black people;
- responses to black people by white people, and vice versa;
- the fight against colonialism, racism and discrimination;
- black positive achievements and contributions to British society.

The history of the British Empire taught in schools and colleges has emphasized the glory of British conquest, philanthropy and that of missionaries, who against all odds were able to convert the 'African pagans'. Black people are not regarded as having a history until they came in contact with the white man through the slave trade and other colonial exploits. The cultural, social and economic development of Africans before and after slavery are always either distorted or ignored. They are never treated with the same respect and appreciation as that of the early socio-economic development of the white world. Many Africans have also tended to cast doubt on the importance of their early civilization and contribution to world progress because of the social constructs imposed and popularized by Europeans. All talk of slavery becomes an embarrassment. Like many people, both black and white, they have not been informed about the valuable contributions black people have made to society prior to and after slavery, nor of the fact that black people were at the forefront of the emancipation struggle, or that slavery forms an intrinsic part of British heritage and that the profits made from the labour of Britain's black slaves and from investments in slavery formed the most essential part of Britain's economic power and influence. It was the involvement of Britain in the slave trade, and the need to justify slavery, that encouraged writers, scientists and others to look at Africa as a nullity, a continent devoid of orderliness until European intrusion. They saw Africans as having no ability to perform fully as human beings; Africans were savages running around naked in the bushes. English literature and history is replete with these examples of denigration which has entered into the world view of an overwhelming number of people.

This attitude and belief gave rise to colonialism where a small white minority created and justified minority rule over an African majority, on the popular assumption which has again persisted up till today, that the intelligence of the white person is superior to that of a black person. These assumptions have been shown to be false, but continue to flourish for ideological reasons based on race. Basil Davidson has shown that the spirit of African independence and self-respect was broken 'not by military prowess but by the long ensnarement of the slavery years' (Davidson, 1991). Furthermore, Chancellor Williams (1974) has shown in his book *Destruction of Black Civilisation* that Africa was colonized for economic reasons.

The stereotypical perception of black people firmly ingrained in British and European beliefs is that of the black savage being civilized by a white man. This fallacy is many, many centuries old, yet it continues to find expression in contemporary reportage where the natives are introduced to civilization by the white aid worker or by the shining light of the Christian religion. The myth of savages and hence violence has instilled fear and mistrust among white people so that all black people are regarded as threatening and/or dangerous. The expressions of that fear today are: the black male is a criminal or mugger; the black community is associated with drug abuse and therefore deviant; the black male is promiscuous and endowed with vast sexual prowess.

Remarks made in May 1995 by the Metropolitan Police Commissioner that young black males commit the largest number of violent crimes, without publishing the research findings on which his comments were based, give credibility to these stereotypical views. Another standard view of black people is of good dancers and singers and good sportspersons with innate qualities to excel in the entertainment and sports industries, but not in cerebral matters. Implicitly put, it is that black people can excel in the physical but not in the intellectual, which is clearly the domain of the white person. These images of black people can surely be rebuffed by evidence collected in a black cultural museum.

If the cultural heritage of black people becomes an acceptable aspect of British heritage and culture, it will imply:

- the destruction of the popular myth of the superiority of white heritage and culture, or of a pure white culture;
- the acceptance that British heritage and culture is a mixture of the heritage and culture of many people, including the English;
- that the black population, though numerically small, has contributed significantly to British heritage and culture.

The issue of heritage has now become a matter of national importance and current debate. For many white people, any other form of cultural expression other than white is alien and therefore should be controlled or forbidden. These views are often inward looking and parochial. In the same way as white travellers in past centuries have described African artefacts as exotics or curios, there are many in contemporary life who refer to black peoples' culture as interesting, but unequal and inferior to British culture. The persistence of these views is an indication of the importance and urgency of the need for a black cultural museum in Britain.

## Multiculturalism and education

The erroneous view of a pure white British culture and heritage has wide support, and this has encouraged the disseminators of culture and heritage in Britain to exclude the black contribution.

The exclusion of these contributions is a dereliction of duty on the part of policy-makers, who are responsible for the gross mis-education of the whole mass of people. The effect of this mis-education is felt most by children both black and white, but more so by the black child, who has to face an agenda set by society based on the colour of his/her skin. In the case of the white child, he/she does not have to face a colour bar or deal with the white sense of superiority. The black child has got to struggle to gain recognition and acceptance for reasons to do with his/her race and colour (Hall, 1985).

Museums in a pluralistic, multiethnic and multicultural society must reflect that plurality and diversity without any form of hegemony. Museums must act as repositories of objects which represent the cultural values of the people in the country. These objects should be used for exhibitions, study and education. An intermix of objects in an exhibition will not only indicate the various cultures within a society, but also their ability to coexist and live together without friction or animosity. Attempts have been made at various times by national museums at exhibitions to promote cultural diversity, cultural awareness and multiculturalism. Whilst these attempts should not be undervalued, they have existed at the margins. Museums in Britain need to display materials that not only deal with the correction of imperceptible but systematic bias, but also that place Africa and black people in their proper historical context. It is not impractical for any of the British national museums to change philosophy and start a new selection and display ethos to reflect the black contribution. Such a change in philosophy and ethos must involve the participation of black people to select, interpret and display objects. This change, if it occurs, will not get the total support and confidence of black people, who are aggrieved at the extent of the marginalization of black contribution to society. What is now needed is a specially built museum which is run by black professionals who will devise a selection and display policy from an African perspective. Such a development will help in destroying racist imagery which is so commonly perpetuated by mainstream institutions, including current national museums.

It was the declared aim of educators in the 1970s and 1980s to pursue the principle of multicultural education. Their enthusiasm was, however, ill-conceived. The resources needed to teach so sensitive a subject were not available. Although many schools take their pupils to see African artefacts in state museums, school textbooks or other books that children use for their study show stereotypical images of black people, as they 'incorporate and perpetuate racist assumptions'. For example, geography 'uses explanatory frameworks which fail to mention the trade relationships between the First and Third World as a reason for the relative poverty of the latter. Population growth, if mentioned in textbooks at all, is rarely linked explicitly with levels of economic development, more often with hints that the uneducated are failing to use contraceptives. Developing countries are presented as places which are important only because they provide Europe with certain commodities. Urbanisation is considered a major problem, its cause being immigration into cities, immigration is presented as the main cause of inner city decline' (Gill, 1982).

This is another reason for many black children in Britain today to reject any suggestion of their links to Africa. A black cultural museum will exhibit objects and artefacts and other visual materials which will show the great civilization of places like Ghana, Mali, Zimbabwe, Songhay and others. Such a museum will put Egypt and the Nile Valley civilization in its rightful place in Africa. The achievements of these civilizations will dispel the myth that Africans have not made any significant contribution to world civilization.

As Anthony Browder noted, 'The manipulation of African history has been so thorough that many people now mistakenly believe Egypt is not in Africa. It is as if Egypt has mysteriously detached itself from the continent and floated off to a nebulous place called "The Middle East"' (Browder, 1992, p. 41).

The achievement of Egypt and other ancient African civilizations will dispel the myth that Africans have not made any significant contribution to world civilization. Today, people quite rightly ask the question: what about the black contribution in contemporary times? That contribution has also become invisible. The main reason for this is the same as in ancient times; black people do not own or control the channels of information. This is what George Orwell had in mind when he said in paraphrase 'whoever controls the image and information of the past will determine what and how future generations will think;

and whoever controls the information and images of the present, will also determine how those same people will view the past' (Browder, 1992). A black museum will initiate steps and be the vanguard for disseminating the role of black people in every area of life.

## The lost contribution of World War I and World War II

The role of black people since the 1930s in Britain has nearly been lost. Black contribution is not a feature in main textbooks. In the national museums, the black contribution is either placed in some corner where it is difficult for visitors to see, or it is marginalized.

Black people remained invisible during the VE and VJ Day celebrations. At the Imperial War Museum display of World War II, black people's contributions were largely ignored. The same is true for the contribution of black people in World War I. Yet these two wars marked a pivotal point in British history.

Recent historiography has presented World War II as merely a European affair, but the British pulled in the colonies to fight on their side and black people died in their thousands fighting for the Mother Country. Some of these black people paid their own way to Britain to make a contribution to the war effort, others served in the Merchant Navy, Scottish Forrestry Camps, the northern war production factories and in other areas. Some were enlisted in the Army, Royal Air Force, the Auxiliary Imperial Service and Women's Auxiliary Air Force.

From the 1930s to the present, there have been thousands of black people who have come to Britain and helped to reconstruct British society in the post-war depression. Hundreds were recruited to take up jobs that white people considered unacceptable. They came to work in the National Health Service, London Transport and in other skilled and semi-skilled jobs. Some after many years of struggle joined the Trades Union Movement and attained the highest position, such as Bill Morris of the Transport and General Workers Union; others joined political parties and later became parliamentarians; others became mayors in local councils throughout Britain. Sam King returned to Britain in 1948 on the SS *Windrush* after World War II. He became Mayor of Southwark between 1983 and 1984. Bishop Malachi Ramsay came to Britain in 1968 and founded his own church, The Shiloh Church of Christ Apostolic. He has branches in London, Birmingham, Sheffield, Ghana, Sri Lanka and India.

The first generation of British-born black, though very appreciative of the efforts of their parents, were not as complacent. Many became very active within their communities, demanding equal rights at work, in education and especially in housing. One such activist was Olive Morris, of Brixton, who died at the young age of 27. She was an active campaigner for the poor and homeless. Because of her indefatigable efforts and campaigns, the local council decided to name one of their buildings in her memory. The Olive Morris House in Brixton Hill is a testament to her hard work and determination for equal rights for all. These are some achievements under the great struggle against racism and discrimination, and it shows how resilient black people can be in spite of adversity.

When national institutions do not encourage or make provision for these efforts and achievements to be shown or displayed, which will ultimately lift the veil of ignorance, is it any wonder that the man in the Clapham omnibus will continue to remain ignorant, perceiving that black people's contribution to the development of British society and Western civilization was negligible or non-existent? The post-war migration of black people to Britain should be seen as a continuum of relations between Mother Country and colonies, and not as a concession based on the benevolence of England.

## The African People's Historical Monument Foundation

In 1981 a group of parents, teachers and others met to discuss the causes of black children's failure in the education system in Britain, and to suggest ideas for improving the situation. After several meetings they agreed to research the content of history and geography teaching in schools and the place of black people within these subjects. They were disappointed that there was hardly anything taught in schools about black people. Slavery was the only topic that was mentioned – in a very negative and patronizing sort of way. There was no mention of the positive contributions of black people. In interviews with teachers it became evident that there was a paucity of historical documentation and social data for school use. It was at this point that these parents decided to form the African People's Historical Monument Foundation. This foundation was given the remit to establish a black cultural archive/museum as a serious attempt to recreate a sense of historical base and framework for the following actions:

- collecting, documenting and disseminating the history and culture of black people in the diaspora;
- encouraging and supporting liberating interpretations of black people's history so that everyone, especially young people, will understand the central and indispensable role that Africans have played in the evolutionary processes of world civilization;
- promoting links which will restore, unite and strengthen historical association with the African continent, by establishing a centre to act as a memorial and institute to our ancestors who perished in the

middle passage and those lost under the plantation system and the colonial and post-colonial eras;

- giving recognition to the work of black people in Britain and everywhere through a programme designed to identify and give credit to their individual and collective work.

The archives have begun to reawaken black people to the strong historical connections with Africa through lectures, exhibitions, seminars and research. The museum aims to have a comprehensive technical facility which will contain the most important events, developments, personalities and struggles in black people's history. Special attention will be given to the middle passage, the resistance to enslavement and the consequences of this trade to the present day. The Atlantic slave trade will not be treated as part of a pre-determined routine evolutionary development. The museum will hopefully facilitate a process whereby black people will begin to use history in the same way as others have done. For example, many black people in Britain are uneasy with their African ancestry in the same way as black Americans were, but in 1988 leading black Americans, among them Reverend Jesse Jackson, challenged the description of black people as black Americans. It was pointed out that such a term was vague, lacked coherence and was terminologically incorrect. In 1989, the name African-American was officially adopted at the African-American Summit in New Orleans, because it reflected a stronger racial and cultural identification. The new name describes black people in the USA as peoples of African descent currently living in America in the same way as there are Brits (British Americans), Jewish Americans, Polish Americans, Irish Americans, etc.

The Jews have been able to use the event of the holocaust during the past 50 years to create a cohesive political culture. The symbols continue to be used as weapons to arouse a unified collective action. Indeed the shared symbolism of Jews makes it possible for individuals within the Jewish community to subjugate their individual interest for the collective good. Their solidarity and shared sense of history has been effective in soliciting international support. A black cultural museum will begin to inculcate a sense of historical pride and worth among black people, young and old.

In 1994, a small child of seven and of African ancestry returned from school one day and reported to his father that some of his classmates called him an African and he was upset. He was upset because of the negative connotations to black people and Africa. A denial of black people's experience and history is a denial of the existence of black people. Malcolm X once wrote that: 'A people without a knowledge of their history, is like a tree without roots.' Adam Clayton Powell, the

American educationist, has also said that 'there is no future for a people who deny their past'.

There are now some black people whose perception of Africa is changing and are gradually accepting their African ancestry. Rejected by society at large as outsiders and aliens, they are now seeking to adopt an identity which is distinct, but finding it difficult to locate a point of reference in Britain where that identity finds expression. A black cultural museum will provide that point of reference. It will provide evidence of black people's great advances in the collection and documentation of black African-Caribbean social history in Britain, as well as advances in other areas of excellence. A black museum will also show that black people have not only been receivers of 'good things' from white people, but that they have been providers of 'good things' for Europeans to this day. A black cultural museum will emphasize the benefits of the Atlantic slave trade to Britain, such as:

- Barclays Bank – this bank was founded by two brothers, Alexander and David, who were Quaker slave merchants and sugar plantation owners;
- the Bank of England – the family fortunes of most of the bank governors and directors were augmented through slavery;
- the nucleus of the paintings in the National Gallery were donations from John Angerstein, who had slave interests in the West Indies. He was also a Lloyds Underwriter (Fryer, 1984, p. 46).

Black people need to focus on their shared history and unify around a common set of symbols. The symbolic importance of a black cultural museum in Britain will be complemented by its use by scholars, research students and teachers, who will develop curricular materials and interpret history and contemporary experience from the perspective of black people. In America the Schomburg Centre in New York is a repository for the collection of black history. It is a source for reference, study and research of the black experience. It is international in scope and covers every phase of black activity. The black cultural museum has similar objectives to the Schomburg, but with an emphasis on the black presence in Britain and the connections to Africa, the Caribbean, USA and Europe. The archive collection will fall into these categories:

- black contemporary life history (1960 to present);
- present history of black people in Britain (1900–1950);
- the Atlantic slave trade;
- history of black people in Europe (AD 208–1890s).

The time has come for all good people to rally together and challenge the fallacies and distortions about the history of black people which had been based very largely on stereotypical images depicted in Western historiography of black people as savages, slaves and poverty-stricken when there is evidence that there have been black people as noblemen, saints, priests, kings and queens. In order to stop the distortions about black people and their history being reinforced in the young minds in our schools and colleges today, progressive people all over Britain must ideally subordinate their bias, prejudice and bigotry to the lofty goals of disseminating truth for the advancement of humankind. A national black cultural archive/museum in Britain will be the vehicle to enable that process.

I will conclude this chapter by quoting to you one of the most challenging remarks I have ever come across. It was made by an eminent African-American scholar, Carter G. Woodson, and quoted in *Ebony Magazine*, February 1994:

> the [African] in his native country ... produced in the ancient world a civilisation contemporaneous with that of the nations of the early Mediterranean, he influenced the cultures then cast in the crucible of time, and he taught the modern world the use of iron by which science and initiative have remade the universe. Must we let this generation continue ignorant of these eloquent facts?

## References

Ajayi, A. (1993) Philosophy and history of the crusade for reparations, paper presented at the *First Pan African Conference on Reparations*, Abuja, Nigeria, p. 22.

Ali, A. and Ali, I. (1992) *The Black Celts. An Ancient Civilisation in Iceland and Britain*, Punite Publications.

Barley, N. (1990) *The Black Image. Representations of Africans in Europe throughout History*. A video production by the Association for Curriculum Development.

Browder, A. (1992) *Nile Valley Contributions to Civilisation*, p. 17.

Davidson, B. (1991) *Africa in History*, Phoenix Press.

Fryer, P. (1984) *Staying Power. The History of Black People in Britain*, Pluto Press.

Gill, D. (1982) *Multicultural Education*, Vol. 10, p. 3, no. 3, National Association for Multiracial Education.

Hall, S. (1985) *Professor Stuart Hall Assesses the Implications of Educational Resources at the Afro-Caribbean Education Resource Project*. A video production.

Hughes, J.C.A. and Larkin, J.F. (1969) Acts of the Privy Council XXVI, 1596–7, Licensing Casper Van Sanden to deposit negroes (1601), in *Tudor Royal Proclamations 1588–1633*, p. 221, Yale University Press, New York.

Iziren, A. (1994) In the camera's distorting eye, article in the *Voice* newspaper, issue number 597, dated 26 April, p. 24.

*Multi-Ethnic Educational Review* (Summer/Autumn 1985) ILEA Vol. 4, no. 2, p. 22.

Pieterse, J.N. (1992) *White on Black. Images of Africa and Blacks in Western Popular Culture*, pp. 23–24, Yale University Press, New York.

Sherwood, M. (1992) *Black Peoples in the Americas. A Handbook for Teachers*, The Savannah Press.

Williams, C. (1974) *The Destruction of Black Civilisation*, Third World Press.

# 3

## Contextualizing the black presence in British museums: representations, resources and response

### STEPHEN SMALL

### Introduction

In November 1992 Peter Moores announced his intention to fund a permanent gallery on the history of Transatlantic slavery, to be located at the Merseyside Maritime Museum. This was to be the first permanent gallery of its kind in Britain, to be established under the auspices of an Advisory Committee headed by Lord Pitt of Hampstead, and funded with a donation of over £500,000 from the Peter Moores Foundation. At the public announcement, attended by members of the black community, and representatives from black organizations in Liverpool and nationally, Peter Moores indicated that he wanted the gallery to be based on the best scholarly research, not to shy away from controversy, and to be objective and impartial. He was doing this, he said, because slavery was a taboo topic and needed to be addressed.

Peter Moores was no doubt taken by considerable surprise when he heard some of the criticisms that were offered by many black people present. These criticisms concerned the process by which the gallery had been established, particularly the decision-making process, the choice of location and the choice of topic. Mr Moores was criticized for failing to consult meaningfully with black organizations in Liverpool and across the country. Although many decisions had already been made, the majority of black people present had heard about the gallery only when they were invited to the launch. It was argued that the National Museums and Galleries on Merseyside (NMGM) had made little contribution towards an accurate representation of black people in their existing exhibits, where there remained many negative images and representations, in particular of black women, and had ignored or marginalized efforts to rectify this, in particular efforts by the local black community to establish a black museum. The proposed location of the gallery, in the Albert Dock, was also criticized because it represented an environment which was hostile to black people – there are few black employees in that vicinity, and young black people innocently shopping are often subjected to harassment by store guards and patrol guards. The Merseyside African Council (MAC) wanted to know why the first important gallery about Africans was to be about slavery rather than about the rich and textured history of African civilizations prior to European conquest.

The secretary of the Consortium of Black Organizations (CBO) argued that white people should not have responsibility for the gallery because so much of what has been written in books or presented in museums by whites was distorted and abusive. The CBO proposed that the gallery should be from a black perspective because it was black people who had been exploited, raped and murdered. Several black organizations – including the CBO and the Federation of Liverpool Black Organizations (FLBO) – called for a boycott of the gallery.

Peter Moores and Lord Pitt of Hampstead promised to look at the many issues raised, to ensure that all voices would be heard and that black concerns would be taken into account. During the course of the following months a series of public meetings took place, numerous concerns were registered and some significant changes occurred. In particular, the scope of the gallery was extended to include a section on African society and culture prior to European intrusion, and the initial proposal to have one guest curator was changed to a group of guest curators, numbering 11 in total, which included four black men and three black women. Some people felt that their concerns had been addressed, though others still argued that the changes had been too little, too late, and had all been done on the terms of the Peter Moores Foundation and NMGM. Among black organizations in Liverpool, the MAC played an active role throughout the establishment of the gallery, the FLBO was intermittently involved, while the CBO effectively boycotted the discussions. The gallery was opened in October 1994, entitled Transatlantic Slavery: Against Human Dignity.[1]

What this episode exemplifies is that one cannot begin to discuss black people and museums unless one understands something about the history and current experiences of black people in this country, as well as our collective memory of past treatment; that is, unless we understand something about the facts and legacy of slavery, colonial history and black immigration to Britain since World War II. What a review of these areas indicates is that the experience of black people has been, and continues to be, one characterized by racialized hostility in the form of violence, victimization, exclusion and misrepresentation.[2] Clearly museums alone cannot be held responsible for these experiences, but any review of the evidence indicates that most museums, their professional staff and related professionals (such as anthropologists), have been culpable and duplicitous in much of this hostility (Ramamurthy, 1990; Coombes, 1994). Indeed, some of the most demeaning and vile representations and images of black people in general, and black women in particular, have occupied places of glory and pride in the heart of British museums (Mehmood, 1990). This has also been the case elsewhere in the West (Bachollet *et al.*, 1992; Turner, 1994). Black people have fought vigorously and persistently to challenge racialized hostility in general; and we are increasingly challenging it in the institutional domain of museums.

It is true that much has changed in British society generally, especially in the last decade, as well as in museums. Many museums now aspire to offer a wider range of exhibits than ever before, and to appeal to more diverse class, racialized and gendered audiences. This has resulted from the pressure exerted on museums to come out of their ivory towers, to increase exhibits that address the experiences of other groups, and from the initiatives of a small number of museum professionals. Many of these changes, and some of their results, are documented in the chapters that follow. Black people – and other groups – now have a significant number of exhibits where they can see accurate and varied representations of black humanity, culture and lifestyle.[3] These initiatives demonstrate the potential for transcending the narrow and stereotypical representations of black people, for extending the processes of decision-making, and for changing the structures that permit such caricatures. They demonstrate the very real possibilities for significant and extensive change, and for alliances between common-minded people from diverse racialized and ethnic groups.[4]

Yet what I want to suggest is that these efforts have not led to any fundamental transformation in the institutional principles or practices of museums in this country, nor in the essential structures, decision-making processes, or overall representations of black people that continue to prevail in most museums. The initiatives just mentioned have been far too marginalized to have had that success. Racialized hostility remains pervasive in British museums, and many grotesque caricatures of black culture and humanity, as well as inaccurate accounts of encounters between non-blacks and blacks, as well as black achievements, continue to adorn their halls and corridors. Black people continue to suffer the consequences. So too do non-blacks.

In this chapter I provide a background and a context for interpreting the black presence in museums, and black attitudes and behaviour toward museums. Clearly this cannot be an exhaustive treatment, but I hope that by highlighting some of the major issues this can provide a framework within which the remaining chapters might be read. My main focus will be on Africans and African-Caribbeans, but I will also speak of some issues around the experience of Asians.[5] I outline some aspects of racialized hostility that continue to obstruct black aspirations and endeavours generally, as well as, more briefly, in museums today. I then turn to some black initiatives currently under way to counter these problems. Many other initiatives are described in subsequent chapters. In the final section I propose that many of these gains can be consolidated and expanded, but that, in order to achieve substantive and sustainable goals at more fundamental levels, museums need to make greater efforts to remove the obstacles to black involvement in decision-making, and to increase the involvement of black organizations in these processes.

## Racialized hostility in contemporary Britain

What is the context within which black people in Great Britain approach museums? In Britain today black people face pervasive racialized hostility and experience entrenched 'racialized' inequality (Skellington *et al.*, 1992). These problems are manifest in the areas of immigration legislation, employment, education and housing, as well as in our interactions with the police and the welfare state (Braham *et al.*, 1992; Wrench *et al.*, 1993). Racialized inequality in resources, and in these institutional areas, is paralleled by racist representations and images in film, television and print media. As a result of these problems, black people experience levels of psychological attack and abuse (stereotypes, misrepresentations of culture, scapegoating, insufficient acknowledgement of black achievements) to a far greater degree than other communities. Many scholars argue that black people are still wearing the 'psychological chains' of slavery (Akbar, 1984). The evidence collected about racialized hostility in Britain demonstrates that systematic racialized discrimination and injustice are largely to blame for these inequities.[6] Elsewhere I have characterized these problems as constituting *racialized barriers* to black aspirations (Small, 1994b).

Successive governments have encouraged and manipulated white fears of black people for purposes of electoral success, and immigration control has been, and remains, predicated on the notion that black people *per se* are undesirable. For example, immigration legislation in Britain in the 1990s continues to be articulated around this principle, which is captured in Roy Hattersly's contention in 1965 that:

> Without integration, limitation is inexcusable; without limitation, integration is impossible. (Miles and Phizacklea, 1984, p. 57)

This 'clever little syllogism', as Miles and Phizacklea call it, insisted that white British people should 'love thy neighbour, who shouldn't be here in the first place'. Completely ignoring the facts that black people constituted a tiny proportion of the population – then and now – and that the majority of immigrants to Britain were white – then and now – politicians, media and public alike have widely, and wildly, employed notions of 'floods' and 'tidal waves' to describe black settlement. As a result of British attempts to exclude black people, there are now three types of British passport in 1990s Britain, and black people are more likely to hold a passport that offers them no right of entry or abode in Britain (Jones, 1993). There have also been several recent highly publicized incidents around immigration control which exemplify the problems which confront black people. Most notable was the incident around Christmas 1993 in which several hundred Jamaican nationals who arrived in Britain to spend Christmas with friends and family were detained, and a significant number of them returned without good reason.

The best way to understand the economic and political circumstances of black people in Britain is to say that a 'colour line' prevails, that is, compared to white people, black people are at a disadvantage by just about every major economic and social indicator.[7] Data from the 1990s indicate that this is as true in wealth and health as it is in education, employment and housing. Black people are more likely to be unemployed or to receive low pay, and more likely to be claiming welfare benefits. Black males earned 10–15 per cent less than whites at the start of the 1990s, while almost twice as many black households as white were likely to be reliant on child benefits (Brown, 1992).

Compared to white people black people are less likely to be self-employed and more likely to be in manual and lower paid jobs, while white men are more likely to be employed as corporate managers and in skilled and semi-skilled jobs (Owen, 1992). Black people are generally less likely to receive educational qualifications (Gill et al., 1992). Similarly, whites are more likely to live in owner-occupied housing than blacks (66 per cent of whites own their own homes while 42.3 per cent of blacks do) (Owen, 1992), and black households are more likely to be overcrowded and to share a bathroom.

Our problems do not end at economic injustice. Racist murders have always threatened our very existence, and in recent years they have been on the increase; racist violence and abuse continue to prevail (Hesse et al., 1991; Francis and Matthews, 1993). Nor do those who are required to protect us fulfil their responsibilities. Interaction with the police continues to be an area in which black people in general, and young black people in particular, experience racialized hostility first hand. From stereotypes and verbal abuse, to random stopping and searching, police continue to intimidate black lives. When black people are the victims of violence, the police have failed to respond with the urgency and vigour that other communities command, and there have been a number of highly publicized deaths in police custody or at the hands of police officers – the tragic case of Joy Gardner being the most visible.

Black people continue to be subjected to the most pernicious degradation and vilification of our colour and culture, to charges of the so-called primitiveness of Africans and African-Caribbeans, and accusations of black family pathology. Images like these continue to be disseminated by press, television, literature and in popular culture (Gilroy, 1987; Small, 1994b). Several incidents highlight the continued ways in which manipulation of racist stereotypes remains an important element of state activities, for example, suggestions by government ministers that 'foreign scroungers' are burdening the welfare system. In 1993, Winston Churchill, MP, argued that 'ethnic minorities' formed a majority in many northern cities and were responsible for most crime. In 1995 the Metropolitan Police Commissioner issued statistics in a highly distorted and unprofessional manner, criminalizing young black men in particular, and stigmatizing the entire black community. This corresponds almost identically to the release of racialized data in the early eighties (Small, 1984).

It would be inaccurate to suggest that all the problems typical of British society are reproduced in British museums. But when we look at museums we find, *mutatis mutandis*, a similar range of problems (Coombes, 1994). The power and decision-making infrastructure of British museums is overwhelmingly white, upper and middle class, and male; decisions made about museums and their exhibits are made by this tiny and unrepresentative group. When we look at exhibits we find that racist and racialized representations are pervasive (stereotypes, savagery, etc.) (Mehmood, 1990); and black people continue to enjoy limited access to, and are less likely to visit museums (because we do not see museums as places that are friendly or inviting environments). Clearly many of these problems reflect class and gender obstacles, but all of them remain, despite the many significant successes of multicultural initiatives.

Many of these problems are reflected in what happened in the gallery on Merseyside. Objections were raised about who controlled NMGM, about the lack of black employees in NMGM, and about the negative images that existed throughout NMGM's exhibitions. Many of these criticisms have been documented by Gifford, and some of them acknowledged by NMGM (Gifford *et al.*, 1989). The MAC's view that more work should have been done on African culture, as African history did not begin with slavery, is a case in point; had black people been involved in discussions from an earlier stage, this possibility would have emerged. It is true that NMGM had already begun to make efforts to rectify this situation, especially the 'Staying Power' exhibit, and saw the gallery as offering greater opportunities to go further. Other initiatives currently under way indicate continued commitment, but the decision to have a gallery on slavery had already been decided by the Peter Moores Foundation, and it was clear from the start that this decision would not be changed. It may be only fair that Foundations should decide what to do with their money, but they should not expect black people to like them, nor to offer unequivocal support, around these decisions.

Similar experiences are illustrated for the nation as a whole when we look at the instance of the Benin bronzes. In February 1897, 1500 British troops raided the city of Benin, and plundered the royal court of several thousand pieces of treasure and sacred artefacts (Coombes, 1994). These artefacts are now held on display in museums throughout England (in Liverpool, London and Oxford), as well as in Europe. This attack, named the 'Punitive Expedition' by the British, was ostensibly to punish the Oba (King) of Benin for the murder of a small party of British officers who had attempted to enter Benin City, despite a flat refusal of access by the Oba, but this cannot be understood apart from the increasing encroachment by the British upon the Oba's trading territory, and their efforts to enforce a treaty they had tricked the Oba into signing, granting them sovereignty of his lands (Coombes, 1994, p. 9). I have visited the Museum of Mankind and the Liverpool Museum to inspect the accounts of the 'Punitive Expedition'. These accounts emphasize punishment for uninvited wrongdoing and completely ignore, or significantly downplay, the economic and political interests of the British. Visitors come away with partial and biased perspectives.

These problems have long historical precedent – precedent with which many black people are familiar. Black people have been in Britain at lease since the middle of the sixteenth century (Walvin, 1973; Shyllon, 1977), and they have contributed to British economic, political and cultural development in a myriad of ways, institutionally, ideologically and materially, through our presence in Britain and through the labour and lands acquired by Britain through conquest (Williams, 1944; Fryer, 1984). Black people almost invariably faced problems – discrimination and denial of access to resources – across the British Empire as well as in England (Ramdin, 1987). Ubiquitous negative representations have been part and parcel of this experience –

in art, literature and, in this century, in film, television and the press (Fryer, 1984).

Similarly, in British museums many of the problems today have long historical precedent (Small, 1994a). From the plunder and looting of the Benin bronzes, to the reconstruction and mocking of African village life and culture; from the show-casing of the bodies of black men and women as spectacle, for example the so-called 'Pygmies' (Coombes, 1994), to the marginalization of black art and creativity (Dixon, 1991).

The obstacles and hostility that confront black people in British society generally shape the experiences and attitudes of black people who visit, or consider visiting, museums; and our experiences in museums affect our attitudes more generally. Problems around decision-making, control, access and the creation of images also shape one another. For example, the discrimination and mistreatment that we experience perpetuates inequality, which in turn results in negative images and representations. At the same time, representations and images create and fuel stereotypes which affect how non-blacks interact with black people – expecting black men to be violent and aggressive (Asian men to be illegal immigrants, corrupt and deceitful), black women to be sexual 'creatures' and promiscuous (Asian women to be passive, or 'good mothers', enslaved in their own community traditions).

In light of these concerted attacks upon our humanity and our communities, black people have not sat idly by, but have sustained communities of resistance, which have drawn upon the strengths of our community organizations as well as their diasporic links (Ramdin, 1987; Small, 1994b). Black people thus remain systematically disadvantaged, but our resolve to survive and succeed has never deserted us (Sivanandan, 1990). What these experiences, and knowledge of them, mean is that when a museum exhibit takes place, black and white audiences are likely to approach it from very different standpoints. Their respective appreciation of the extent and causes of racialized inequality, and their commitment to changing this inequality, is demonstrably different.[8] This has to be taken into account.

## Black initiatives around museums in contemporary Britain

Restructuring the nature of museums and exhibits has never been a priority for most black people in Britain. With one or two exceptions, we have been too concerned with more immediately life-threatening obstacles around immigration, violence, police intimidation, injustice and widespread discrimination in employment, education and housing.[9] Today, these latter problems remain our priorities in improving our life chances, but increasingly our attention has turned to the area of museums. This in part is linked to our many efforts to challenge the pejorative images of Africa and black people which have been ubiquitous in film, television and the printed media. Consequently, it is possible to identify key organizations, key initiatives and key demands within the black community.

At the forefront of demands for a fundamental change in the nature of representations of black people in British museums, and for redressing the imbalance in who controls the resources and the institutions in which such representations take place, is the African Reparations Movement (ARM). ARM arose out of an international meeting of black politicians, academics and concerned individuals in Nigeria in 1993 (Small, 1994c; *Voice*, 1995). The central demand of ARM is that the governments of those countries that benefited from slavery and colonialism acknowledge the damage done and the gains made, and make payments for this damage. Reparations can be made by cancelling financial debts, or transferring capital, or offering training and education to those they have victimized, or finding some other way of making restitution (Ellis, 1992). ARM argues that there are thousands of artefacts in British museums that were illegally and illegitimately acquired during slavery and colonialism; that the display of these artefacts brings financial benefit and kudos to Britain; and that such revenue and kudos is thus lost to the countries from which they were stolen. ARM believes that reparations must involve the return of artefacts, treasures and other property of historical value and cultural heritage now being held in public and private collections (Small, 1994c; *Voice*, 1995).

ARM has been working for reparations in a variety of ways, and the return of African artefacts is a major aspect of its work. Working with a small group of volunteers, ARM has carried out several types of work, including raising awareness via boycotts, lectures, public meetings and the dissemination of information; in addition, ARM has begun the long and time-consuming work of documenting the many artefacts held in British museums. Bernie Grant, MP, has held a series of public meetings in the House of Commons, chaired a national conference in Birmingham in 1993, and has lectured, and written, on the issue of reparations throughout the country and internationally (Reparations Now, 1993). Throughout 1994 the author lectured to African and African–Caribbean societies at several British universities, a key concern of ARM being to encourage people of African origin to become more involved in researching, documenting and writing the history of African men and women).[10]

Although this is in its early stages, a great deal has been done to raise awareness of the importance of cultural and religious artefacts in the black experience, of the many illegitimate ways by which some of the most important artefacts in British museums were acquired, and in mobilizing action to bring about change. Many issues remain to be decided but, under the leadership of Bernie Grant, MP, ARM has made important first steps.

Many other black initiatives have been under way for some time, including the efforts of the Black Cultural Archives to establish an African National Museum and the work of a wide range of black organizations that touches upon museums directly or indirectly in a number of ways. Black women's centres and educational groups that are concerned with the pejorative images of black people that assault our community's youth, such as Osaba Women's Centre in Coventry, the Charles Wootton College in Liverpool, African Caribbean Families and Friends in Nottingham and Kemetic Educational Guidance (KEG) in Manchester. Magazines and journals and/or reports that focus on black art and culture specifically (Dixon, 1991), or that deal with black life generally and include special sections on art and culture, such as the weekly journal, *Voice* (which has special sections of culture, history and museums), and *The Alarm*. All these activities testify to the increasing extent to which black people have addressed the control of cultural resources as a key factor in shaping our lives.

These efforts are all the more praiseworthy in light of the widespread racialized hostility that we have always faced, and the considerable obstacles such hostility has presented in our lives. They are all the more impressive given our limited resources and the small size of our community upon which we can draw. In discussing the size of the black community in Britain, the popular media and politicians on all points of the spectrum have generally subscribed to a view that the fewer black people there are in Britain the better it is, and to a primary concern to reduce the numbers in Britain (see details in Miles and Phizacklea, 1984). This has made discussion of numbers highly problematic. However, it is important to have information on the general position of black people in Britain, in terms of our demographic, economic and social profiles for several reasons.

One important reason is that our limited size, and our relatively disadvantaged position, means that we have tended to lack the resources or the means to redress many of the problems that we face. Racialized hostility means that we are more preoccupied with matters of survival and success, and that issues of representations and images in museums often take a low priority. This has led me to argue elsewhere that alliances between blacks and whites are indispensable in any black efforts to counter racialized hostility (Small, 1994b, Chap. 5).

At the present time, blacks number just over 1.5 per cent of the British population, all people of colour number less than 5 per cent.[11] The 1991 Census counted nearly 54.9 million people in Britain, of whom the total number of black people was 890,700 (Owen, 1992, p. 1, Table 1). This included 500,000 black Caribbean (0.9 per cent of total population), 212,400 black African (0.4 per cent of total population) and 178,400 black Other (0.3 per cent of total population) (Owen, 1992, Table 1). There are more Asians than blacks nationally and in all regional concentrations; the total number of Asians in Great Britain is 1,479,600 (that is, 2.7 per cent of the total population) (Owen, 1992, p. 2, Table 2). The Asian population is more economically and ethnically diverse than blacks, with significant proportions of educated and occupationally advantaged groups.

Differences between blacks and Asians in occupation and education, voting preferences and cultural institutions, mean different priorities will continue to prevail in those communities. Africans, African–Caribbeans and Asians are currently working out alliances and associations on a range of common concerns. Strong alliances have been developed in key urban areas, especially around white racists, racialized violence and community needs (Hesse et al., 1991). Younger people, especially those born in Britain, show signs of solidarity and commitment to a shared common identity, across cultural and national identities, though this is not entirely free from tension.

So the black population remains a tiny proportion of the British population, but is nevertheless highly visible because of the politicization of 'racism' and because black people are overwhelmingly concentrated in urban areas. Despite our small numbers, and the plethora of problems that continue to confront us, some of the initiatives described here indicate that we have increasingly seen museums as a focus of our concern.

## Conclusion

When one looks at the current contours of British society, at the experiences of black people in general, and of museums, it is clear that much has changed, while much remains the same. Many steps can be taken to improve the representation of black people in museum exhibits; to increase the number of black people that visit museums; or even to increase our representation among museum staff. Museums can certainly begin to change some of the more explicit, hostile and degrading representations of black people, of working-class whites and of all women. Some of these measures will require no extra financial outlay, others will require some outlay, but if museums stop after simply increasing black visibility among exhibits, visitors or employees, then they miss the point. One important goal may be to make museums more diverse, more multicoloured, more multicultural. But another important goal is to challenge and change the goals, nature and philosophy of museums as the promoters of upper- and middle-class culture in narrow ways, and to the detriment of the cultural and creative products of the vast majority of the population in this country, and across the world.

In order to understand black peoples' attitudes and behaviour towards museums we must look at their experience of British society, and their attitudes towards this experience, including the historical background. For black people the collective memory of colonialism and the British Empire is more pronounced than for white people, and takes a very different form. Black people are more likely to have negative views of this experience, and to see it as playing a significant role in shaping the hostility that we face in Britain today (Small, 1994b). We also see it as a primary explanation for the inequality which we must endure. A central reason for this is the current circumstance of entrenched racialized inequality, the psychological abuse black people continue to confront and the racialized hostility which underlies both.

Black people have refused to accept the maltreatment we have had to face, or to give up in the face of adversity and we have fought in a myriad of ways, during slavery, colonialism and in contemporary Britain (Small and Walvin, 1994; Sivanandan, 1990). Similarly black people have fought against museums, though this has always been less of a priority. Black people are sick and tired of white people being indifferent, unwilling or unable to tackle the additional obstacles that we must confront (*Voice*, 1995). This shapes our interaction with 'white' institutions and is one of the primary reasons that black people are working steadfastly to develop and expand our own institutions, whether schools, cultural centres, bookshops or museums. Black organizations, first and foremost, are safe spaces in which we can decide our priorities and work towards them without hindrance by those hostile to our goals, or by those with good intentions who don't share our priorities.

Museums alone cannot be held responsible for all the pejorative images of black people which pervade British society, nor for the very many problems which we continue to face. Negative images pervade the media – in television, cinema and newspapers – and these continue to have a detrimental impact on the quality of black lives. Racialized hostility continues to constrain black efforts to survive and succeed. Nor can museums be expected to provide solutions on their own, but museums have certainly been part of the problem – a major part in some periods of British history – and they certainly play a role in the perpetuation of problems that continue to plague black people (Coombes, 1994; Small, 1994a). Similarly, they can certainly be part of the solution – and this volume offers testimony to many of the sincere efforts dedicated to how this might be done. Museums must continue to take action to ensure that their activites are inclusive, fair, accurate and impartial.

The climate for change in the 1990s is not the most auspicious for two reasons. The economic climate, and the response to it, is threatening, with high levels of unemployment, homelessness and poverty, and low levels of investment in health and education. Secondly, the move to the right, to conservatism, has necessarily entailed a rejection of any pro-active efforts to combat racialized hostility and the advocacy of colour-blind policies. There has been a general mood-swing back to a climate of colour-blindness, accompanied by increasing privatization and a withdrawal of resources from cultural institutions. This has been part of the move to so-called 'free-market' principles, with all the competitive and individualist philosophies and ideologies inextricable from it. This has affected museums adversely in a number of ways, particularly in resources. Many now find they have to stand on their own. However, institutions, organizations and individuals have not simply acceded to such forces, and there are many exemplary efforts to counteract these negative forces. Such initiatives must be identified and supported, and efforts redoubled.

Black people will no longer be satisfied if the door to museums is opened only slightly. The issue for most black people is how do we recapture our past? How do we influence the processes by which the past is described, interpreted and explained – in museums and galleries, as well as in film, cinema, television and education? Most black people don't have high expectations that significant change will come about if we are not involved, and involved integrally, in decision-making processes. In the past most black people have primarily wanted an end to the pejorative stereotypes, inaccurate and distorted representations of African lives, cultures and achievements. We have achieved far greater success in areas that fall outside the domain of sport, music, food and dance, and we want it acknowledged. We want accurate images of black life that satisfactorily reflect the variety and vitality of African contributions, and today we want more. We are no longer prepared to leave it to the hands of non-blacks, to let them dictate what and when and where. We want access to and control of representations and resources. And we want the black organizations which currently play such a role in our lives to also play an integral part in these processes. This is a central platform of ARM. Only in this way can we begin not just to rectify the damage done to black people's lives, but to rectify the damage done to white people's views and attitudes.

The chapters that follow describe some of the sincere and genuine efforts of museums to make their decision-making processes and activities more inclusive of the diverse constituencies that they serve. To consolidate and expand such initiatives I believe that museums need to make greater efforts to remove the obstacles to black involvement in decision-making and to increase the involvement of black organizations in these processes. Black people with the relevant knowledge, skills, expertise, experience and qualifications are available to work on these goals. In part this will require a greater understanding of the broad range of problems which confront black people in this country. This, I believe, is one of the lessons learned from the gallery at the Merseyside Maritime Museum.

## Notes

1. I attended the initial public meeting, and subsequently served as both a guest curator and a member of the Advisory Committee. During this period I was also an active member of the Consortium of Black Organizations, the Federation of Liverpool Black Organizations and the Merseyside African Council. In the publication that arose out of the gallery, I wrote two chapters, and co-wrote a third (Tibbles, 1994). In writing this chapter I have only drawn upon information and documents that were publicly available.

2. I introduced the concept of 'racialized hostility' to describe and delimit the range of activities, institutional and individual, that act to constrain the lives of black people in Britain. I argued that we should see hostility 'not in its usual sense of aggressive, explicit action. Rather I use it to refer to attitudes and actions where the intentions and/or outcomes are detrimental to black people' (Small, 1994b, p. 210, footnote 6). The term 'racialized' derives from the work done by a range of authors working within the 'racialization problematic'. What these authors share in common is a belief that 'race' is not a fixed biological category, but a socially constructed category which serves a variety of interests. An early introduction to this work is that of Michael Banton (1977). Robert Miles has written extensively on this framework, while work has also been carried out in the US (Miles, 1982, 1989; Omi and Winant, 1994). I have articulated theoretical and empirical aspects of the framework in several contexts (Small, 1989, 1991, 1993, 1994b).

3. One early example was the exhibition 'Staying Power' at the National Galleries and Museums on Merseyside, opened in 1991. The Black Cultural Archives has also organized exhibits.

4. There are no 'races' in the sense of naturally occurring biologically distinctive groups. Historically, Europeans have defined themselves as a racialized group, that is, 'white', in opposition to a racialized Other, that is, 'black', and various racialized ideologies have been central to this process (see Banton, 1977; Miles, 1982, 1989).

5. I believe that much of what I say in terms of exclusion and stereotypes has general applicability to the experience of Asians, but I do not profess a specialist knowledge of Asians, nor can I provide details of their particular experiences with museums.

6. For evidence of 'racialized discrimination' over the last three decades in England, see McCrudden *et al.* (1991).
7. This conceptualization of the 'colour line' deriving from Dubois' famous statement – 'the problem of the twentieth century is the problem of the color line' – is described further in Small (1991, 1994b).
8. For details of surveys documenting these divergent racialized attitudes and explanations, see Small (1994b, Chap. 5).
9. These exceptions include the work of the Black Cultural Archives.
10. This included Birmingham University, Leicester University and the London School of Economics.
11. I use the term 'people of colour' in preference to the more commonly used term 'ethnic minorities'. I find the former eminently preferable to the hostile and demeaning phrase 'non-white' which defines us negatively in relation to a presumed white majority.

# References

Akbar, N. (1984) *Chains and Images of Psychological Slavery*, New Mind Productions, Jersey City.

Bachollet, R., Debost, J.-B., Lelieur, A.-C. and Peyriere, M.-C. (1992) *NegriPub L'Image Des Noirs Dans La Publicite*, Somogy, Paris.

Banton, M.P. (1977) *The Idea of Race*, Tavistock, London.

Braham, P., Rattansi, A. and Skellington, R. (eds) (1992) *Racism and Antiracism. Inequalities, Opportunities and Policies*, Sage, London.

Brown, c. (1992) 'Same difference': the persistence of racial disadvantage in the British employment market, in Braham, P., Rattansi, A. and Skellington, R. (eds) *Racism and Antiracism. Inequalities, Opportunities and Policies*, Sage Publications, London, pp. 46–63.

Coombes, A. (1994) *Reinventing Africa. Museums, Material Culture and Popular Imagination in late Victorian and Edwardian England*, Yale University Press, New Haven.

Dixon, R. (1991) *Black Arts, Poverty and The Issue of Equity – a Study of Art and Creative Culture Within Toxteth*, University of Liverpool, Race and Social Policy Unit, Liverpool.

Ellis, R. (1992) Africans want millions in slavery 'reparations', *Sunday Times*, 5 January, p. 6.

Francis, P. and Matthews, R. (eds) (1993) *Tackling Racial Attacks*, Centre for the Study of Public Order, University of Leicester.

Fryer, P. (1984) *Staying Power: the History of Black People in Britain*, Pluto Press, London.

Gifford, Lord, Brown W. and Bundey R. (1989) *Loosen The Shackles. First Report of the Liverpool 8 Inquiry into Race Relations in Liverpool*, Karia Press, London.

Gill, D., Mayor B. and Blair M. (1982) *Racism and Education. Structures and Strategies*, Sage Publications, London.

Gilroy, P. (1987) *There Ain't No Black in the Union Jack. The Cultural Politics of Race and Nation*, Hutchinson, London.

Hesse, B., Rai, D.K., Bennett, C. and McGilchrist, P. (1991) *Beneath the Surface: Racial Harassment*, Avebury, Aldershot.

Jones, T. (1993) *Britain's Ethnic Minorities*, Policy Studies Institute, London.

McCruddon, C., Smith, D.J. and Brown C. (1991) *Racial Justice at Work*, Policy Studies Institute, London.

Mehmood, T. (1990) Trophies of plunder, *Museums Journal*, September, 27–30.

Miles, R. (1982) *Racism and Migrant Labour*, Routledge & Kegan Paul, London.

Miles, R. (1989) *Racism*, Routledge, London.

Miles, R. and Phizacklea, A. (1984) *White Man's Country: Racism in British Politics*, Pluto Press, London.

Omi, M. and Winant H. (1994) *Racial Formation in the United States. From the 1960s to the 1980s*, 2nd edn, Routledge & Kegan Paul, London.

Owen, D. (1992) Ethnic minorities in Great Britain: population totals for countries, regions and local authority areas, *Centre for Research in Ethnic Relations*, University of Warwick, Coventry, November.

Ramamurthy, A. (1990) Museums and the representation of black history, *Museums Journal*, September, 23.

Ramdin, R. (1987) *The Making of the Black Working Class in Britain*, Gower, Aldershot.

Reparations now (1993) *Journal of Nigerian Affairs*, November/December, 6–7.

Shyllon, F. (1977) *Black People in Britain, 1553–1833*, Oxford University Press, London.

Sivanandan, A. (1990) *Communities of Resistance. Writings on Black Struggles for Socialism*, Verso, London.

Skellington, R., Morris, P. and Gordon P. (1992) *'Race' in Britain Today*, Sage Publications, London.

Small, S. (1984) The criminalization of the black community, *Christian Action Journal* (for Prison Reform Trust), 22–24.

Small, S. (1989) Racial differentiation in the slave era: a comparative analysis of people of 'mixed-race' in Jamaica and Georgia, unpublished Ph.D. dissertation, University of California, Berkeley.

Small, S. (1991) Racialised relations in Liverpool: a contemporary anomaly, *New Community*, 11(4), 511–537.

Small, S. (1993) Unravelling racialised relations in the United States of America and the United States of Europe, in J. Wrench and J. Solomos (eds), *Racism and Migration in Europe*, Berg Publishers, Oxford.

Small, S. (1994a) Concepts and terminology in representations of the Atlantic slave trade, *Museum Ethnographers Journal*, December, 1–14.

Small, S. (1994b) *Racialised Barriers: the Black Experience in the United States and England*, Routledge, New York.

Small, S. (1994c) The general legacy of the Atlantic slave trade, in T. Tibbles (ed.), *Transatlantic Slavery. Against Human Dignity*, pp. 122–126, Merseyside Maritime Museum.

Small, S. and Walvin, J. (1994) African resistance to enslavement, in T. Tibbles (ed.), *Transatlantic Slavery. Against Human Dignity*, pp. 42–49, Merseyside Maritime Museum.

Tibbles, T. (ed.) (1994) *Transatlantic Slavery. Against Human Dignity*, Merseyside Maritime Museum.

Turner, P. (1994) *Ceramic Uncles and Celluloise Mammies*, Routledge, London.

*Voice* (1995) 15 August, pp. 18–19.

Walvin, J. (1973) *Black and White: the Negro and English Society 1555–1945*, Allen Lane, London.

Williams, E. (1944) *Capitalism and Slavery*, Andre Deutsch, London.

Wrench, J., Brar, H. and Martin, P. (1993) *Invisible Minorities. Racism in New Towns and New Contexts*, Centre for Research in Ethnic Relations, University of Warwick.

# 4

# Background notes: Ajay Khandewal in conversation with artist Shaheen Merali

## EDITED BY PAMELA MERALI

'The formulation of authenticity, which has been an integral function of Western museums and galleries, has marginalised the creative and critical aspects of Black experience. However, the emergence of the colonised object as critical subject has problematised the notion of a spatially located, homogeneous and ahistorical black culture.'[1] The Predicament of Culture is reflected in the life story of the artist Shaheen Merali. As art speaks to the soul, it also draws from it – the sum of experience revealing itself in work and thought.

### Q. What were your first experiences of Britain?

I was born in 1959 in Dar-es-Salaam, Tanzania, where I was educated to primary level. I came over to this country with my mother in 1970, just before the troubles started in East Africa with the Asian community.

Whilst much difficulty may be experienced by those wishing to enter the UK, my mother had a British passport and this allowed us rights of residency. My elder brother and sister, studying in India, joined us later, but my father was refused entry for the following two years – a situation which led to a deepening depression in my mother. The stress of working in this country, looking after five children, not having the ability to speak very good English and the economic pressures mounted on her and after they granted a visa to my father she just let go, subsequently dying of cancer.

My first experience of Britain was living in an area of North London

abandoned by the indigenous population to a succession of new
immigrants and asylum seekers; a polyglot society living unhappily in
juxtaposition with its original owners. The latest arrivals shouldered
the wrath of the marginalized – the 'pecking order' of new British
society urging the previous tenants to mock the estrangement of the
Asians rather than unite in a common anti-racist front.

Ironically, our MP was Margaret Thatcher, a name which evokes
bitter personal memories of my mother's futile banging at the closed
doors of Finchley Civic Centre. The attempt to win a right to entry to
the UK for my father frustrated the whole family and further
debilitated my mother. Her sense of powerlessness, both as a woman
and as an Asian, overwhelmed her. Whilst a close family member gave
support, it was tacitly acknowledged that his personal struggle to
survive in this hostile environment prevented him from offering little
more than advice in the initial stages of settling in. The strength of the
extended family network, taken for granted in East Africa, was sorely
missed.

My father's financial contribution to our new life, smuggled into
Britain in my sock, had to sustain the family group until his ever-
delayed arrival. My mother sought work, and like many newly arrived
immigrant women before her, was only able to procure the most menial
of factory jobs, of the type commonly eschewed by the indigenous
population. Testing flash bulbs for a firm in North London lacerated
her fingers and threatened her hearing. The factory owners, knowing
that its workers were not aware of employment laws or health and
safety guidelines, like the denizens of the Victorian society which had
created the empire and its dependants, mercilessly exploited their
mainly female, Asian labour force.

Furthermore, the social stability experienced by most Asian families
in the long-settled communities within East Africa ill-prepared us for
the several crises we weathered in England in regard to our
accommodation. Six of us huddled against the unknown vagaries of
the British climate in a room in Palmers Green, let to us by a landlord
bedevilled by personal tragedy. Days before our arrival, his wife had
doused herself with kerosene and committed a particularly vicious form
of self-annihilation. This incident appeared menacingly prophetic to
our somewhat battered family; the fate of the Asian woman in this new
promised land writ large for all our community to see.

## Q. How has the education system affected you and your family?

Education was the source of several different problems for the family.
Most of us had rudimentary English; my mother from knitting patterns
in women's magazines, whilst drive-in Disney movies and the

improbable popularity of Elvis Presley and Cliff Richard had initiated the younger members of the family to the structure and sounds of the language. Fluency, however, was yet to be achieved and school became an area of personal distress on more than one level; firstly the struggle to perfect the langauge and secondly, and most importantly, a battle with the constant feelings of fear and inadequacy, engendered by the horrific bullying experienced by young Asians in the UK at this time. This was the era of 'Paki-bashing', when every last poor white, the disaffected Londoner under-educated after a century of free schooling, poured out his scorn on the newly arrived. Real physical damage was done, both in school and on public transport. Not wishing to add further problems to an overloaded situation, the pain and bitterness had to be swallowed at home and alone. The horror of the comprehensive school, immortalized in memory in the shape of the three biggest bullies, Tony, Paddy and Mario, left lifelong scars. Whilst vowing that the next generation should not have to suffer the same torments, a general interest in education was born out of this period in my life.

Bullying creates a climate of fear, in which to stand out from the norm is to seek the wrong kind of attention. Many Asian children belittled their academic achievements and suppressed their curiosity in class in order not to further ignite the wrath of the bullies by winning teacher approval. School life was informally organized to avoid problems wherever possible – break time and lunch time were an endless source of potential violence; the classroom at least held the teacher as a sometime intermediary.

A code for day-to-day existence had to be formed – where to stand in the playground or the lunch queue was enormously important. Once out of the sight of the teacher the field was open for the bullying to start. This method of survival in the UK is still found today. As Asians it is vital to understand that the UK is not how it was envisaged. This great domain of knowledge, this centre of empire from which everything emanated did not equate with the raw windy streets of downtown Edmonton and the outstanding prejudice of the local community *vis-à-vis* their new neighbours.

## Q. What effects did these events have on you?

At one stage, the inmates of Friern Barnet psychiatric hospital inspired me to a suicide attempt – avoiding the bullies at any price had become the main thrust of my life. Further the family was living above a defunct butcher's shop, now overrun with worms. The fabric of our life was rapidly deteriorating and still my father struggled to assert his right to citizenship.

Around this time, I began to forge links with the Turkish-Cypriot students I met when I left school to attend Barnet College. Although we were from different countries, we were all from a Muslim background and faced similar situations in Britain. At that point we could discuss and make links and create a platform for ideas. I came to understand that there were other cultures in Britain which were co-existing with the Asian one, cultures with similar boundaries and experiences. I had received inklings of that when I was in school but it became more evident as I moved into higher education.

It was really good for me to have relationships of this sort; it grounded me and made me see that one did not have to move within the narrow confines of the family network of the immediate language structure and that one could make contact with people outside an institution. I realized that people of different tongues could share similar experiences, historically as well as contemporaneously. Two years in college went very quickly. I developed a strong interest in international films, which is still very much part of my makeup today. It was the start of an international discourse.

## Q. How did you respond, artistically?

My own art became much more experimental. I think that the anger built up earlier was released somewhat whilst taking art A level. I remember doing a piece of work, which was a head I had constructed. It was a life-size piece – head and shoulders. I broke up a lot of glass and made the whole head from the broken shards, cutting myself ridiculously in the process, but it was fantastic. This must have been around 1977, at about the time that I began to hear stories about Johnny Rotten and the Sex Pistols and the alternative white struggle.

It came to be more and more meaningful. A student, Angela, who was the cousin of Johnny Rotten, used to bring news about the punk movement. Rotten had not made the Bill Grundy show at that time and was not known to the general public. An energy started to creep into me and I began experimenting by going to see some of the shows – late sessions in the small venues of the punk movement. Before this period I had dressed soberly: James Dean haircuts, pointed shoes and drainpipe trousers, but now I started to respond to new waves of youth culture and then the whole punk thing exploded. I was on the edge of something, here in the UK, the beginning of inclusion in cultural movement.

I remember an A level project about cartoons for which I made a series about the Joker, a man on the outside of society. For me, Batman was not the central character, which made me realize that I was looking at the periphery of culture. Most students would work with clay but I would work with glass. These were difficult times, but ones which I felt were more in tune with the way I was growing up and with my surroundings. I started to experiment with three-dimensional imagery as well. I enjoy working in multimedia, rather than two-dimensional drawings, paintings and illustrations. I remember making plaster forms at the age of 16, projecting slides on them and then photographing the whole thing, letting it become layered. I was becoming more aware of processes that would evolve into another image about experience, away from a literal reading.

## Q. After school, how did you manage to procure a foothold in the art world?

My first interview for a place at art school was with Middlesex Polytechnic and had typically disastrous results. In my portfolio there were a series of images about horse racing as a metaphor; instead of a horse I had put a black person with a white jockey riding him as a commentary on racism and slavery. I was asked, 'So why exactly do you draw images of black men?' My reply 'Because that's what I am', elicited a curt response, 'That's not good enough'. After a brief argument with the interviewer I walked out. There was no room in my life for people who would not consider anything outside European culture.

My second interview was at Newport College of Further Education, which had a very strong documentary and mixed-media tradition. I thought I would be the first Asian person in Newport, but a community of Somalians had lived there for something like 120 years. There was also a large community of Punjabis in this small Welsh port. It made me feel very good to go and discover a new part of Britain, and to have the possibility of being part of another community which had existed before the 1960s' wave of Asian arrivals which I knew in London. I needed that space, to be out of London and out of my family's reach, to be able to carry on doing what I wanted to do. It was very important – it was my break for independence.

## Q. It seems that much of your work deals with immigration and injustices. How is it grounded into cultural terrains?

After a few months I started to plan a trip to India. Although culturally an Indian I had never set foot on the subcontinent. Armed with a Super-8 camera, sketch-books and diaries, I intended to cover as much as possible.

I had a wonderful time in India and got myself completely lost. I came to terms with being in India and being an Indian. I was completely enthralled and came back with an incredible amount of inspiration and ideas and new formats of working. My work became very inspired by tantric formations and also the architecture of India. I started to make work using only natural materials and hand-made tools.

## Q. How did it affect you, on your return to Great Britain?

At that point I also made a vow not to comb my hair for nine years. I was very involved with Shiva, as a godhead, as a deity. I felt a great deal of empathy and strength with that figure and it all became entwined with my personal life, reflecting the tantric way of life. Prior to that point I had become a vegan and was doing an immense amount of searching which lasted for many years. I had a group of friends, who were outside college, people from the town of Newport. Some wore dreadlocks because of Rastafarianism and some wore dreadlocks for other reasons. I had little to do with traditional society at this point, I was involved with my work and with living an alternative type of life which was reflected in the making of my work.

This was a journey initiated in previous generations; my family were originally Hindu, converting to Islam within reasonable memory. At one point Hinduism, especially Shivism was very, very strong in me, an energy I could not put down. I went to all sorts of places to discover more about Shiva, to discover more about that whole life and what it meant. I went to places like Hardwar, to Benares and I stayed with the sadhus, bathed in the Ganga at four o'clock in the morning on Pooranmasi, which was at full moon, and entered all sorts of rituals. When I was in India I was seen as a saint, a holy man, because of my locks; when I was in Britain I was seen as a troublemaker, because of my locks, some sort of radical, especially in the early eighties (however, locks are now a fashion accessory, worn by fashion designers and musicians). At that time, the late seventies to early eighties, it was very much seen as some sort of anarchic statement, which the white community considered a return to tribalism. It was not my aim to re-create this sense of a passive past. It was very much about integrating a past history which I had links with somehow – and I'm not sure how – within me, and was manifested by making a statement which would tie me to that.

The statement was putting my hair in locks, something which I had vowed to do in India and which resulted in my being pursued by another community when I returned to this country. Rastafarianism was part of that and through this movement I came to know the Caribbean culture very well, while always maintaining my links with my own religion and avoiding becoming involved with Haile Selassie and the cult of the Emperor. I could not believe in the Emperor and his majesty played a very strong role in eighties' Rastafariansm. In a sense I was Other within the Other.

My trips to India were potentially the most shattering experience that I went through. More so than the racism here, because it was an experience which cannot be equalled or repeated – the first time of going back to the culture of origin. It involved, for me, very strong decisions about how those links were going to be maintained. At that time I had not yet conceived the idea of maintaining a link through an archive or an organization or through an art form. It was very much a link through change in direction of the development of the personality. My decision to pursue this direction cut me off from the family, which had to be accepted as I was going through a very individualistic path anyway. I tried to discuss my feelings with my siblings, who were very supportive. They saw my individualism as a facet of the fragmentation which occurred when we came to Britain.

## Q. When did you start making fabric-related art, especially batik?

A friend from a brief spell at Portsmouth Polytechnic introduced me to batik, which is a process using wax and dyes which originated in Asia and Africa. I started experimenting with a fellow sojourner, Carl Clark. We got into a routine together, working all day on our art. It was just about manageable to make small pieces of work in our tiny living place. I found a job in an Indian restaurant and the restaurant owner put a couple of pieces of our work up. Eventually we got an exhibition for the 'One Islington' campaign against racism and were asked to do workshops as part of this at the Central Library. The workshops became very successful and since that day I have never lacked work teaching batik in various capacities in schools, colleges and universities. Also, of course, I was going back and forth to India quite a lot at that time to collect information, inspiring Carl Clark to start going to India. Carl was of part Afro-Caribbean descent and started to make work about his experiences in India, whilst I, an Asian person, was making work about my time in Africa.

After being advised by George Kelly, an elder black artist, that signing on the dole leads to laziness, I stopped signing on and wanted to make a living from my art. Some of my work I made in batik was for sale and some was to make statements about multinationals' involvement in India. I used to work with researchers who would produce textual and photographic information. I made a series of work on the role of Unilever which was later shown at the 3rd Havana Bienalle (Figure 4.1). I also had a one-person show at the Tom Allen Centre in East London, *The Fire and the Garden*, which explored the

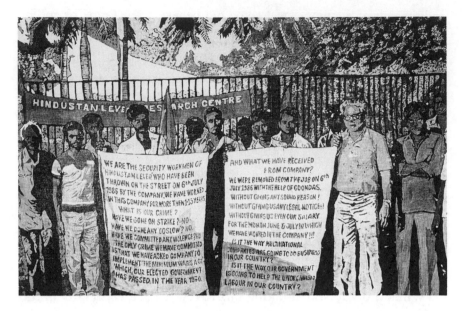

**Figure 4.1** *Shaheen Merali, 1987; 'The Unilever strike', batik on cotton, 6 ×
5 ft. © Shaheen Merali.*

relationship between economics and the misdevelopment of the Third
World. The visual metaphors worked well, but were marginalized due
to the subject matter and the medium employed.

### Q. So in a sense you raised what would normally be a textile or decorative art into a political art form?

That was the good part of it and that is why it was being picked up by
other Asian and African cultural workers, but at the same time the
mainstream galleries, except the Chisenhale Gallery, sidestepped my work.

### Q. What was the first piece of installation you made?

It was for 4 × 4, an exhibition curated by Eddie Chambers, which had
four artists in four galleries, therefore 16 in total. I had been to see
the Tamil refugee centre in Camden and collected a lot of
information from them: photographic information, statements and
press cuttings.

    From this interaction I started working on 'It Pays to Buy Good
Tea', which is a title drawn from the side of a tea chest. The whole
piece was based on the atrocities in Sri Lanka and the role of the
multinational in both the civil rights and civil war situation. I made this
work as a kind

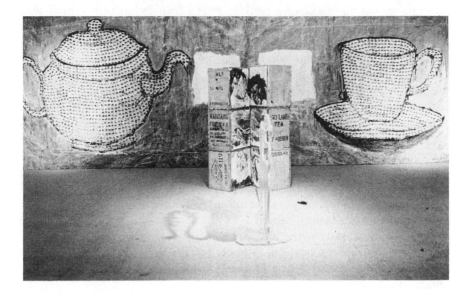

**Figure 4.2** *Shaheen Merali, 1990–1991; 'It pays to buy good tea', sculpture, sound and slide projectors, variable size. © Shaheen Merali.*

of artist/journalist to expose the situation, which I found relevant to my being, not only as an artist but as an Asian (Figure 4.2).

Central to this piece were six tea chests, three a piece, which were stacked like a building and parted. Within the parting were photographs of two children who had been murdered; but they looked like they were sleeping, with dried blood on their faces. In front of that stood a wooden cutout of a yellow lion, which is a symbol on the flag of Sri Lanka, except the lion holds a sword upright and in the installation the sword was thrust downward, as if it could splice open the tea chest to expose the image of war.

This installation was aimed at alerting the audience to the true cost of a cup of tea, because the British and tea are synonymous. It was about looking at the relationship between the British audience and the country of origin of a product. I had a theory that countries are known by their products to the British. The Empire Marketing Board had introduced cultures through their products, things like New Zealand lamb, Ceylon tea or Tanzanian sisal. In this way I was identifying and analysing how countries are known by their economic wealth. It was about making tea, which is a relevant experience for the British, bringing that experience into the work, and then taking it further into where that tea actually originates, and at what cost.

I followed it with three other installations based around the Sri

Lankan war. One was conceived as part of an exhibition which was curated by myself with Allan de Souza, *Crossing Black Waters*. My installation was called 'In Health and Sickness' and was conceived and created at a time when all the hospitals were on alert to accept American soldiers during the Iraq crisis, 'Desert Storm'. There was a whole debate going on with the National Health Service (NHS) and the lack of facilities, so I decided to recreate a hospital ward, and I wanted to use only original furniture from a closing hospital, if possible. I was lucky to know people who worked in a hospital which was being affected by the Tomlinson Report, where whole wards were closed overnight and furniture, often donated by bereaved relatives, was being relegated to the rationalization scrap-heap. I managed to get unwanted beds, lockers and other paraphernalia to do with hospitals and used them for my installation, which was about a ghost ward in which the beds were covered with mosquito nets. These were basically a metaphor for the colonial experience, for the protection from disease only obtainable for those who could afford the bed and the house around it.

The installation worked on different levels. One was the historical notion of the mosquito net, keeping 'the Other' at bay: the colonial shrine, similar to the hoodahs and pallaquins used by rajahs. The metaphor for disease in this piece was the keeping out of refugees of a certain country, out of the NHS, which was supposed to be part of the welfare state – yet it was available for American soldiers fighting in the Gulf. The installation discussed the colonial system which gives its resources to countries it wishes to work with. I projected images, used in the previous installation, onto the hospital bed, thus the photos of the massacred became the patients of my recreated ward, specifically images of people who looked like they were sleeping but were actually dead and deteriorating. I projected them onto the bed in a ghostly remaking of what would happen if refugees were given that space and the health system gave some of its resources.

There was also a sound track of someone breathing; this was my wish for the presence of these refugees to be a reality within our institutions, which are available to help people and to cure them.

The installation was successful in that a lot of people found it scary to enter because it was so realistic and hard-hitting. As well as the sound track, the 'ward' also had the smell of Dettol, a sensation of being in hospital that a lot of the audience were familiar with.

## Q. What considerations do you bring to bear to create links with the audience?

Coming to terms with a British audience, knowing the expectations of a

British audience, creating pieces in museums and galleries so that their visitors can relate to something which is basically from outside Britain, is a huge undertaking – especially when the issue is so serious. It made me feel like an outsider again, this process of creating something from outside their culture.

For instance the next installation I did was for an exhibition called *Trophies of Empire* which was shown at the Arnolfini (Bristol) and the Bluecoat Gallery (Liverpool). The exhibition 'Trophies of Empire' was put together as a response to the quincentennial celebration of Columbus by British artists. Most of the artists were black British and my installation 'Going Native' was about Columbus actually looking for India and Japan. Most artists responded to Columbus 'discovering' the Caribbean and North America. So what I wanted to discuss was Vasco da Gama, who ended up 'discovering' India, and at the same time not just Vasco da Gama, but also contemporary India.

The installation was about tourism and about the beach, the activities of the beach, the local communities, the economic dependencies on the British and Europeans and about tourism being the neo-colonialist arm of colonialism. For the installation I had about 30 deck chairs, covered in white cotton and black and white slide images shot in Goa as well as at the Baghwan Rajneesh centre in Pune; of white people being in India and how they interact in contemporary situations. I had a collection of slides projected onto those deck chairs. I composed a specific piece of music with a young Asian musician, Oni Das, using the sound of the beach and Anglo-Indian popular music. There was also a very large video production, about 20 × 15 ft, of Franciscan monks crossing from right to left on the beach in Goa. They would just keep on coming, invading.

It is a repetitive, seductive installation about the history of Goa and India. I was looking at how Vasco da Gama introduced Christianity to Goa, and I used that as a key into a whole culture and also to the colonial process and an analysis of contemporary tourism. The performative aspect of the piece was that people could sit on the deck chairs to see the video, and therefore the projected images would be projected onto them and they became part and parcel of the whole process – 'Going Native'.

I try and find one very simple symbol within the work which has to jar with the British audience. It was tea in 'It Pays to Buy Good Tea', the mosquito nets in 'Health and Sickness' and the deck chairs in 'Going Native'. These are simple basic metaphors that link their experiences to a wider critique.

**Q. You have been involved in lens-based and new media for a long time now. What does the process involve?**

I have been working for the last two years photographing myself and four other people in my studio. I have something like 500 images on slide. Three of the models are European women and two of the models are Asian men. It began as a discourse on Asian men and European women and their relationship both historically and in contemporary society. This is a biographical piece, in that I am married to a European woman and most of the relationships I have had in the past have been with European women. It was about looking at what that means. I felt that a lot of discourse around sexuality and gender had come from a homosexual perspective within art and theory and very little from heterosexual discourse, especially within a black and Asian perspective. So I wanted to do something about sexuality and about the discourse of relationship between genders. Out of the 500 images I have chosen 15 to be in the exhibition. *Channels, Echoes and Empty Chairs* (Figure 4.3).

Over the last six years I have also been collecting racist objects or objects of stereotype which can be found in flea markets. I am juxtapositioning these two images in a digital collage. Objects like sambos, mammies, Indian rag dolls, Indian Barbie dolls, gollywogs – these are all toys which depict non-European people stereotypically. I have got 15 images of these objects which have been analysed by their place and time of purchase by an astrological computing programme. They have acquired an objective presence through astrological language.

The sound score for this work has been produced in collaboration with the composer Philip Chambon. A sound beam is projected and, whenever it is broken by the audience, a sound is activated on the sampler, so the composition will occur through the audience's reaction to the images. The astrological reading will be within the text. It is about connecting the visual and the sound with another language which has not been drawn upon in contemporary post-modern discourses, yet which has a familiar feeling to most people because they have a link with astrology in newspapers, books and magazines, especially within the Asian subcontinent, where it is part of the religious as well as the political system.

My hope for my work is that, for the first time, critics and curators will look at my work more openly as part of the post-modern discourse, or post-colonial discourse, and that my work will be looked at professionally on a par with people with whom I began my career. This has always eluded me, in part because of the medium I have worked in and the subjects I have explored. I hope that the language and imagery I have employed will have enough substance to activate a

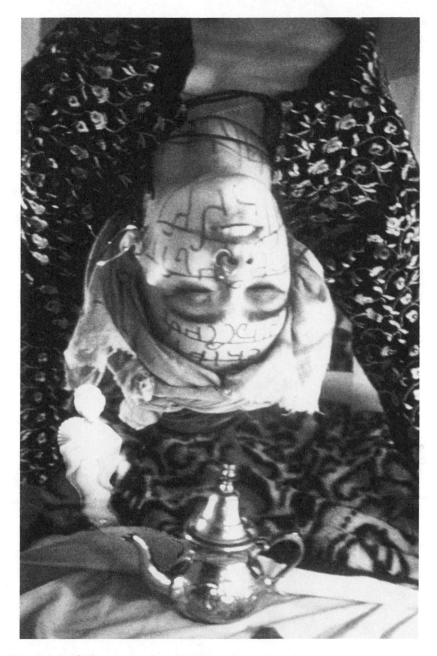

Figure 4.3 *Shaheen Merali, 1993–94; 'Channels, echoes and empty chairs', duratran prints, lightboxes, sound beam, astrological charts and texts, size variable. © Shaheen Merali.*

discourse around them. This is my real dream – not to make a fortune, but for my images to make an impact. I feel that all the components are there and it has been worked on for long enough for it to come together at some point in the future. I remain an optimist.

## Note

1. Clifford, J. (1988) *The Predicament of Culture*, Harvard University Press.

# 5

# *Analysing macro- and microenvironments from a multicultural perspective*

JULIAN AGYEMAN AND PHIL KINSMAN

## Introduction: environment and multiculturalism

Man [*sic*] consciously responds to his environment as he perceives it: the perceived environment will usually contain some but not all of the relevant parts of the real environment, and may well contain elements imagined by man and not present in the real environment ... The real environment ... is seen through a cultural filter, made up of attitudes, limits set by observation techniques and past experience. By studying the filter and reconstructing the perceived environment the observer is able to explain particular options and actions on the part of the group being studied. (Jeans, 1974, p. 36)

Aside from the seemingly gender-specific nature of his observation, one aspect of what Jeans (1974) calls a 'cultural filter' which still remains largely unexplored, is the influence of ethnicity on perceptions and meanings of environment, despite commentaries and critiques of the cultural experience of the environment based on class, gender, nation and religion (Daniels, 1993; Rose, 1993; Lowenthal, 1991; Agyeman, 1995). The multiple meanings of the word 'environment' and their roles in building the environmental movement and constructing environmental organizations has also excluded a variety of groups, including ethnic minority groups in Britain (Agyeman, 1990a).

Since the mid-1980s, however, there has been a developing debate both among black[1] and ethnic minority people who wish to become active within the heritage, environmental and conservation movement,[2] and within this movement itself, concerning the potential for defining or developing a meaningful common ground for these different groups. Black and ethnic minority people have experienced powerful cultural forces which have made both the heritage, environmental and conservation movement and its objects of concern, highly problematic (Agyeman, 1995). These initial encounters have not been painless for the heritage, environmental and conservation movement either, but genuine and meaningful cooperation and an altered level of partici- pation by black and ethnic minority people seems to be developing (Agyeman *et al.*, 1991).

What we intend to do in this chapter is to briefly explore some of the issues which are of concern in these encounters and the scales at which they come into play. We would perhaps also stress that what Jeans (1974) calls a 'cultural filter' is the beginning of an understanding of the complex manner in which environmental perceptions are formed, and that 'the real environment' (Jeans, 1974, p. 36) is a very elusive concept indeed. In many ways it is perhaps as important to disturb settled notions of environment or history by introducing the concerns of black people as it is to search for the real environment or the real history, in order to produce a critical understanding of such concepts which are continuously redeveloped and renegotiated. It is also important to recognize that environmental perceptions are both actively constructed as well as passively received. The recent introduction of ideas of multiculturalism is taking place at a number of levels, within different locations and kinds of spaces, and it is this process which we would like to begin to open out by exploring some of the widely varying ideas and issues which come together under the heading of multiculturalism, heritage and environment.

## Environmentalism, conservation and the language of the natural world

What are the implications of Jeans' (1974) statement in terms of differing perceptions of the environment by different ethnic or cultural groups? There has been little work specifically on this in terms of macroenvironments in the UK, except for those of Agyeman (1989) and Malik (1992) in relation to gaining access to the countryside, and that of Environ (1994) in terms of communicating environmental ideas with the Asian community.

Malik (1992) investigated working-class inner-city white and Asian attitudes towards the countryside, and compared these to suburban middle-class Asian and white attitudes. She found that, whilst both the white and Asian inner-city residents were less likely to use the countryside than their white and Asian suburban counterparts, that is, class was important, there were significant cultural differences. This was especially so in terms of both obtaining information and choosing where to go. Amongst inner-city Asians, word of mouth was a very significant way of obtaining information. In terms of where to go,

Snowdonia and the Lake District were popular with suburban Asians because it reminded them of Indian hill stations.

Environ (1994, p. i) found that amongst Asians in Leicester, 'crime, unemployment, the economy and racism are of the greatest concern, but the environment is firmly on the agenda, particularly the quality of local living space (clean, uncongested streets and pollution free air and water). Asian people are more likely to become involved in initiatives relating to these issues'.

The primary environment of multicultural Britain is the urban or built environment, not the rural one. However, is the urban environment perceived as the 'real' Britain? Lowe (1983, p. 349) notes that 'from the turn of the century period comes an aesthetic and spiritual identity with the wild, strong anti-urban and anti-industrial sentiments, and a sense of stewardship, associated on the one hand with an appreciation of the web of life and its fragile balance, and on the other hand with a patriotic attachment to the indigenous flora and fauna'. The friction between rural, that is, 'native' or indigenous Britain, and urban, that is, 'alien' Britain, is being played out in many arenas, including conservationist discourses about native and alien plants, and in heritage conflicts.

Nicholson (1987–1988, p. 4) assessed conservationists' attitudes to alien plants. He noted that: 'sometimes they are disliked simply because they are "foreign" and therefore out of place in native plant communities'. Wright (1992, p. 6), in discussing conifers in the British landscape, notes that 'they are ... alien imports, plainly lacking the cultural credentials of the native broadleaf' and 'like other immigrants these fir trees all look the same to the affronted native eye'. Fenton (1986, p. 22) is even more direct: 'dislike of alien species is indeed similar to racial discrimination – wanting to preserve the culture and genetic integrity of one's own stock (a natural human failing). Alien species are welcome in strictly defined areas (gardens), but must not be allowed to pollute the native culture (the wider countryside)'.

Journalists, such as Schoon (1992, p. 7) in the *Independent on Sunday*, have attempted to popularize the conservationists' native–alien debate by appealing to peoples' xenophobia. His choice of archaic and pejorative phrases is wide-ranging and unguarded. One can only assume that his sources fed him their own prejudices, which he then adapted into emotional populism.

He talks of 'encroaching foreigners', 'running riot', 'ferocious, fast growing foreign plants', 'the villainous and the benign', 'acceptable aliens', 'staggering penetration', 'ruthlessly ousting the natives', 'pink and green Japanese terror' and plants which 'brutalize the native flora'. This language betrays an abject xenophobia, including a sexual metaphor ('staggering penetration') and is an indication of the depth of feeling (and fear) which the issue raises.

More recently, *Scotland on Sunday* ran an article entitled 'Ethnic cleansing in woods roots out non-Scots pines' in which the Forestry Authority were cutting down trees because it was deemed that they were not 'sufficiently Scottish in origin' (Davidson, 1994). Similarly, the *Independent on Sunday* ran a headline 'Hitler law used against UK oaks' in which it was argued that an EU Directive on Forest Reproductive Material, derived largely from the German Forest Race Law of 1934, ensured that nurseries could 'breed only from perfect and pure-bred examples of a species' (North, 1994, p. 7). Not to be outdone, the *Daily Mail* ran a title 'Beast of the moor is hacked to death' about efforts to halt rhododendron encroachment on British moorlands (*Daily Mail*, 1995). The practice of rhododendron control is euphemized as 'rhodobashing' by some conservationists. Doughty (1978, p. 28) documents the popular comparison between alien plants or animals and human immigrants. He discusses the feelings of Americans to the immigration of the English house sparrow into the US in the nineteenth century and notes that 'sparrows and immigrants had "low morals", reproduced at amazing rates, and appeared to be plotting and conspiring to exploit the United States at the expense of native-born Americans. In contrast, native birds were clean, tidy and hardworking who preferred country living and fulfilled the "yeoman myth"'. Doughty (1978, p. 28) continues by noting that, according to Berrey's *American Thesaurus of Slang*, 'Irishmen were also nicknamed sparrows because they were so numerous and prolific'.

This fear amongst Doughty's Americans is viewed from 'the other side' by Agyeman (1989). He investigated the forces at work in alienating people from ethnic minority groups from the British countryside, including their popular conceptions. The words of the photographer Ingrid Pollard articulate this shared experience of the English countryside: 'it's as if the black experience is only lived in an urban environment. I thought I liked the Lake District, where I wandered lonely as a black face in a sea of white. But a visit to the countryside is always accompanied by a feeling of unease, of dread' (Pollard, 1989).

Niemann (1992, p. 10) summarizes the prevalence of xenophobia in 'environment-speak' when he states that 'properly controlled elsewhere in society, overt racism runs unfettered throughout environment-speak, as we are taught about the need to promote native species and remove aliens which are bad for wildlife'. Yarrow (1994, p. 21) agrees: 'am I the only person to think this is a nonsense, reflecting our island mentality and a politically correct form of xenophobia? Racial and religious discrimination is no longer acceptable, yet substitute 'people' for plants in a sentence such as 'plants of non-local, and especially foreign, origin are no longer acceptable' and you see what I mean.'

## Microenvironments and multiculturalism

In terms of use of microenvironments, such as museums and heritage centres, Merriman (1989a, p. 167), of the Museum of London, notes that (similar to countryside visits), 'museum visiting reflects social divisions in British society, and that cultural barriers which deter certain groups from participating in them lie deep within our socialization process'. In his paper on the *Peopling of London* project, Merriman (1995) argues that, while over 20 per cent of London's population classified itself as belonging to an ethnic minority (1991 Census data), only 4 per cent of the Museum's public could be so classified.

Heritage conflicts with a cultural focus, which effectively delineate the disputed territory between urban multiculturalism and rural monocultures, are becoming frequent. In 1993, the *Guardian* published an article entitled 'In Pursuit of the Suffolk Maharajah' (Bunting, 1993). It provided a fascinating insight into what can only be described as a 'heritage clash' between the villagers of Elveden in Suffolk, and members of the Sikh community in Britain. Since the 1960s Sikhs have been travelling from London, Bradford and the West Midlands to Elveden, to pay homage to the last Sikh Maharajah, Duleep Singh, who, as friend of Queen Victoria and one time owner of Elveden Hall, is buried in the local parish church. He owned the Elveden Estate, where he hosted George V for a shooting weekend and was one of the most prominent individuals in developing driven shooting in Britain in the 1850s and 1860s (Ruffer, 1977). The *Guardian* article explores the contradictory meanings of his burial site for England's Sikh community and the local villagers, and identifies a rural brand of racism. It takes the story, quite appropriately, as an engagement over national identity, and 'a tale for our times' (Bunting, 1993, p. 3).

The centenary of the Maharajah's death was in 1994, and the Sikhs wanted to commemorate it with a carnival in Elveden. Harbinder Singh, a member of the centenary committee, said that the carnival aimed 'to take away this veil of anonymity about our history and get people to realize that the link between the British and the Sikhs is not just as immigrants but as equal partners' (Bunting, 1993, p. 3). The committee offered a sweetener of donations to a local charity of the villagers' choice, a travelling exhibition and the endowment of a chair in local history at the University of East Anglia.

Despite this, the villagers were reluctant to allow the centenary events: 'I have to say the Sikhs are a bit of a nightmare' said one villager; another said that 'they walk all over other graves and leave plastic swords about'. A 22-year-old said: 'I'm not interested in learning about Sikhism' and the chair of the local parish council, who probably speaks for most villagers, said: 'I know very little about Sikhs' (Bunting, 1993, p. 3). Here, the *Guardian* claimed to have identified a particularly rural brand of racism, but also gave the impression that such values and issues were somehow inappropriate to a rural setting. However, this heritage conflict has not been entirely acrimonious, reflecting our earlier contention that a dialogue is developing. Indeed, Duleep Singh's son, Prince Frederick, became a noted local historian in Norfolk and Suffolk, donating his collection of portraits and his library to the Ancient House Museum, Thetford. Norfolk Museums Service co-operated with Harbinder Singh and the centenary committee to commemorate the Maharajah's centenary, and the 70th anniversary of the opening of the Ancient House Museum, also in that year. It is proposed to erect a statue to the Maharajah in Thetford, and the museum produces a leaflet in Punjabi in order to encourage and welcome Sikh visitors.

In both the arenas of environmentalism and heritage/conservationism, deeply felt concerns are expressed in languages which mobilize sentiments drawn from attitudes to race.[3] This is seen in both the anthropomorphism of ecology, where social and cultural values are projected onto the living world, and in the naturalization of the social world where socially constructed categories such as race are made concrete through being seen as natural. As can be seen from the above, the disentangling of these linguistic collisions demonstrates the strength of the bonds between language and its concrete impacts. In addressing such issues, complex relationships are revealed and 'taken for granted' categories are questioned in ways that can be very threatening for people involved in implementing policy or maintaining institutions on a day-to-day basis. It is important to recognize that this is an area where emotions and questions of identity are powerfully at play.

## Black experiences of the landscapes of heritage: the countryside as a macroenvironment

Given the status of people from ethnic minority groups in Britain, there is little sense of 'ownership' in terms of both macro- and microenvironments. This severely limits the sense of ease which people might feel, should they decide to visit such environments.

Access to what is perceived as being 'someone else's' possession (whether it be to the 'macroenvironment' of the countryside or urban greenspace, the 'microenvironment' of a heritage facility or an environmental campaign meeting) comprises both 'physical access',

that is, getting there, with its attendant economic and time requirements, and 'mental' or symbolic access, that is, 'yes, it's for me, I can go
there' (Agyeman, 1995). More fundamentally though, physical access
has to be preceded by mental or symbolic access. In Britain, gaining
mental or symbolic access amongst people from ethnic minority
groups, and others who feel alienated from the mainstream, is difficult,
for the reasons mentioned above.

In visiting the countryside, people from ethnic minority groups can
be seen by locals (and other visitors) as different, unusual. This feeling
does not need to be communicated to people in ethnic minority groups:
it is palpable, and it affects their perception of the countryside. Many
people in ethnic minority groups would wonder why they should go
somewhere where blackness stands out, when the city offers
anonymity, and therefore comfort. As David Dabydeen, the poet,
novelist and academic, commented in a 1992 Anglia TV programme
'Black People White Landscape', 'you don't confront England in the
city'. However, whether the reception of people in ethnic minority
groups on visiting the countryside will invariably be as it is perceived,
that is, hostile and racist, is a matter of conjecture. The start of an
exploration of this issue has come not from the gatekeepers of these
landscapes of leisure, although it has been revealed through their own
research, rather it has come from black people's own experiences and
the various means they have found of articulating them.

One person who has been raising these kind of issues in her work as
an artist is the photographer Ingrid Pollard, who, since the mid-1980s,
has been documenting the sense of unease she experiences in the
countryside, but also how it has a powerful attraction for her and
comprises some of her sense of self. 'Pastoral Interludes' is one of her
best known works which addresses these kinds of issues (Kinsman
1993a, 1995).

The countryside is for her a place of childhood memories and
continued pleasure as an adult, albeit at a high price. Her reasons for
visiting the countryside are much the same as many other people's, for
pleasure and refreshment, and she finds herself identifying with certain
places as she returns to them and develops a sense of intimacy with
them (Kinsman, 1993a, p. 30). However, her experience as a visitor to
various British landscapes has involved racial abuse, expressions of
surprise and shock at her presence there as a black person, intrusive
curiosity at the appearance of her hair (which is in dreadlocks), and
most poignantly in terms of her work, the constant visual attention of
other, white visitors and residents, who look away in embarrassment
when the gaze is returned (Kinsman, 1993a, p. 31). This has resulted in
a greatly heightened sense of visibility for her, even surveillance.

Her personal experiences of the landscapes of Britain have resulted in their becoming 'landscapes of fear', in contrast to the city being a stereotypical contemporary landscape of fear, and despite violence and fear in the countryside having a substantial historical tradition (Tuan, 1980). Her fear is very much a product of a unique combination of circumstances.

It can be partly explained through her experience of the African diaspora, as she has a healthy respect for the rural environment of Guyana, her country of origin. The 'bush' is perceived as a place of danger that you do not venture into unprepared, although it is still an environment that she finds beautiful (Kinsman, 1993a, p. 23). These residual perceptions of rural environments as dangerous or backward go some way towards explaining what has been a collective experience of lack of interest in, or fear of, the English countryside by migrants from less domesticated landscapes (Agyeman, 1989). However, the sense of threat articulated by Ingrid Pollard is not merely due to a received impression of other landscapes: it is the marginal place that black people are ascribed in Britain and the racism that they experience in their daily lives that makes the landscapes which are so powerful within national iconography, insecure spaces for them. It inverts the dominant, presumed 'normal' experience of rural Britain, which has mythologized the countryside as an Eden, resulting in a fear which unquestioning, common-sense categories find hard to acknowledge. The fact that such perceptions seem so strange to white Britons indicates the gulf which exists between white and black experiences of the environment.

Her work is a retelling of black experiences at the collective level, to make black people visible within the daily life of Britain. This expression of collective experience is how her personal experiences are translated into a political artefact. Her sense of identity does not exist at an individualistic level, as she endeavours to represent those with whom she has a collective affinity through the experience of racism.

Although she disavows the idea that her work is about challenging stereotypes or producing ideal images, a stereotypical image of black people in Britain which has come to interest her is that of their being perceived as entirely urban (Kinsman, 1993a, p. 28). Their identity is partly configured by the environments in which they are imagined to be both present and absent. The construction of black identities involves the more localized geographical environments of the urban and the rural as well as the global diaspora. It is not considered part of the black experience to visit the countryside, and if they do decide to go there, black people still face barriers of confidence. She stresses that going to the countryside is a cross-cultural activity; there is a country code that has to be learned, and which proves to be a barrier to black people (Kinsman, 1993a, p. 24). Although there are also very material barriers preventing black people from going to the countryside, much of what impedes them is ideological (Agyeman, 1989, 1995), and part of this is the way black people think about themselves and this issue. She has expressed her desire to challenge stereotypes with her work in terms of a geographical metaphor – 'boundaries shifting' (Kinsman, 1993a, p. 30), making people think again about where different groups of people are located in society.

Through photography, therefore, the landscape has become a means of exploring her identity whereby she is also able in some way to take possession of a space in which she feels insecure (Sontag, 1979). If the act of photography can be seen in some way as an appropriation, then the spaces she has depicted are in some way familiarized for her, and the cost to her of being there is recorded and made known. She is able to say that she has been there, and that, perhaps, is also a means of making these spaces secure.

## Black experiences of the landscapes of heritage: the stately home, the museum and the gallery as microenvironments

Another kind of space that Pollard has more recently begun to explore has been that of the stately home and country park. As a visitor to these kind of places, with a particular kind of knowledge relating to the history of black people within Britain and its imperial experiences, she wonders what might be the hidden histories of the places she visits, which are absent from the tour guides and largely invisible in the physical presence of the houses and gardens (Kinsman, 1993a, p. 30). She shares a concern with David Dabydeen, also from Guyana, who recently presented a series of radio programmes about precisely these kinds of invisible histories, in which Ingrid Pollard also took part.

In some recent photographic work, part of which appeared in *Museums Journal* (Agyeman, 1993), she places images of black people in historical settings such as the Sackville family home of Knole, alongside words which speak of the hidden, erased presence of black people in such places. To accompany the picture of Knole, now a National Trust property, is something from the journal of Vita Sackville-West describing how there was a black page there who 'had always been called John Morocco regardless of what his true name might be' (Agyeman, 1993, p. 23, quoting Sackville-West, 1958).

Pollard is not alone in addressing these kind of issues. She is part of a group of practitioners who have redefined what has been called 'black photography' and who have worked within a number of collective organizations, such as D-Max and Autograph (the Association of Black Photographers) (Gilroy, 1987b; Bailey 1987). They have self-consciously taken on a variety of issues, such as aesthetics, realism and political and theoretical discourses in photography. Another has been the very institutions which present photography and define authorized practice.

David A. Bailey explored these kind of issues during his residency at the Sheffield Museum. He has also done work in the British Museum, which he describes in the following way:

> it is a Brechtian statement on photography in relation to realism, power and knowledge. Lacking the sensitivity of the human eye, the camera fixes an image and removes and preserves it from the flow of images. The image is taken out of its social, historical and spatial context. A photograph of the British Museum is merely an image of the British Museum, whereas the reality of the British Museum is in its history, in the forces and relations of its production and in its political and financial power. It is the combination of these which has enabled the British Museum to appropriate black historical artefacts and treasures and to contain them physically, in the glass cabinets, as well as within a specific ideological discourse – that of British anthropological culture ... However realistic a photograph of the British Museum might be, it will not offer any knowledge of this truth, for we cannot photograph history or social structures. Therefore, the real power of the British Museum hides itself in its visible appearance. (Bailey, 1989a, pp, 35–36)

He has also participated in D-Max and Autograph, as well as in initiatives within the more established arts world, in projects such as INIVA (Institute of New International Visual Arts) and the Arts Council initiative of the 'New Internationalism'. His photographic work has been accompanied by writing, where he has consistently argued that the arts world is exclusive of black artists, and constrains the range of activities in which they are perceived as legitimately participating (Bailey, 1987, 1989b, 1990). With Stuart Hall he co-edited a special issue of the photographic journal *Ten.8* which placed black photography at the centre of the renewal and politicization of photographic practice during the 1980s (Bailey and Hall, 1992). He has actually come to be in a position within the world of photographic and artistic institutions to influence their construction in relation to cultural production by black people, its patronage, presentation and reception.

He has also exhibited alongside Ingrid Pollard under the title of *The Cost of the English Landscape* as part of the 'Beyond Landscape' photography festival in Derby in 1992, contributing pictures about urban landscapes and the representation of black people in such places. This perhaps demonstrates the importance and subtle complexities of the places and spaces in which cultural products appear, and illustrates the special implications when issues of race are involved.

The 'institutional spaces' that photographs occupy have been recognized as a prerequisite for their fuller understanding (Solomon-Godeau, 1990, p. 69). The spaces where photographs are exhibited place them alongside images from other photographic genres, so that the debates of aesthetics and practice carried on elsewhere in writing are played out within the geographical environment.

The aspirations of the 'Beyond Landscape' festival's organizers are illuminating and provocative. The photography festival, according to Hayward (1991, p. 3) aimed to present 'new landscape photography which challenges the conventional notion of what that term means' and to reveal the tensions they clearly perceived between 'our understanding of the landscape of our country and our country.'

> The landscape of Britain, and the way we see it, is changing. The old industrial order has declined and new 'sunrise' industries have developed outside the confines of the city to encroach on greenfield sites. Currently the histories of our industrial and agricultural past are being usurped by a new realm of consumerism in which the lived experience is forgotten in favour of the currency of an imagined cultural heritage. The landscape is no longer a simple site of pleasure, it is a troubled territory for photographer and visitor alike. (Hayward, 1991)

This paragraph, from the introduction to the programme, seems to have the work of photographers like Ingrid Pollard and David A. Bailey very much in mind, which questions the concepts of nation and landscape, although it still conflates the countryside and landscape, hinting at an oppositional relationship between an authentic old industrial order and an inauthentic post-industrial one. It also has a conservationist tone which leans away from more radical ideas about the landscape.

The relative locations of their work in what was described as a 'city-wide' festival are revealing (Hayward, 1991). Ingrid Pollard's work, under the title of 'The Cost of the English Landscape', was shown at the Derby African and Caribbean Arts Centre in Rosehill, some way out of the city centre. Whether this would have deterred those likely to be interested in art/exhibition photography cannot be said, but it could seem to indicate a strong bracketing of the subject, the photographers and their assumed audience, as well as potentially peripheralizing the exhibition. The choice may have been the result of constraints in finding venues, but the other exhibitions were concentrated around the city centre, and the centrepiece of the festival, the John Blakemore retrospective, was shown in the more hushed surroundings of the Derby Museum and Art Gallery. This was no doubt due to his appeal as an internationally recognized landscape photographer and his status as a local artist, but the content of his work seemingly presents less disturbing ideas to its audience (Kinsman, 1993b).

It is in ways such as these that microenvironments (stately homes, museums and galleries) actually affect the meanings of the objects, artefacts, images and messages they display, through the environments they create and the meanings which are shared about them. Objects are transformed according to this level of their contextual setting. Such spaces of representation have a microgeography which contributes partly to the perceived exclusivity of these cultural experiences, and have been the subject of attempts of control and manipulation by the bodies which govern such places. These spaces have actually been described and discussed by black critics in the US and UK as 'white', i.e. exclusive, and the need for alternative, 'black' (or multicultural) spaces, has been articulated (Araeen and Chambers, 1988; Chambers, 1991). There are a number of potential dilemmas and opportunities which this problematic situation of defining spaces offers to museums and galleries; either segregation, a thorough-going and non-tokenistic multiculturalism, or maintenance of the status quo.

This is but one aspect of the influence gallery and museum spaces have upon the materials they present, but one which is increasingly pressing for such institutions as they seek to become more responsive to the populations they serve. Therefore, these issues will not be resolved simply by introducing more exhibitions which are thought to be relevant to black people, but require a more meaningful presence of black artists, curators and decision-makers within these institutions.

The representation of history is an international concern for black people, because it is in spaces such as stately homes, museums, galleries and heritage parks that history is dramatized and its meanings are contested, as well as being very popular locations of leisure activity. These ideas concerning the current situation of black people within the artistic environment have been more extensively developed in the US (Berger, 1990; Failing, 1989), where there have been exhibitions and attendant publications drawing attention to the presence of black people in Western art, and in particular American art (Honour, 1989; McElroy, 1990). These issues are an international concern for black people. Yet despite a vigorous debate in Britain over the nature of what has been called 'black art' and over black artists' relationships to their viewing audiences, to artistic institutions and to their perceived constituencies (Araeen and Chambers, 1988; Chambers, 1991; Gilroy, 1988, 1989), such issues are only just beginning to have an impact on the presentation of the arts, heritage and history at a grassroots institutional level.

## Ethnic minority participation/visitor rates in macro- and micro-environments

Reasons for the under-representation of people from black and ethnic minority groups in macro- (Agyeman, 1989; Malik 1992) and microenvironments (Merriman, 1989b) can be linked, as we have shown, to the global black diaspora and the appropriation of black lives and their history into 'white' spaces in what is now a post-colonial Britain.

However, other factors, such as the cost of such visits, whether (and where) they are advertised, positive imagery and consultation and whether such leisure/educational activities fall within the range of activities which are perceived as appropriate or relevant to black people, also need to be considered.

In terms of countryside visits, Agyeman (1989) questions the role of cost in barring access to the countryside. He argues that cost may be significant in terms of getting out of inner London, but that many ethnic minority communities live in smaller cities and towns, often in outer urban estates, which may be close to urban fringe sites, such as country parks. The Bolton Initiative (1993, p. 3), a Countryside Commission-funded project which was set up to 'gain a dispassionate understanding of the attitudes of Bolton's minority communities to their local countryside and to establish demand for focused events and information designed to improve their awareness and confidence in enjoying the countryside', is a case in point. The Moses Gate Country Park is 'on the doorstep of many ethnic minority families, with easy access by public transport' (p. 6) yet, prior to the initiative, few if any ethnic minority families used the site. Clearly, other factors are of greater importance.

Agyeman (1990b) and Malik (1992) have emphasized the importance of whether, where and how information about the local countryside is advertised. Agyeman (1990b, p. 3) questions 'how many people from black or ethnic minority groups read or even know of the existence of *Countryside Commission News* or similar publications? Why not publicize them in youth clubs, community centres and in the widely read black press?' Malik (1992) highlights the importance of word-of-mouth contact for Asians from lower socio-economic groups.

Agyeman (1990b, p. 3) develops the theme of positive imagery in relation to countryside access. He argues that the Countryside Commission 'could help to ensure that more (some?) black staff are employed and trained in roles which are visible to the public and at a decision-making level' and that 'it could put forward positive images of black and ethnic minority groups in the countryside'.

Consultation, and whether such activities fall within the range of activities which are perceived as 'appropriate' or 'relevant' to black people, also needs to be considered. The Bolton Initiative (1993, p.6) found that 'when black people get together to do typical white customs they are a source of amusement and spectacle'. This is, however, not necessarily always true in terms of countryside access. Several ethnic minority cultures do view countryside access and picnics as a tradition.

In terms of microenvironments, especially museums, and specifically the Museum of London, Merriman (1995) notes that 'one of the reasons for this (low ethnic minority participation rate) was the fact that there is hardly any mention of the city's long history of cultural diversity in the permanent galleries, and in particular, there is currently no post-war gallery. Thus there was no real incentive for anyone from an ethnic minority community to visit the museum, as their history had no place in the story of London presented there. Clearly the museum was failing to address the needs of up to a fifth of its potential constituency.' Merriman continues that, in terms of consultation, 'involving the communities themselves as much as possible' is vitally important. This is a point that Agyeman (1993, p. 23) has emphasized. He argues: 'imagine, however, that black British heritage ... was not overlooked and abused; that it was portrayed positively and marketed in collaboration with those who are presently excluded. Aside from the moral rectitude of such a policy, the revenue implications for Britain's ailing stately homes, monuments and other heritage facilities, including museums, would be significant'.

## Conclusions

There is clear evidence, despite exhortations to the contrary from the gatekeepers of heritage and 'environmental access' (to the countryside or environmental organizations), that people from black and ethnic minority groups are still infrequent users (Merriman, 1989b; Agyeman, 1989; Malik, 1992). However, there are young black people, who, in the course of their current education, are being drawn to issues of heritage, environment and conservation. Some will emerge in the future as environmental, conservation and heritage professionals; others will own them as leisure activities and personal concerns. This has already happened to a small extent, and can only increase in the future. The publication of a book such as this is a welcome part of this process of change. It is imperative that responsible contributions are made in defining the spaces where such different and varied groups can meet and continue to develop a meaningful exchange of perspectives.

## Notes

1. The term 'black' is used in this paper to denote people of indigenous African, Afro-Caribbean and Asian descent, and therefore as a political grouping rather than as a racial signifier (Miles, 1989). The term 'ethnic minority' is used in a similar way.
2. What we have referred to as the heritage, environmental and conservation movement should not be seen as a singular and distinct organization. Rather it is a large number of groups with seemingly diverse, overlapping and sometimes contradictory interests and methods, but which have in some way offered a shared experience for black and ethnic minority people in that they have been largely excluded from them. In thinking of the ideas of museums and the presentation of history, for example, the concerns of the curators and administrators of museums have broadened out over the past 20 years to encompass the preservation and appropriate presentation of entire landscapes and settlements, as seen in heritage centres all over the world. The coalescence of the interests of traditional museums, conservation groups and environmental organizations cannot be ignored.
3. Race is a concept fraught with conceptual difficulties and will be treated here as an 'essentially contested concept' (Gallie, 1962). It is now widely held to be a meaningless category, a second-order abstraction that uses phenotypical variation to ascribe status and roles rather than allow their achievement (Banton, 1983, p. 8). This does not mean, however, that it can simply be dismissed, as it is an elaborately constructed ideology which releases powerful political forces, and it is the very emptiness of racial signifiers which makes them vulnerable to appropriation, and their contradictions which give them power (Gilroy, 1987a, pp. 38–40). As a concept it has a particular history and geography (Banton, 1977, 1983; Livingstone, 1992a,b), which is mutable and contested within specific locations and times (Poliakov, 1971; MacDougall, 1982; Barkan, 1992). It is emphasized here that race is a relative and negotiated process which takes black people outside history, constructing them as problems or victims, paradoxically by reworking past images and ideas within a new context (Gilroy, 1987a, pp. 27, 44–69).

## References

Agyeman, J. (1989) Black people, white landscapes, *Town and Country Planning*, 58(12), 336–338.

Agyeman, J. (1990a) Mind your language, *New Ground*, Summer, 20.

Agyeman, J. (1990b) A positive image, *Countryside Commission News*, 45, September/October, 3.

Agyeman, J. (1993) Alien species, *Museums Journal*, 93(12), 22–23.

Agyeman, J. (1995) Environment, heritage and multiculturalism, *Interpretation: a Journal of Heritage and Environmental Interpretation*, 1(1), 5–6.

Agyeman, J., Warburton, D. and Wong, J.L. (1991) *The Black Environment Network Report: Working for Ethnic Minority Participation in the Environment*, BEN, London.

Araeen, R. and Chambers, E. (1988) Black art: a discussion, *Third Text: Third World Perspectives on Contemporary Art and Culture*, 5, 50–77.

Bailey, D.A. (1987) D-Max, *Ten.8*, 27, 38–41.

Bailey, D.A. (1989a) From essential black subject to cultural black subject(s): exploring the photographic practices of Rotimi Fani-Kayode, Ingrid Pollard and Maxine Walker, in *US/UK Photography Exchange Catalogue*, Camerawork, London.

Bailey, D.A. (1989b) The black subject at the centre: repositioning black photography, in M. Reeves and J. Hammond (eds), *Looking Beyond the Frame: Racism, Representation and Resistance*, Links Publications, Oxford.

Bailey, D.A. (1990) Photographic animateur: the photographs of Rotimi Fani-Kayode in relation to black photographic practices, *Third Text: Third World Perspectives on Contemporary Art and Culture*, 13, 57–62.

Bailey, D.A. and Hall, S. (1992) Critical decade: an introduction, in D.A. Bailey and S. Hall (eds), Critical Decade: Black British Photography in the 80s, *Ten.8*, 21(3), 4–7.

Banton, M. (1977) *The Idea of Race*, Tavistock, London.

Banton, M. (1983) *Racial and Ethnic Competition*, Cambridge University Press, Cambridge.

Barkan, E. (1992) *The Retreat of Scientific Racism: Changing Concepts of Race in Britain and the United States between the World Wars*, Cambridge University Press, Cambridge.

Berger, M. (1990) Are art museums racist?, *Art in America*, September, 68–77.

Bolton Initiative (1993) *An Evaluation of the Project by Bolton College for the Countryside Commission*, Bolton College.

Bunting, M. (1993) In pursuit of the Suffolk Maharajah, *The Guardian*, 3 March, pp. 2–3.

Chambers, E. (1991) Black art now, *Third Text: Third World Perspectives on Contemporary Art and Culture*, 15, 91–96.

*Daily Mail* (1995) Beast of the moor is hacked to death, 6 January.

Daniels, S. (1993) *Fields of Vision: Landscape Imagery and National Identity in England and the United States*, Polity Press, Cambridge.

Davidson, H. (1994) Ethnic cleansing in woods roots out non-Scots pines, *Scotland on Sunday*, 30 October.

Doughty, R. (1978) The English sparrow in the American landscape: a paradox in nineteenth century wildlife conservation, *Research papers 19*, School of Geography, Oxford.

Environ (1994) *The Asian Community and the Environment – Towards a Communications Strategy*, Environ Research Report 16, Environ, Leicester.

Failing, P. (1989) Black artists today: a case of exclusion, *ARTnews*, 88, 124–131.

Fenton, J. (1986) Alien or native? *ECOS*, 7 (2), 22–30.

Gallie, W.B. (1962) Essentially contested concepts, in M. Black (ed), *The Importance of Language*, pp. 121–146, Prentice-Hall, Englewood Cliffs, NJ.

Gilroy, P. (1987a) *There Ain't no Black in the Union Jack: the Cultural Politics of Race and Nation*, Hutchinson, London.

Gilroy, P. (1987b) Introduction, in *D-Max: photographs* (exhibition catalogue), Ikon Gallery, Birmingham.

Gilroy, P. (1988) Nothing but sweat inside my hand: diaspora aesthetics and black arts in Britain, *Black Film, British Cinema: ICA Documents 7*, pp. 44–46, ICA Documents, London.

Gilroy, P. (1989) Cruciality and the frog's perspective: an agenda of difficulties for the Black Arts movement in Britain, *Third Text: Third World Perspectives on Contemporary Art and Culture*, 5, 33–44.

Hayward, L. (1991) Introduction, in *Beyond Landscape* (exhibition catalogue).

Honour, H. (1989) *The Image of the Black in Western Art:* Vol. iv, *From the American Revolution to World War I*; part 1, *Slaves and Liberators*, Harvard University Press, Cambridge, MA.

Jeans, D. (1974) Changing formulations of the man–environment relationship in Anglo-America geography, *Journal of Geography*, 73(3), 36–40.

Kinsman, P. (1993a) Landscapes of national non-identity: the landscape photography of Ingrid Pollard, *Working Paper 17*, University of Nottingham, Department of Geography.

Kinsman, P. (1993b) Photography, geography and identity: the landscape imagery of John Blakemore, *The East Midland Geographer*, 16(2), 17–26.

Kinsman, P. (1995) Landscape, race and national identity: the photography of Ingrid Pollard, *Area*, 27(4), 300–310.

Livingstone, D.N. (1992a) 'Never shall ye make the crab walk straight': an inquiry into the scientific sources of racial geography, in F. Driver and G. Rose (eds) *Nature and Science: Essays in the History of Geographical Knowledge*, Historical Geography Research Group Series, Vol. 28, pp. 37–48.

Livingstone, D.N. (1992b) *The Geographical Tradition*, Blackwell, Oxford.

Lowe P. (1983) Values and institutions in British nature conservation, in A. Warren and F.B. Goldsmith (eds) *Conservation in Perspective*, Wiley, Chichester.

Lowenthal, D. (1991) British national identity and the English landscape, *Rural History*, 2(2), 205–230.

MacDougall, H.A. (1982) *Racial Myth in English History: Trojans, Teutons and Anglo-Saxons*, Harvest House, Montreal.

Malik, S. (1992) Colours of the countryside – a whiter shade of pale, *ECOS*, 13(4), 33–40.

McElroy, G.C. (1990) *Facing History: the Black Image in American Art, 1710–1940*, Bedford Arts/The Corcoran Gallery of Art, New York.

Merriman, N. (1989a) The social basis of museum and heritage visiting, in S. Pearce (ed.) *Museum Studies and Material Culture*, Leicester University Press, Leicester.

Merriman, N. (1989b) Museum visiting as a cultural phenomenon in P. Vergo (ed.), *The New Museology*, Reaktion Books, London.

Merriman, N. (1995) The peopling of London project, *Museum International* No. 187, 47(3), 12–16.

Miles, R. (1989) *Racism*, Routledge, London.

Nicholson, B. (1987/1988) Native versus alien, *London Wildlife Trust Magazine*, Winter issue.

Niemann, D. (1992) A greater community for conservation, *The Wildlife Trust Magazine* (Beds and Cambs Wildlife Trust), 5, 10.

North, R. (1994) Hitler law used against UK oaks, *Independent on Sunday*, 20 November.

Poliakov, L. (1971) *The Aryan Myth: a History of Racist and Nationalist Ideas in Europe*, trans. Edmund Howard, Chatto/Heinemann, London.

Pollard, I. (1989) Pastoral interludes, *Third Text: Third World Perspectives on Contemporary Art and Culture*, 7, 41–46.

Rose, G. (1993) *Feminism and Geography: the Limits of Geographical Knowledge*, Polity Press, London.

Ruffer, J.G. (1977) *The Big Shots: Edwardian Shooting Parties*, Debrett-Viking Press.

Schoon, N. (1992) The barbarians in Britain's back yards, *Independent on Sunday*, 17 May.

Solomon-Godeau, A. (1990) Living with contradictions: critical practices in the age of supply-side aesthetics, in C. Squiers (ed.) *The Critical Image: Essays on Contemporary Photography*, pp. 59–79, Lawrence and Wishart, London.

Sontag, S. (1979) *On Photography*, Penguin, Harmondsworth.

Tuan, Y.F. (1980) *Landscapes of Fear*, Basil Blackwell, Oxford.

Wright, P. (1992) Lexicon of life for the common man, *The Guardian*, 4 July.

Yarrow, C. (1994) Make our flora multiracial, *Horticultural Week*, 16 June, p. 21.

# 6

## Speaking other voices

### HELEN COXALL

Until the lions have their historians, tales of hunting will always glorify the hunter.

This African proverb highlights the difficulty faced by Western museum curators when making exhibitions about cultures that are not their own. Recently, there have been many examples of exhibitions whose staff have tried to overcome this perceptual difficulty – some more successfully than others.

The controversial exhibition, *Into the Heart of Africa*, which opened in 1989 at the Royal Ontario Museum (ROM), Toronto, drew attention to several key areas of difficulty. The exhibition, which displayed items borrowed from other museums and many from the ROM itself, was seen by its curator as celebrating 'the rich cultural heritage of African religious, social and economic life' (Cannizzo, 1989, p. 62). The curator's purpose was to criticize colonialism, missionaries, collectors and museums. However, by giving a platform to the colonialists (albeit an ironical one) without a comparable one to the Africans, this implicit intention was misunderstood. In fact, it appeared to some sections of the audience to be examining the impact that colonialism had on Africa through the eyes of colonial Canadian missionaries. According to Schildkrout (1991, pp. 16–23) the museum embarked on the project without undertaking an appropriate public relations programme with Canadians of African descent, or approaching their African historians for contributions and advice. The unfortunate result was that Africans were seen by many as passive recipients of colonial oppression: as victims without a voice.

Conversely, at the Museum of London, when embarking on the temporary exhibition, *Peopling of London*, the curator appointed a freelance black researcher onto the staff. Her efforts made a considerable difference to the co-operation received – in the form of support, information and exhibits – from the 19 different ethnic groups involved. The very extensive programme of performances and seminars, which involved members from many of the groups, was an extremely important part of the exhibition and an African artist-in-residence was employed during the time that the exhibition was running. The catalogue consisted of a collection of essays written mostly (although not entirely) by members of the groups they were writing about. *Peopling of London* was not a permanent exhibition. However, the museum is now committed to further representing all the communities in London in its permanent collections, which would suggest that the time has come to appoint permanent, rather than temporary, staff representative of this cultural diversity. Several reviews and evaluations have already been written about these and other similar exhibitions, some of which are included in this publication. I want to concentrate on the somewhat neglected area of the special importance of exhibition text to this kind of exhibition.

It is vitally important that curators are aware of the significance of what they choose to say and what they choose to leave out, and of the implications in the words they use to tell other people's stories because:

> We see and hear and otherwise experience very largely as we do because the language habits of our community predispose certain choices of interpretation. (Sapir, 1941, pp. 75–93)

As children we are taught the language of our family which is already shaped with ways of saying that denote attitudes and value judgements that are specific to our community and culture. When we use these words we speak those preconceptions innocently – that is without being aware of them, so incorporated are they into our knowledge of our language as 'common sense' assumptions. I would contend, along with Roland Barthes and many others, that there is no such thing as 'common sense': perceptions of it vary and are even diametrically opposed, depending upon where we are coming from (by this I mean where we come from culturally, educationally, philosophically, politically, economically and geographically). In other words, rather than universal 'common sense', such assumptions are examples of ideologies that denote power relations within our particular cultural group. Curators of exhibitions about cultures not their own would be well advised to remember that language itself is a source of power that contributes to ideological domination. Implicit in this premise is the understanding that language is a site for the negotiation and renegotiation of meanings by readers/visitors, and different visitors will read meanings differently depending on where they, too, are coming from.

> There isn't a single theory about the way the world works, and just as crucially and relatedly, there isn't a single theory about the way language

means. Following on from Derrida, there is no such thing as *the* single meaning, the *correct* meaning, the *right* meaning. There are many meanings associated with many theories of reality. (Birch, 1989, p. 25)

I will return to the issue of differing interpretations in a moment, but I want to look briefly at the linguistic classification of reality embedded in one crucial word that is central to the subject of this essay – the ways in which Western museums articulate 'Other' peoples cultures. In this context I am using the term 'Other' to indicate any culture that is likely to be misrepresented if seen from a purely Eurocentric perspective. Eurocentric visions of the world are not restricted to the interpretation of cultures situated geographically at a distance from the country in which the museum is situated. In fact, the people whose culture museums represent are often resident in the same country as the museum itself. One example of such an exhibition, *Peopling of London*, has already been mentioned.

The term 'Other' indicates a fixed perspective on cultures, that is, it implies that any culture that is not the speaker/writer's own is classified simply according to its difference. This traditional, often colonial, way of seeing the world persists – in some cases unconsciously, so deeply embedded is it into shared consciousness – in the minds of Europeans in general, and museum curators in particular.

Edward Said's work in *Orientalism* and *Culture and Imperialism* draws attention to Eurocentric supremacist notions of measuring all cultures that are not Western as being 'Other', as if Western culture were the norm and anything else a mutation. In an essay 'The text, the word, the critic', he said:

Monocentrism is practiced when we mistake one idea as the only idea, instead of recognizing that an idea in history is one among many. Monocentrism denies plurality, it totalizes structure, it sees profit where there is waste, it decrees the concentricity of Western culture instead of its eccentricity, it believes continuity to be given and will not try to understand instead how continuity as much as discontinuity is made. (Said, 1979, p. 188)

However, a recognition of the concept of 'Otherness' has a deeper significance than an acceptance that people have different perceptions of the world and different ways of talking about themselves. It is as well to remember that the practice of measuring people against a fixed perception of identity can be motivated by a feeling of paranoia and threat to individual identities: the extreme outcome being xenophobia. Xenophobia is born out of such unacknowledged fear of the unknown that has progressed into a projection of that perceived threat into fierce animosity against individuals.

Even more fundamentally, the Eurocentric concept of 'Otherness' assumes the existence of 'pure' cultures – that people can be identified in a stereotypical way as representative of their specific cultures historically. In Britain today this perception is far from valid. As Homi Bhabha points out, our multicultures have influenced each other, making strict divisions no longer possible. English people born and brought up outside England could easily find themselves less at ease with contemporary British culture than people of African or Asian descent born and brought up in Britain. And people of African and Asian descent who have never lived anywhere other than Britain often feel themselves to belong neither to the culture of their parents/ grandparents nor to that of Britain, but to an evolved culture influenced by both, and by others as well.[1] And yet Western notions still persist in labels which are predominantly based on visual differences.

To return to the premise that different audiences re-interpret meanings differently, Valentin Volosinov said:

> Orientation of the word towards the addressee [reader/audience] has an extremely high significance. In point of fact, *word is a two-sided act*. It is determined equally by *whose* word it is and *for whom* it is meant. . . . A word is a bridge thrown between myself and another. If one end of the bridge depends on me then the other depends on my addressee. (Volosinov, 1973, p. 86; my emphasis)

Thus it is clearly problematic for writers (in this case of exhibition text) to write without an audience in mind because there is no such thing as a hypothetical audience. 'Real readers . . . are living people; social beings with different backgrounds, different contexts in which they read or view texts . . . . *Text as meaning is produced at the moment of reading, not at the moment of writing*' (Meinhof, 1994, p. 213; my emphasis).

Meanings made at the moment of reading may not be those intended by the writer. In a society where such a variety of cultures and sub-cultures receive mass-mediated messages this is inevitable. The intended and 'dominant' reading of a text is one that seems to be self-evident or 'common sense' to the majority culture based on shared values, knowledges and ways of saying. However, readers who do not accept the dominant reading will negotiate a compromise or construct a completely 'resistant' (oppositional) reading. For example, for many years Nelson Mandela was labelled by the previous regime in South Africa as a *terrorist*, whereas those he represented, and many other people too, made a resistant reading of that word as they perceived him to be a *freedom fighter*. Stuart Hall gives the example of a possible oppositional reading of the term *in the national interest* as used frequently in the press, as to be a euphemism for *class interest*.[2]

These are very extreme examples, however it is precisely because of the potential for resistant readings that museum staff and advisors can, quite innocently, and with the best of intentions, put together a proposal for an exhibition that is destined to be taken for granted as a 'true picture' by themselves and the majority of their audience, whilst being interpreted as yet another example of Western supremacist attitudes by the very group of people whose history the exhibition intends to deal with. As Moira Simpson wrote in the *Museums Journal* after controversy over Christopher Columbus quincentenary exhibitions in Canada: 'From bitter experience, museum curators in Canada and the United States are becoming increasingly aware of the need to be more sensitive and responsive to the views of those whose culture is being represented' (Simpson, 1992, p. 31). Homi Bhabba quotes Clifford Geertz as saying that the experience of understanding other cultures is 'more like grasping a proverb, catching an illusion, seeing a joke, than it is like achieving communion' (Geertz, 1983, p. 70). The need to work closely with advisors of the cultures being represented is clearly crucial and is the concern of other essays in this publication.

Research into communication with audiences in the media highlights the need for acceptance that there is no such thing as a passive, hypothetical audience. Audiences are diverse and demanding. If people produce meanings that are directly influenced by their own social and cultural history, they will reject anything that has no direct relevance to them. That is not to say that writers/exhibition organizers should strive to include all possible audiences, but that they should be much more aware of their potential audiences, because it is not possible for any writer to assume an audience of singular culture any more than it is possible to assume uniform gender or age. Many visitor surveys have found that few Asians or Afro-Caribbeans visit museums.[3] However, exhibitions about these peoples' histories are likely to be an exception and require very close attention to their ways of saying.

## Transatlantic slavery: against human dignity

In order to illustrate some of the issues that arise when writing such museum text I want to examine some examples of texts written for 'Transatlantic Slavery: against Human Dignity', which opened at the Merseyside Maritime Museum, Liverpool, in October 1994, for which I acted as language advisor.

I would like to thank the Maritime Museum for their permission to use these working texts to illustrate the process of writing texts for exhibitions which attempt to speak other voices and hope, together with the curator, that this information will help others to short-cut some of the difficulties encountered on the way by the exhibition team.

Producing text panels for such an exhibition was a daunting task for the curators for several reasons: first, they were not themselves of the culture being represented; second, the high expectations generated by the need – long overdue – to tell a politically sensitive story that had not previously been fully related either in schools or in museums in Britain; third, the limiting expectations of the sponsor; fourth, the pressure of conflicting demands of advisory groups; fifth, the large numbers of writers involved. There were 11 guest curators (both black and white historians) engaged to write the texts, all of whom were knowledgeable in their fields but only one of whom was familiar with writing museum text. Professional copywriters, advisors and, of course, the exhibition staff, were also involved.

It is not my purpose to discuss these issues in detail. I cite them only as examples of the many factors that can influence exhibition-making in general and text-writing in particular – indeed they can be seen reflected quite clearly in the various drafts of the texts of this particular exhibition. With exhibitions of this nature it is clearly not advisable to leave the writing of information until last, and the exhibition staff of 'Transatlantic Slavery' were well aware of the importance of the textual information to this exhibition. The texts went through several stages. First, the exhibition briefs: two draft briefs were drawn up after discussion with the 11 guest curators/writers. The preferred one was edited seven times after discussion with advisors. Second, the exhibition text: the guest curators produced researched essays about the individual topics outlined in the brief. Third, this material was edited into the form of draft summaries by curators. Fourth, professional copywriters reduced the information into panel-sized format. Fifth, these panels were further edited and shortened by museum staff. Sixth and last, the final information panels were written after consultation with guest curators and advisors.

## Exhibition briefs

Exhibition briefs are vitally important because they define the intended aims of any exhibition at the outset. Briefs/guidelines that a museum works with, and the language that is used in them, will define a reading of history. Writers will just go away and write the section they have been requested to write. After consultation with advisors the overall aims of the exhibition, therefore, have to be absolutely clear in the minds of the museum staff first of all – as does their own reading of the history involved. When they are clear, they can be written into the brief and the resultant texts will reflect these attitudes and intentions.

An ability to regard the subject from the viewpoint of those whose history is being told is essential when writing a brief. In the case of

'Transatlantic Slavery' the necessity for the focus to be people-centred as opposed to trade-centred is self-evident as these two positions have close correlation with being Afrocentric as opposed to Eurocentric. Difficulties in the focus with this kind of exhibition often occur at this early stage and can result from several sources. Insufficiently considered language use and gaps in the story over politically sensitive areas are prime causes. A lack of awareness of the relevance of seeing the story being told in the context of the people's previous histories – not just as an isolated episode – is another. The compartmentalization of issues into separated topics allows cause to be separated from effect and the fragmentation, or even complete loss of the reality of the people's experience. All of these issues have direct implications on opportunities for the articulation – or conversely – for the suppression of voices in an exhibition.

I would suggest that a crucial factor in 'getting it right' lies with the implications of the details curators decide to leave out. Issues that are referred to briefly in passing or not mentioned at all can send a message about a preferred reading of history. Obviously space is a limiting factor and no exhibition ever seems to have enough – especially for the texts – because too much text can simply put people off. So the decision about what to leave out when shortening information to fit a panel-sized format is crucial. In the light of these observations I am going to trace the progress of selected topics through different stages of development to the final exhibition panels.

## Placing the peoples discussed in the context of their own and world history

### Guest curator's first draft

The general sequence of African history as slavery, followed by colonialism then independence is undoubtedly a misrepresentation and distortion of the defensible facts.

An array of political arrangements emerged in the constellation of African civilizations. These included the earliest nation-state in human history, Kemet (the Egypt of the Pharaohs) in the Nile Valley region of North East Africa. It is from this region that most of the various nationalities in West Africa claim their descent, and where, as science confirms, human life began.

The variety of political arrangements that emerged in West Africa included city-states, kingdoms and territorial federations. Significant amongst these were Akan, Bambara, Dohomey, Hausa, Ngola, Mossi and Yoruba states. Moreover, literate and well-recorded empires emerged in West Africa which cemented inter-ethnic relations and formed large federations from diverse nationalities; some of which were as large in size as the entire Western Europe. The most noted of these Empires were Guana, Mali, Songai and Karnem-Bornu.

This curator also wrote about the people's expertise in medicine, literacy, science and technology, mathematics and languages. He also wrote about accounts by Christopher Columbus himself that recorded the presence of Africans in America upon his arrival, and discussed archaeological evidence of African presence in ancient and medieval Honduras, Mexico and other places in South America: 'The bulk of these were unearthed between the 1880s and the present century, many of which were found at the very centre of the Olmec civilization.'

## Reduced text at first draft stage

The reduced text refers to trading between kingdom states before the advent of the slave trade. It also acknowledges that many different languages were spoken, literacy was encouraged, and writing, mathematics and medicine flourished. Also it adds that:

> Africans had travelled to America in the 14th century; archaeology attests their presence, while Columbus himself records encountering black merchants from West Africa in the Caribbean.

This text also identifies that the kingdom-states of Mali, Benin and Kongo were large and powerful, with elaborate monarch-led political structures governing hundreds of thousands of subjects.

Although the text is considerably shortened, the issues from the original text are covered. However, the origins of human life on earth have been left out, as has the significance of ancient Egypt (Kemet), which preceded Ancient Greece – which Europeans have hitherto regarded as the seat of civilized culture. The implications of these omissions are very significant both to the historical perspective on Africa and the deletion of information about which little is known in the West.

## Final text

The final text takes great care to identify the expertise of the West Africans prior to slavery, mentioning art, learning, technology, medicine, mathematics and astronomy. It adds information about specific trade goods that the copywriter's text had not mentioned:

> As well as domestic goods they made very fine ivory, gold and terracotta for local use and for trade.

This text also describes the political arrangements, including the kingdoms and city-states, and goes on to say:

> The empire of Songhai and the kingdoms of Mali, Benin and Kongo were large and powerful with monarchs heading complex political structures governing hundreds of thousands of subjects.

Although it could be argued that the omission of the meaningful size comparison between these states and Western Europe makes the text less graphic, the meanings are still present. However, not only have the previous omissions with regard to human origins and Ancient Egypt been upheld, but the reference to Africans' presence in America before Columbus has also been deleted. What remains of all references to their previous history is this one sentence:

> The people of West Africa had a rich and varied history and culture long before European slavers arrived.

Although this is certainly true, because all concrete details have been removed, the historical significance of Africa as regards the world prior to slavery has been silenced. The Afrocentric perspective of the original writer has been lost, which effectively denies the people a voice in this respect. Clearly these omissions have been made because of the pressure of word length on the final text panel, which is a very real consideration. Nevertheless, if the intentions to place the people in the context of their own history and not to isolate the period of slavery from its context had been given priority at the brief stage these omissions would probably not have occurred.

## Language use and gaps

Another issue that arises when trying to shorten texts to fit information panels is the choice of appropriate language. There are convenient 'ways of saying' that help anyone attempting to produce a summary, but one that is sometimes chosen can also sound very evasive without intending to: 'the institutional voice'. This is a mode of writing frequently adopted by professionals such as lawyers, diplomats, news readers, doctors and politicians, and (significantly in this instance) by academic historians. It lends itself to representatives of an institution speaking not as 'I' (Lerman, 1983, p. 77), because it enables the speaker to maintain apparent objectivity, to remain distanced from both him/herself, from the topic and often from the reader/listener too.[4] Its distanced arguments that avoid selected facts are unanswerable because of the use of the presence of an unidentified authoritative voice which utilizes sweeping generalizations, euphemisms, model auxiliaries (would, might, will), the deletion of personal pronouns, names and dates, and the persistent use of the agentless passive construction. It is a style of writing that permits 'blanket' statements which appear to be irrefutable without the need to provide detailed information or to identify the source of the authority.

The institutional voice is also frequently used in museums for convenience because it enables curators/exhibition teams to remain anonymous, to easily avoid unknown issues (gaps in the collection for example) and to remain silent about the task they undertook in putting the exhibition together. However, it can also effectively distance them from their topic/story and from their audience/readers. This does not have to be the case and there are several examples that adopt a more self-conscious approach with the result that the meanings have not been 'closed down'. The next example taken from a section dealing with the process of enslavement in the Caribbean has already been through two processes to shorten it, but is still copying the academic style of its original source.

### Second draft exhibit panel

**Seasoning**
Newly arrived Africans were forced to adapt to new working and living conditions by their owners. They *were also made* to adapt to new customs and languages. This was known as *seasoning* and could last for two or three years. Many Africans *died* during this period.

Owners sought to obliterate the former identity of their slaves and to break their will and any bonds with the past. Each African *was given* a European name and *might be* marked with their owners' initials by branding with a hot iron. People of a common language and tradition *were frequently separated* from one another, as owners believed that slaves unfamiliar with each other's languages would be unable to plan rebellions or escapes.

'Many Africans *died* during this period.' The intransitive verb *died* was probably used originally, out of convenience, in the interests of brevity, because it requires no object (you can't 'die someone' but you could use the transitive alternative and 'kill someone'). However, its use permits the avoidance of why they died. Therefore, the use of intransitive verbs can contribute to the impression that responsibility is being avoided.

Similarly, euphemisms enable a writer to speak of sensitive subjects without drawing up mental pictures of them.[5] '*Seasoning*' is a classic euphemism which would need to be drawn attention to as the process of 'breaking in' slaves emotionally, mentally and physically, unless it too appears to be avoiding identifying a reality.

The use of the modal auxiliary *might be* also contributes to this effect. Similarly the passive construction has been used – 'Each African *was given* a name ... People *were* frequently *separated*.' This further contributes to the impersonality of the text and to the impression that identification of those responsible is being avoided, because the passive does not require an active agent. Another more obvious example in the section about the enslavement of the Africans (also from the second draft of the exhibit panels) shows clearly how the use of the passive can give an impression of an attempt at avoidance:

> Most enslaved people *were captured* in battles or *were kidnapped*, though some *were sold* into slavery for debts or as punishment. ... One at the coast they *were imprisoned* ... *Some were held* in elaborate forts.

All of which prompts the question 'By whom?' If the active construction had been used it would not be possible to avoid identifying those responsible. For example, 'Portuguese and English slavers imprisoned the Africans in forts', etc. It is advisable to delete as many agentless passive constructions as possible in the interests of presenting more accurate histories. Occasionally the passive is useful if one really doesn't know who the perpetrators were, but it is as well to remember that the passive allows gaps in the information which tend to look like a deliberate evasion of the truth.

The final re-write for the information panels was not concerned with further shortening the text, but with filling in gaps and altering the language style. The deletion of the institutional voice here has immediate effect.

## The final exhibition panel

**Seasoning**
Owners sought to obliterate the identities of their newly acquired slaves, to break their wills and sever any bonds with the past. They called this process 'seasoning'.

Owners and overseers forced Africans to adapt to new working and living conditions, to learn a new language and adopt new customs. They gave each person a European name and branded many with their owner's initials with a hot iron. They deliberately separated people of common language and tradition to prevent rebellions.

For Africans weakened by the trauma of the voyage, the brutality of this process was overwhelming. Many died or committed suicide. Others resisted and were punished. However, slaves appeared to conform and developed ways of survival which preserved their dignity.

Here the process of 'seasoning' has been more clearly defined with the use of verbs from a field of discourse associated with violence: obliterate, break and sever. They are also active rather than passive formations of the verbs, which of necessity identifies the direct involvement of the slave owners. The passage starts with the action of the overseers not with the effect on the Africans. Thus the active 'Owners sought to obliterate' has replaced the passive 'Newly arrived Africans were forced'.

Having identified the owners' and overseers' precise involvement, their presence is maintained throughout the second paragraph with the use of the pronoun *they* and the continued use of active verbs to describe their actions. Thus the passive: 'Each African was given a European name' becomes 'They gave each person a European name'.

The intransitive verb 'died' has been used again, but not in order to avoid explaining the reasons for the deaths. In fact new information spells out the causes in the last paragraph:

> For Africans weakened by the trauma of the voyage, the brutality of this process was overwhelming. Many died or committed suicide.

Partly because of the use of the institutional voice, the message of the first draft was that of the dominant ideology of which the Africans are not a part. Rather, they were positioned as what the anthropologist Edwin Ardener calls a 'muted' group without a voice (Ardener, 1975). Yet people of African descent in Britain are part of present-day society and, as John Fiske points out, although representation is used as a means of exercising power, this does not mean that it will not be resisted (Fiske, 1987). Deletion of the institutional voice has completely altered this perception and ensured that other voices are heard.

## Politically sensitive issues

There is no consensus on the number of Africans who were enslaved or who lost their lives during the transatlantic slave trade – even among historians. In fact African historians and African-American historians quote completely different figures from European historians. With reference to the previous discussion about the need for museums to avoid perpetuating a Eurocentric perspective of other people's histories, this was clearly a contentious issue for the museum to deal with. There are those who argue that only existing records, such as ships' logs, can be used as evidence of numbers, and there are others who regard these as limited and woefully inadequate. An examination of the texts as they progressed through the editing stages makes interesting reading with regard to the subject of numbers and the dilemma that this presented to the museum.

### Guest curator's draft text: an Afrocentric historian's view

Figures for the number of deaths attributed to the Atlantic slave holocaust alone ranged from 10 million to 150 million, depending on the authority one consults. It promoted inter-ethnic divisions where inter-ethnic relations existed. The slave system through its destructive character encouraged the denial, distortion and erasure of African contributions to history.

The Atlantic slave system, which has proven to be the most peculiar and expensive of all slave systems in human history, even led to the denial of the African as a human being. It impaired the identity, purpose and direction of African societies.

The use of terms like holocaust to name the slave trade is one that white Europeans may not be familiar with, but it is commonly used by Africans and by Europeans and Americans of African descent. The use of the term highlights the different feelings associated with the practice of transatlantic slavery, and shows quite clearly why the people's own story needs to be told from their perspective and not just from a Eurocentric view. This is also clear in the claims made about the attitudes to Africans as not even human.

## Another guest curator's text

Political instability resulting from the slave trade had disastrous consequences for many Africans ... This political instability reinforced the slave trade because it was always the major source of slaves ... Large numbers of people, perhaps more than caused by wars, were actually forcibly moved to the Americans, died in war and raids within Africa, or were killed rather than be taken prisoner, because they were too old or too young to be sought as slaves. Many died from disease and famines that were induced by these wars and raids, and others still died in the long marches to the coast or in slave markets in the interior. It is difficult to know the scale of this demographic catastrophe. Approximately 11.8 million Africans were sold to European slavers and forcibly removed from Africa. At least as many more remained as slaves within Africa, and probably as many more again were killed or died in the conduct of war of slave raiding.

This text is attempting to come to terms with the numbers who were enslaved, died or were killed in Africa. It does not, however, deal with the numbers who died in America, Brazil and the Caribbean subsequently.

## The first draft exhibition panel

### The impact of slaving on Africa

The warfare and political instability contrived by white slave traders had disastrous consequences for West Africa. Some states were completely destroyed – subsumed by rivals and annihilated by the loss of the cream of their population ...

> Millions of slaves *were removed* from Africa. At least as many
> remained slaves within Africa, and probably as many again *died* or *were*
> *killed* in slaving wars. The demographic changes were enormous. Large
> areas *became depopulated*.

This summary has clearly taken its information from the previous one
quoted, but has not included information from the first one. Also all
references to specific numbers have been deleted. It could be claimed
that this is a convenient way out of the numbers dilemma. However,
such generalizations as 'Millions', 'at least as many' and 'probably as
many again' are generalizations if not actually euphemistic in their
avoidance of detail. Such generalizations are associated closely with the
evasiveness of the institutional voice, as has already been observed.

The repeated use of the term 'slave', which occurs in several other
texts, throughout the text writing process is problematic. Clearly used
as a shorthand, it unfortunately robs the Africans of their identity. This
word gives no clue as to the sex, age, nationality, status or even
humanity of the people being named. Linguistically this term would be
known as a 'naming device'. All naming devices give the impression
that they reflect the attitude of the person doing the naming. The first
Africans who were enslaved were not born in captivity, and when they
became slaves this state was imposed upon them. Calling them *slaves*
from before they were captured and repeatedly thereafter unconsciously perpetuates the common Eurocentric terminology that is taken
for granted, due to the familiarity by those people of a Eurocentric
view. However, there are others who would make a resistant reading
and see it as a label which denies the people's humanity.

Later in the same draft the subject is referred to again: this time using
particular figures.

*The scale of transatlantic slavery*
The number of Amerindians and Africans involved in the saga of
Atlantic slavery is hotly debated, and the true toll will perhaps never be
agreed. A broad consensus, however, maintains that between 12 and 20
million Africans were shipped westwards.

These figures have clearly not considered the original text quoted in
their consensus figures, which represents a problematic oversight in
view of an almost certain resistant reading. Historian Dwight Lowell
Drummond, in his book *Anti-Slavery* (1990), gave figures of 100 million
captured and 75 million deaths. The importance of these figures is that
they were ones that Malcolm X spoke of widely and they are now
considered to be common knowledge by many of African descent.

## The final exhibition texts

*The impact of slaving in Africa*

The demands of European slave traders and firearms they supplied increased warfare and political instability in West Africa ...

Many states, including Angola under Queen Nzinga Nbande and Kongo, strongly resisted slavery. However, the interests of those involved in the trade proved too great. Millions of Africans were forcibly removed from their homes, and towns and villages were depopulated. Many Africans were killed in slaving wars or remained enslaved in Africa.

*The scale of transatlantic slavery*

Historians do not agree on the number of Africans who were transported across the Atlantic. Some accept a figure of about 12 million based on European shipping records. Others argue that these records under-estimate the numbers and put the figure at nearer 20 million.

In addition, many more millions were enslaved or were killed in Africa during the wars encouraged by slave traders and at every stage of transatlantic slaving.

Scholars of an Afrocentric perspective believe this total number could reach between 50 and 100 million. Whatever the figure, this African holocaust involved death and dislocation of an unimaginable scale. Its full impact will never be known.

Being aware of the need to address this politically sensitive issue, the final text repeats the acknowledgement of the controversy over the figures, but it adds the crucial observation that these numbers would have been increased 'at every further stage of transatlantic slaving'. This allows more appreciation of the numbers controversy because the numbers of Africans shipped, killed or enslaved in Africa would not include the fate of those people born into slavery in America, the Caribbean, Brazil, and so on. The naming device 'slaves' has been replaced with Africans.

Finally, it has given details of the differing numbers instead of just offering a consensus based on European records and has referred to the scale of the disaster with the Afrocentric (and semantically accurate) term holocaust. This term was also used as a section heading in the exhibition itself.

I would like to remind readers that the examples quoted above were intended to highlight some of the issues that arise during the process of text production for such a large venture. There were far too many texts to give a more comprehensive overview. Also that the exhibition itself supplied information that was not contained in the texts – in the form of exhibits and labels, audio-points, maps, videos, a model ship and an installation aimed at re-creating the feeling of being in the hold of a slave ship. However, the information panels carried the bulk of the information and therefore would carry the meaning for the majority of visitors. It is easier to miss an audio-point or a small exhibit label than a large panel. When the exhibition opened, a brochure was available whose text was based on the finalized information from the text panels, which meant that the text was doubly important and all the care taken over it was justified.

Curators who work very closely with advisors and make the effort to acquaint themselves with the way language speaks their own voice will be able to speak other voices too. And this is of vital importance because:

> In a society that has consistently failed to come to terms with its historical relationship with less industrialized societies and the nature of its own cultural identity in a newly aligned Europe, museums are in a unique position to encourage public debate about such issues, since they are the custodians of the fragmentary evidence that provides the greatest contradictions to prejudiced misconception. Education, in the widest sense of the word, is an essential condition of good citizenship. Exhibitions are well-placed to ensure a level of public awareness that is as equal in sophistication to the times in which we live. (Shelton, 1992)

## Notes

1. For further reading see Bhabba (1994).
2. See Montgomery *et al.* (1992) on resistant readings and Hall (1993) on negotiated and oppositional readings.
3. 'Museum visiting in the U.K. remains primarily a white upper/middle class pastime', Eckstein and Feist (1992), p. 77.
4. See Lerman (1983), pp. 75–103.
5. See Orwell (1972), p. 366.

## References

Ardener, E. (1975) Belief and the problems of women, in S. Ardener (ed.), *Perceiving Women*, Malaby Press.

Bhabha, H. (1994) *The Location of Culture*, Routledge, London.

Birch, D. (1989) *Language, Literature and Critical Practice*, Routledge, London.

Cannizzo, J. (1989) *Into the Heart of Africa*, Royal Ontario Museum, Ontario.

Drummond, D.L., *Anti-Slavery*, quoted in Malcolm X (1990) *Afro–American History*, p. 39, Pathfinder.

Eckstein, J. and Feist, A. (1992) *Cultural Trends*, Vol. 12, Policy Studies Institute, London.

Fiske, J. (1987) *Television Culture: Popular Pleasures and Politics*, Methuen, London.

Geertz, C. (1983) *Local Knowledge*, Basic Books, New York.

Hall, S. (1993) Encoding, decoding, in S. During (ed.), *The Cultural Studies Reader*, p. 103, Routledge, London.

Lerman, C.L. (1983) Dominant discourse: the institutional voice and control of topic, in H. Davis and P. Walton (eds), *Language Image Media*, Blackwell, Oxford.

Meinhof, U.H. (1994) Double talk in news broadcasts, in D. Gradda and C. Boyd Barrett (eds), *Media Texts: Authors and Readers*, Multilingual Matters/The Open University.

Montgomery, M. *et al.* (1992) *Ways of Reading*, p. 227, Routledge, London.

Orwell, G. (1972) Politics and the English language, in D. Lodge (ed.), *Twentieth Century Literary Criticism*, Longman, London.

Said, E. (1979) The text, the word, the critic, in J.V. Harari (ed.) *Textual Strategies: Perspectives in Post-structuralist Criticism*, Cornell University Press, New York.

Sapir, E. (1941) in L. Spier (ed.), *Language Culture and Personality: Essays in Memory of Edward Sapir*, Sapir Memorial Publication Fund, Menasha, WI.

Schildkrout, E. (1991) Ambiguous messages and ironic twists: into the heart of Africa and the other museum, *Museum Anthropology*, 15 (2), 16–23.

Shelton, A. (1992) constructing the global village, *Museums Journal*, August, 25.

Simpson, M. (1992) Celebration, commemoration or condemnation?, *Museums Journal*, 92 (3), 28–31.

Volosinov, V. (1973) *Marxism and the Philosophy of Language* (first published in 1930), trans. L. Matejka and I.R. Titunik, Seminar Press, New York.

# PART 2

# *Inclusive strategies: exhibitions and educational programmes*

# 7

## The Peopling of London project

NICK MERRIMAN

### Introduction and background

It is an undeniable fact that Britain today is a culturally diverse nation. What is not often recognized is the long presence that many communities have actually had in this country. The acknowledgement of both of these facts is slowly having an impact on museums. First, museums are realizing that, in order to maintain their claims to be responsive to the needs of their communities, they must make themselves relevant to the diversity of populations that make up their constituency. Second, some museums are beginning to realize that, in the interests of historical balance, they must begin to represent the previously neglected presence and contribution of minority ethnic communities in their areas.

London is a cosmopolitan city on a global scale. Some 20 per cent of its citizens identify themselves as belonging to a major ethnic group of non-European origin, and a much larger percentage belong to Irish, Jewish, Italian, Spanish, Cypriot, Polish and other groups. Some 200 languages other than English are spoken in London homes.[1]

This chapter describes a project, *The Peopling of London: 15,000 years of Settlement from Overseas*, which has been undertaken by the Museum of London in an attempt to embrace the concept of cultural diversity within the Museum's work. It is presented as an evaluated case study of some of the issues, pitfalls and rewards of undertaking a project that attempts to present a long history of population diversity to a pluralistic audience. It tries to put into practice some approaches advanced in previous work (Merriman, 1991) to wider museum audiences by dismantling some of the barriers that deter people from visiting.

The idea for the *Peopling of London* project evolved over the course of 1990 in response to a number of different ideas and developments both within and outside the museum. One of the catalysts was the adoption by the museum in that year of a comprehensive and regular programme of market research surveys which established for the first time the characteristics of the museum's visitors. One of the most telling findings was that seemingly only around 4 per cent[2] of the museum's visitors were from 'ethnic minority'[3] groups, compared to the 20 per cent in London's overall population mentioned above.[4] There was rightly a concern that the museum's programmes and displays were not appealing to around a fifth of the museum's constituency in the Greater London area.

Some of the reasons for this lack of interest amongst many of London's communities have been investigated in a survey by the London Museums Service (Trevelyan, 1991) on the attitudes of non-visitors to London's museums. For many members of 'ethnic minority' groups, it is clearly shown that museums are perceived as irrelevant in their content, intimidating in their architecture and unwelcoming in their attendant staff. In the case of the Museum of London, this is borne out by the fact that the permanent galleries (currently) finish at 1945, with the result that the histories of people who have settled in London since then receive no mention. Unconsciously, the museum was giving recent settlers the impression that they were not part of the continuum of London's history. In addition, at the time the project was being formulated, it was extremely difficult to gain any sense of London's long history of cultural diversity when visiting the museum's galleries. There was a small section on the Huguenots, a panel put up in 1989 on eighteenth-century immigration and a small panel on the nineteenth-century Jewish community, but little else. There was no mention of the medieval Jewish community, the continuous black presence since the sixteenth century, the establishment of Asian communities from the seventeenth century, the Chinese, Italians and Germans of the nineteenth century, nor anything on the early twentieth-century communities with origins overseas.

At the same time, work on the redevelopment of the museum's prehistoric gallery was focusing on the need to draw out a theme linking prehistoric times with the present. It was decided that population movement from overseas would be a suitable theme. This sprang from the observation that there was a period around 15,000 BC when Britain was devoid of population because of the severity of Ice Age climatic conditions. When the climate improved, people colonized the empty land again, since which time Britain has been permanently occupied. Settlement from abroad therefore presented itself as a theme which is of contemporary relevance, and which could be placed in a truly long-term historical context by a museum display.

These observations coalesced around the idea of developing a project which aimed at highlighting the neglected history of London's diverse populations by placing contemporary communities in a long-term historical context. The starting point would be the colonization of an empty landscape in the Ice Age, progressing through the varied population of Roman times, and on through London's history to the present. The fundamental aim of the project was to demonstrate that London – or the London area – has always had a culturally diverse population originating from various parts of the globe. Far from being a recent 'problem', immigration from overseas would be presented in the project as a fundamental characteristic of the city since earliest times, and something of which London could be proud. By treating this topic in this way, the aim of the project would be both to inform the museum's existing audience about a neglected aspect of London's history, and to open up the museum to a new audience which up until now had tended not to visit.

A final development made the project even more relevant. While some of the above ideas were being developed, xenophobia and racism were becoming more prevalent across Europe (including Britain) as the fall of the Berlin Wall and the collapse of communism led to large-scale movements of people and the unleashing of long-standing hatreds previously held in check. This was combined with the onset of deep recession amongst the Western industrialized countries, which in turn led to unemployment, increased poverty and the perennial selection of immigrants as scapegoats. Perusal of the rhetoric of racist groups made it clear that much of their message was predicted on the notion that – in Britain at least – there had been a homogeneous white population prior to 1945, bound together by a common history and set of values, and that after 1945 this homogeneity had been overlain by the introduction of – in their terms – alien non-white populations with different histories, values and cultural backgrounds who did not belong to Britain and were the source of many of the nation's current woes.

As museums play a fundamental role as interpreters of public history, the team working on the project felt that they must be able to challenge such abuses of history, and offer an alternative to the myth of pre-war population homogeneity. This would be a significant departure for the Museum of London in that it would be taking a view of a particular issue (i.e. that racism should be challenged), rather than maintaining its usual position of apparent neutrality. Given the growing critical understanding within museums of the impossibility of value-free objectivity in historical discourse, this departure was viewed primarily as a useful and explicit recognition of an existing state of affairs. A fundamental objective of the project therefore became to challenge the view that post-war immigration in London was a recent 'problem', by turning this argument on its head and celebrating the diversity of London's people since prehistoric times.

## The formulation of the project

Having established these basic parameters, a small internal team began to examine the different elements of the project in more detail. It was important to be explicit about the objectives of the project, because it was intended that it should be thoroughly evaluated, particularly in terms of the target audiences. After some discussion the following aims were agreed:

- to widen the focus of the museum by presenting the histories of communities not previously represented in the museum's galleries;
- to make contact with, involve and attract to the museum a new audience who had little or no previous contact with it;
- to make the museum more accessible, both physically and intellectually, to the different people of London;
- to challenge traditional views of what it is to be a Londoner;
- to stimulate discussion of, and interest in, the history of London;
- to encourage new thinking and practice within the museum.

Five target audiences were also identified:

- existing museum visitors;
- people who do not normally visit the museum, especially members of London's ethnic minorities;
- school pupils and teachers;
- tourists, especially those from the countries of origin of some of London's communities;
- museum professionals.

The aim of the project was to challenge the 'them' and 'us' mentality by showing that all communities come ultimately from overseas. As a result, the most important aspect of the project was to give an indication of the great time-depth to the history of London's cultural diversity. It was also clear that if the museum were to develop a broader approach to representing history in this way, the project would have to have long-term aims beyond the production of a temporary exhibition. In a sense, the *Peopling of London* project was to be a 'pilot study' to establish the parameters of a new approach to London's history, the ultimate aim of which was to incorporate the previously hidden history of cultural diversity into the museum's permanent galleries. The new approach was also to emphasize the importance for museums of putting a human face on the past. While original objects were still to be at the heart of the enterprise, they were not to remain ends in themselves. Where possible, it was intended to relate objects to individual people and, in the more recent periods, use oral history and photography to provide a personal dimension to the process being described.

In taking on this subject the museum was confronting head-on some of the more contentious issues in the public representation of history, and needed to develop the project in a manner that was sensitive to the feelings of London's communities, whose histories had hitherto been largely ignored by the museum world. In particular, the issue of community involvement was fundamental to the success of the project. Museum staff felt neither comfortable nor qualified in presenting the history of, for example, the Chinese or Cypriot communities, so a key feature of the project had to be consultation and collaboration. On the other hand, with so many communities in London, this had to be managed in a way that did not over-inflate expectations, given the constraints o the museum's resources and the size of the exhibition space. As relative novices in this area, the team began investigating their approach by holding two brainstorming sessions with museum professionals who had experience of community history projects in London and with academics with an interest in community history or immigration. The experience of those who had worked on the *Museum in Docklands* project was also invaluable. This was a Museum of London initiative to establish a museum of the Port of London and had pioneered community history at the museum. Through its use of oral history, its outreach work amongst schools and local communities, and its use of a mobile museum, it provided a model for the approach of the *Peopling of London* project. One of the 'Docklands' staff, Andy Topping, was later seconded to the *Peopling* project to develop the public events programme, and his experience proved decisive in shaping the project.

Following these discussions a basic programme for the project was established: it should involve extensive consultation and liaison work; it should conduct synthetic research in libraries and archives, review sources of objects and images, and develop a package of activities for the public. The different elements of the project underwent considerable revision as a result of discussion and as the research and collecting process revealed what would, or would not, be possible. The final elements consisted of the following:

- a programme of outreach and consultation, including use of a mobile museum;
- a programme of research amongst archives and public collections;
- a temporary exhibition;
- an accompanying publication;

- a resource pack;
- a programme of activities for schools;
- a programme of events for adults and family groups;
- a related film season;
- a programme of collecting (including oral history recordings) to ensure that the museum's holdings reflected something of London's cultural diversity;
- an archive of information generated by the project to be permanently available in the museum library;
- an evaluation exercise with a final report on the success of the project.

## The research phase

Following this, the team began an extensive research phase. This was particularly important because there were few syntheses of the histories of different community groups available, and in a number of cases – notably amongst recent immigrant groups – there was almost no information at all. Crucial to this process – and to the success of the overall project – was the appointment of Rozina Visram as the project researcher and advisor. A respected historian, teacher, author of *Ayahs, Lascars and Princes. The History of Indians in Britain 1700–1947* (Visram, 1986) and co-author of the Geffrye Museum's report into the *Black Contribution to History* (Fraser and Visram 1988), she already had experience of working in the field of anti-racist and equal opportunities teaching and had a wide network of contacts amongst academics and community groups.

Her role in the first instance was to scrutinize the archives of the Museum of London and to visit the archives of local history libraries and national repositories to search for material concerning settlers from overseas. Each visit resulted in notes on the archives' holdings, which were then incorporated into a synthesis outlining the history of each major community in London, the location and content of historical records and illustrative material, and bibliographical references. This then assisted in the reappraisal of the museum's own object holdings. For example, the discovery that nineteenth-century German settlers specialized in, amongst other things, the sugar-baking industry, led to the use of sugar loaf moulds in the display on the German community in London. A photograph of Italian ice-cream sellers similarly led to the display of a glass ice-cream 'lick' identical to the one in the picture.

Just as important was her role in discussing the project with members of community groups. At an early stage in the project it was decided that community liaison should be done not by a formal committee with nominated representatives, which would be unwieldy given the large number of communities being studied, but on an informal basis using a whole variety of contacts. In this way it was hoped to gather a broad range of views from different age groups, genders and social classes within each community, and from academics as well as non-academics.

Rozina Visram's existing contacts, for example with the Black Cultural Archives and the India Office Library, led to further contacts within the communities, both for advice and for historical information. It had become clear at an early stage that much of the history of recent settlers resided principally in the memories of first and second generation migrants, and that therefore oral history would form an important component of the project. One of Rozina Visram's initial tasks was to identify potential contributors to a programme of oral history recording. This was then followed up by the museum's recently appointed Curator of Oral History, Rory O'Connell.

Rozina Visram's other principal role, together with the leader of the project, Nick Merriman, was in publicizing the project amongst community groups, and in gauging reactions to different approaches. The attitude of the project team[5] was to be as open as possible about its existence and objectives, on the basis that early initial contact and discussion was the best way to generate support and to avoid misunderstandings and antipathy. Partly because of Rozina Visram's credibility as researcher and advisor, and the circumstances of the project's inception (against a background of increasing racism), to the satisfaction of team members the basic concept of the project met with strong approval amongst almost everyone consulted, from community leaders and academics to social workers and oral history contributors. Although many commented that it was 'about time' that the Museum of London remedied its neglect of their history, they were glad that an effort was finally being made, at a particularly appropriate time. In turn, they too passed on many of their network of contacts.

At the same time as this archival research and community consultation was being undertaken, the project team were carrying out research on suitable two- and three-dimensional material for the exhibition, which was envisaged as the centrepiece of the project. One of the first things that had to be demonstrated was that the subject of the project would make a viable exhibition. While many themes make excellent books, videos and lecture series, it is not always easy to translate them into an exhibition where visitors move physically through a space absorbing and being stimulated by ideas and information. As a museum is fundamentally concerned with material culture, it was essential that the exhibition was not simply a 'book on the wall', consisting of text panels and flat photographic images. Initial reactions amongst museum staff were that the museum did not have much material relevant to this theme. In particular it became clear that the museum records were largely silent on the cultural background of the people from whom objects had been collected, no doubt because this information had not been deemed worthy of recording at the time of collection.

Further investigation of the museum's collections, however, revealed material that could be used to illuminate the theme of the exhibition in a number of different ways. First, there was material that was without doubt associated with certain communities, being demonstrably made, used or in some other way associated with the group. This material included Roman tombstones showing the place of birth of the deceased, a tombstone with a Norse inscription, a medieval Italian merchant's seal, Huguenot silverware, an eighteenth-century gravestone from the Dutch Church, various nineteenth-century Jewish items, including a charitable lottery wheel, and nineteenth-century dock labour cards relating to three Irish brothers. Paintings, prints and photographs showing early African-Caribbean, Asian and Chinese inhabitants helped to fill in some of the gaps (Figure 7.1). The second category of material was that which was typically associated with certain processes of certain communities, even though the documentation did not explicitly state that there was a direct association. In the prehistoric

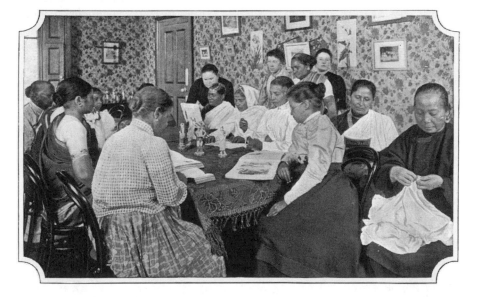

Figure 7.1 *The ayahs' home, Hackney, 1900. The presence of ayahs (Indian nannies) who had travelled to London with British families returning from India, was one of the neglected aspects of London's history that the* Peopling of London **project wished to highlight.** © *Museum of London.*

period, for example, certain stone tools stood as icons for the earliest settlers. In later periods documentary records showed that some communities specialized in certain crafts and industries. Items typical of these crafts could therefore be used to illustrate that fact, even though the particular item exhibited had no definite link (impossible to prove in the case of excavated artefacts). This type of material included leather shoes to illustrate 'Doche' inhabitants in the medieval period, Delft ceramics to highlight the Dutch-inspired development of the industry in London and nineteenth-century tools used in railway construction to symbolize the impact of the rebuilding of London by a predominantly Irish labour force. This second way of using objects, in a generic rather than a specific way, represents a departure from the traditional practice of developing exhibitions that are driven primarily by objects, in favour of one where objects are used as typical illustrations of a theme. This approach has been discussed in detail by Spencer Crew and James Sims (1991) in their account of the National Museum of American History's exhibition Field to Factory. There they encountered the familiar problem that the material culture of disadvantaged ('invisible') communities has rarely if ever been collected by museums, with the result that programmes designed to make such communities visible in the museum must necessarily develop a different way of looking at objects as evidence.

The *Peopling of London* team was relatively fortunate in that the museum's archaeological collections were extensive, allowing a reasonably full treatment of the earliest periods using both directly and typically associated material. Some later communities were relatively well-represented, because their craft products fell within the traditional decorative arts field of museum collecting. The prime examples of this sort of material was that relating to the Huguenot and Dutch communities. Jewish material of a religious nature had also been collected, possibly because of its easy identification with that community through the Hebrew script on the objects. Other communities had been barely, if at all, collected. Three-dimensional material culture relating to the African-Caribbean, South Asian and Chinese communities was absent, and, surprisingly, apart from the one group already mentioned there was almost no material relating to the large and long-established Irish community.

Some of these deficiencies could be remedied through loans from existing institutional collections. Having reviewed the Museum of London's collections, the second task of the project team was to investigate material held elsewhere. Some institutions were obvious sources: the Black Cultural Archives, the Jewish Museum, the London Museum of Jewish Life, the India Office Library, the British Museum (particularly the Prints and Drawings Collection) and the National

Portrait Gallery. Other important material came from less obvious sources. The Royal Albert Memorial Museum in Exeter, for example, had a portrait of the eighteenth-century British black campaigner and writer Olaudah Equiano. The Science Museum had a barometer made by the famous Italian-London firm of Negretti & Zambra and the British Library had copies of books written by eighteenth-century black Londoners. A particularly large source of exhibits was the Public Record Office which lent documents ranging from a bill of sale of around 1220 for a Jew's house in West Cheap to Karl Marx's unsuccessful application for British naturalization.

Despite this extensive trawl amongst public collections, a review of the material available on communities from overseas showed that there were still a large number of gaps, particularly in the more recent periods. It was clearly necessary to embark on a programme to collect or borrow additional material. Before this could commence, we had to be clear about the themes that the exhibition would cover. This involved an extensive review of the evidence available and a consideration of the different approaches that could be explored.

## Exhibition themes

The fundamental question that the exhibition team had to confront was whether the topic should be covered thematically or chronologically. It would be possible to take, for example, 20 of the largest overseas communities in London's history and devote a section to each one, showing its history and impact on the development of London. This would have had the advantage of explicitly recognizing the importance of the history of these communities in the museum context. However, it would also have carried with it several disadvantages. A large number of communities would have been excluded; there would have been a large degree of repetition in the historical information and processes exhibited in each section; and it would have presented each community as a hermetically sealed unit, and not allowed an exploration of the important aspects of interactions between different communities. It is rare in London for any community to live its life insulated from the rest of London's population, so this method of presentation would have produced a false impression of the way in which the city's populations conduct their lives. Finally, it would have been difficult to establish a clear sense of chronology with such a thematic treatment. As the ultimate aim of the project was to demonstrate the great time-depth to cultural diversity in London, this would have been a grave disadvantage. The team therefore decided that the exhibition, like the Museum of London itself, should follow a chronological path, and focus on London and its diversity of populations rather than on specific communities. However, realizing that many first-time visitors would be wishing to see displays specifically on their own communities, the team attempted to develop thematic sections within defined chronological periods which allowed the histories of certain communities to be explored. The broad chronological sections, together with their sub-themes, were eventually as follows:

1 Before London (15,000 BC–AD 50)

2 Roman London (50–410)

3 The Age of Migrations (419–1066)
   a Germanic Soldiers and Settlers
   b Britons, Saxons, Norsemen and Normans

4 Medieval Europeans (1066–1500)
   a Christian Migrants
   b The Jewish Presence
   c Craftworkers (focusing on settlers from the Low Countries)
   d Merchants and Traders (concentrating on Italian, French and German merchants)

5 London and the Wider World (1500–1837)
   a Patrons, Artists and Craftworkers (the role of the court in bringing in overseas artists and craftworkers to London; rulers from overseas such as William of Orange, the House of Hanover)
   b The Early Black and Asian Presence
   c The Jewish Resettlement
   d Refugees and Migrants: the Dutch, Germans and Italians
   e Refugees and Migrants: The Huguenots

6 The Heart of the Empire (1837–1945)
   a Building London: the Irish Connection
   b Living and Working in the Port (including Chinese, South Asian and African settlers)
   c Imperial Citizens (with sections on African, African-Caribbean, Indian and Cypriot settlers)
   d In Search of a Better Life (with sections of the late nineteenth- and early twentieth-century Jewish settlers, Italians, Germans and Americans)

7 After the Empire (1945–present)
   a Invited to Work (1945–1962)
   b Through the Closing Door (1962–present)

Predictably the post-war section caused the greatest degree of debate amongst the project team and the network of advisors. Again, it would have been extremely difficult (particularly given the restricted space available) to have a separate section on each of the communities of overseas origin living in post-war London. On the other hand, treating the post-war period chronologically would be difficult, given its relative brevity in comparison with the other major sections of the exhibition.

The final decision was to treat the post-war period thematically in an introductory section, to set the scene, before visitors began with the prehistoric section (see below). The *chronological* changes within the last 50 years were then covered briefly in the 'After the Empire' section, above. The subjects of the themes themselves were naturally of crucial importance because they would determine the contemporary collecting and oral history programme. They – and the way in which the earlier sections were treated – would fundamentally determine the stance and credibility of the exhibition, both with existing visitors and the new audiences we hoped to attract. The exhibition team and academic advisors were determined that a critical stance should be taken which would not fight shy of tackling issues such as racism, unemployment and discrimination. Consultation with non-academic members of various communities, however, produced a different reaction. The general feeling was that such issues were frequently tackled in the media and would be well-understood by most people visiting the museum. They instead wanted the exhibition to concentrate primarily on showing the long presence and positive contribution of communities from overseas to London's economic and social life. From their point of view the exhibition should be celebratory rather than pessimistic or depressing. This disparity between the critically distanced academic view and the non-academic view has also been noted by Jane Peirson Jones in her analysis of Birmingham Museum's Gallery 33 project. As she notes 'Experience suggests that displays focusing on discord and social conflict will not necessarily be the chosen goal of a community's museum programme' (Peirson Jones, 1992, p. 229).

The museum is itself a culturally high status artefact, and an exhibition in a museum conveys a hidden message of recognition by mainstream society (hence the desire of many 'minority' groups to see their history represented in museums). Understandably there is a desire on the part of many community members to be presented in a positive light in such an institution, which museum workers must be sensitive to. Similarly, some advisors expected a fairly traditional treatment of their history, avoiding – to their minds – gimmicks such as electronic 'games' or cartoons, so that it achieved parity with other mainstream accounts of history in museums. Even though the uncritical and traditional approaches to display technology may be against the instincts of curators themselves, they must be sensitive to these responses. In turn, this raises issues about the degree of influence that community consultation has over the final product in the museum. A range of different attitudes are possible, depending on the nature of the project. In the case of the 'Peopling of London' dealing as it did with a large number of communities and a huge time-span, a reasonably strong degree of direction and central editorial control was required to co-ordinate the many different aspects of the project. As the fundamental aim of the project was to tackle racist beliefs and mythical history, the exhibition team felt that it was important to examine racism in the exhibition, as well as stressing the positive aspects of the peopling of London. We chose, in the light of communities' advice, not to dwell on negative issues such as crime and social dislocation.

The post-war section 'World in a City' was therefore finally displayed along thematic lines which included the following:

## The World in a City

a Coming to London (examining the processes both of leaving the homeland and arriving in London)

b A Liberal City? (noting the existence of racist beliefs and the search for scapegoats on whom to blame economic ills, and the existence of anti-racist movements amongst both the black and white communities)

c A Place of Work (stressing the economic contribution made by post-war settlers from overseas)

d London Lives (a largely photographic section showing the diversity of communities through depictions of children and schools, adulthood and old age)

e Celebration Time (presenting an impression of the diversity of festivals, from the *mela* to the Notting Hill Carnival)

f Leisure (showing the contribution of overseas settlers to London's music, and other leisure activities)

g Religion (giving an impression of the range of religions existing in London)

h A Taste of London (a montage highlighting the revolutionary impact that the presence of overseas settlers has had on London's food)

i Fashion (a market stall displaying a selection of the mixture of dress styles that can be seen in the city which are influenced by traditional clothes from different communities)

j Shopping (a mock-up of a local store, with typical food associated with different communities and a range of community newspapers).

## The contemporary collecting programme

Having decided on the themes of the exhibition, it was then possible to assess those areas where additional collecting was needed. The most obvious gap in the museum's collections was the virtual absence of oral history recordings relating to immigrants. With first generation post-war immigrants now mostly in their sixties and older, it was becoming increasingly important that a record be made of their experiences. The other major gap was a great dearth in the museum's collections of most kinds of material relating to post-war settlers. Thanks to the recent acquisition of a large photographic archive, some communities were relatively well-covered photographically, although many were not. There was some paper ephemera relating to racist and anti-racist groups of the 1970s, but otherwise no original two- or three-dimensional material. Clearly a process of collecting a range of post-war material would have to accompany the oral history campaign. The collecting exercise took the form of several inter-related strands.

## The museum on the move

As part of the desire of the project team to consult widely and publicize the 'Peopling of London' project as extensively as possible, it was decided to mount a series of outreach events using a mobile trailer called 'Museum on the Move'. The 20ft trailer, and the Range Rover used to pull it, were borrowed from the 'Museum in Docklands' project, where they were used primarily for outreach work amongst schools. A small panel-based exhibition was mounted inside the trailer detailing the aims of the 'Peopling of London' project. One wall included 20 questions about little-known aspects of London's cultural diversity (such as a picture of the first known black person living in London in 1511) with lift-up flaps revealing the answer, to give a taster of the kind of information that would be available in the final exhibition (Figure 7.2). The exhibition in the trailer concluded with a request for visitors to come forward to help with the project by sharing their memories with the team, or by lending some items for the exhibition. Leaflets were also produced giving further information and a voucher giving free admission to the museum. Staff were also on hand to talk to visitors and there was a small display on the sort of material that we were looking for, such as passports, letters and diaries.

In selecting venues for the 'Museum on the Move' to travel to, the team targeted areas that market research had shown did not generate many visitors to the museum. These also tended to be areas with a wide variety of ethnic minority groups. In total, 10 venues were visited between October 1992 and May 1993. The locales chosen were ones

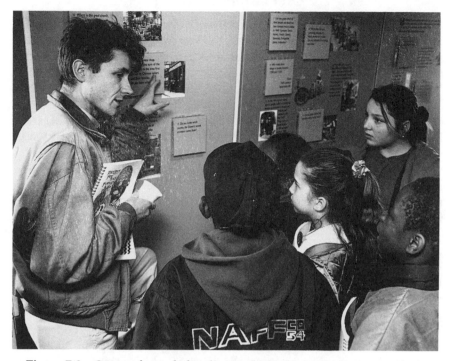

**Figure 7.2**  *Outreach work for the* Peopling of London *project with the 'Museum on the Move'.* © *Museum of London.*

where people already congregated, such as markets, parks and supermarket car parks, so that a ready-made audience was available. These included Ridley Road Market in Dalston, the car parks at the Asda supermarket in Lavender Hill and Tescos in Brixton, Lampton Park in Hounslow, Surrey Quays Shopping Centre in Southwark and a public space near the Westway in North Kensington. Each visit was accompanied by a substantial publicity campaign, with its own press release, targeted particularly at raising local awareness of the project and of the visit of 'Museum on the Move'. This resulted each time in good coverage in the local press, on local and/or ethnic radio stations, and on London television. Over a thousand people visited the trailer on its visits, a good deal of publicity and support for the project was generated, and many people came forward with offers of loans of objects or offers to help by sharing with us their memories of settling in London.

## Oral history collecting

The museum's Curator of Oral History, Rory O'Connell, took up many of the contacts made by Rozina Visram in her discussions with members of different communities and generated his own additional contacts for possible oral history interviewees. Through this, the 'Museum on the Move' campaign, and other people coming forward as a result of general publicity about the project, some 65 individuals were eventually interviewed and some 100 hours of recordings generated. Each individual was given a copy of their own recording, and was allowed to decide him or herself the extent to which the recording would be available to the public. While it was only possible to make brief segments of the interviews available in the exhibition, all of the tapes are deposited in the museum's archive and transcripts of all of the interviews are currently being prepared.

## Collecting of objects, ephemera and images

In order to supplement the photographic material available for communities under-represented in the museum's collections, three principal approaches were followed. The first of these involved a trawl of existing photographers' work conducted both by contacting photographic libraries and agencies and by publicizing our need for supplementary pictures amongst the photographic press. Our aim was, where possible, to use photographers from the communities themselves. This resulted in the identification of a large number of existing bodies of work amongst, for example, the Vietnamese, Somali, Chinese, Greek-Cypriot and Italian communities, that we were able to draw on in the exhibition and publications. The second strand consisted of commissioning a freelance photographer who had experience of photographing a number of communities, and good contacts within them, to photograph certain themes for inclusion in the post-war section of the exhibition. These included images of the Chinese Saturday School in Euston and the Chinese community centre in Gerrard Street, arranged through contacts with community leaders, and photographs of Turkish families at home. The third gap-filling exercise was for members of the museum's photography section to photograph buildings such as synagogues, mosques and restaurants, and general street scenes, to produce images for the photomontages on the wall of the post-war section. Extensive collections were also made of ephemera around the themes outlined above for the post-war section. These included copies of current immigration documents, posters advertising training courses, racist and anti-racist material, business cards, menus and posters of festivals, plays, concerts and clubs. A large range of newspapers was also collected to represent London's role as a centre for the ethnic press. It was decided that all of this material should be disposable, as it was to be displayed and stuck directly on the walls of the post-war section. It was therefore collected without being accessioned. Frequently, two examples of each item were collected so that the one not used in the exhibition could be incorporated formally into the collections in due course.

Collections of three-dimensional objects were a bigger challenge. One the one hand, the museum did not feel it possible to collect 'typical' objects associated with even a range of communities, given that space restrictions meant that any such attempt would inevitably tend towards the stereotypical. On the other hand the material with the greatest symbolic and emotional significance is that intimately associated with the lives of given individuals. Understandably they are usually unwilling to part with the objects, which would anyway tend to lose some of their significance on transfer to a museum.

The project team's policy was therefore to cover most of the themes photographically or with ephemera, and to request the loan of objects from oral history interviewees when these would further illustrate themes that were covered by their oral history testimony. In this way material such as a suitcase brought by a woman from Trinidad and an identification badge worn by a child refugee from the Spanish Civil War were loaned to the exhibition, to illuminate highly personal stories in a concrete way.

The one exception to this policy was in the area of clothing and accessories. The museum's costume section had for some while felt the lack of material illustrating contemporary cultural diversity and was anxious to use the project as an opportunity to enhance its collections. A small project was therefore set up which involved photographing people in the streets wearing clothes that summarized the mixture of ethnic fashions found in London, including combinations such as saris worn with anoraks and training shoes, or white people wearing Rastafarian-influenced clothes. Clothes and accessories similar to those in the photographs were then bought from retail outlets (with their provenance, price and other details documented). In the final exhibition the photographs were made into a montage which formed a backdrop to the mock street market stall on which the clothing was displayed.

## The elements of the project

From all of this huge investment in research and collecting, the details of the individual elements of the project began to come together.

## The exhibition

Always planned as the centrepiece of the project, the temporary exhibition was scheduled to run from 16 November 1993 to 15 May 1994. The six months' duration was dictated by the fact that this was the maximum period for which a number of major lenders were prepared to lend. There was no additional charge for entry to the exhibition, although there is an admission charge to the museum as a whole.

The basic format of the exhibition (the chrono-thematic approach) had already been formulated, and most of the objects and images chosen, by the time that the designer, John Redman of Redman Design Associates, was appointed. The rather awkward configuration of the space led to the decision to begin the exhibition (in the former shop area) with the most recent section, the survey of London's post-war cultural diversity. Visitors then moved down a corridor with a sound track of different languages spoken in London, compiled by multimedia students for a course project, to a small video area where a five-minute introduction to the main themes of the exhibition was played. It was felt important, given the didactic nature of the exhibition, that visitors were primed at an early stage with the basic concepts behind the exhibition which it was hoped would inform their subsequent viewing of the exhibits. The visitor then passed through the main body of the exhibition (divided into the sections described above), with the visit ending with the brief chronological overview of the post-war period 'After the Empire'. After passing a comments book and a panel giving details of further elements of the project, visitors found themselves back where they started, at the entrance to the exhibition. We hoped that, in completing the circle in such an obvious way, we would encourage visitors to look again on contemporary London in a new way, informed by the historical context provided by the exhibition.

The overall feel of the exhibition was intended to be informal, but serious. Generous use was made of bright colours, photographs and ephemera were stuck haphazardly on the wall, a good deal of material was on open display, and music could be heard in most parts of the exhibition. Specially commissioned set paintings above many of the cases gave a flavour of London of the period, while other elements, such as a giant suitcase, provided visual focus. There were four oral history points consisting of pairs of telephone handsets, each with a choice of four different two-minute extracts held on a digital sound store. An upright board provided a picture of each informant, some brief biographical details and an indication of the subject they were talking about.

Graphic panels were designed to be as attractive as possible, with liberal use of colour and illustrations, and text limited to a hundred words. Realizing the power of text to be interpreted in a variety of unintended ways, and of its ability to reinforce rather than challenge stereotypes, the exhibition team consulted extensively over the content and means of expression. All text was written by one person (Nick Merriman) to provide coherence of narrative. It was circulated to all team members, all curators whose periods were covered in the exhibition, education staff and senior management. It was then circulated to the informal networks of advisors who were asked to comment on it from the point of view of their community. This exercise led to some substantial revisions.

The selection of objects and images for the exhibition had largely been carried out in collaboration with advisors and other community members. Where particular images were felt to be contentious, further advice was taken specifically. For example, it was difficult to find images of the nineteenth-century Jewish community which did not have elements of caricature. Discussing possible images with the curator of the London Museum of Jewish Life helped to ensure that appropriate selections were made which would not offend or reinforce prejudices.

The final issue that had to be debated was that of language. Clearly it was impossible to translate all captions and panels into all languages spoken in London, or even the largest language groups. Audio guides would have been too expensive to provide and administer. On the other hand, the project's aim of inclusiveness and expanding audiences would not be assisted by the production of a solely English text. Eventually the decision was taken to provide a free leaflet summarizing the main chronological sections of the exhibition in the eight languages most spoken in London (as well as English): Urdu, Hindi, Gujarati, Arabic, Chinese, Greek, Polish and Spanish.

## The publication

Given that the exhibition was of limited duration, it had been agreed from the outset that an important component of the project would be the production of an accompanying book. After discussion, the project team decided that the publication should not be a traditional catalogue of the material in the exhibition, but instead a series of historical essays on some of the major communities that are, or have been, distinctive in London. This particular approach was adopted because advisors felt that many people would wish to have convenient summaries of the history of their own community, which was something that was less easy to pick out in the more thematic approach in the exhibition.

In selecting authors for the volume, our first concern was with historical knowledge of individual communities. We also wished, where possible, to use historians who were members of the communities about which they were writing, to give the contributions something of an insider's point of view. It turned out that a good proportion of the academics we were using as advisors on the project in general were willing and able to contribute to the book, so we were able to recruit authors relatively easily. The book is introduced by a chapter, 'World in a City', drawing out themes from the long history of London's cultural diversity, followed by a chapter, 'Invisible Settlers', on overseas settlers from prehistoric times to the Huguenots, who are now absorbed into the general population (indeed they *constitute* the general population) and who are not culturally distinctive. The bulk of the book consists of 17 chapters on the larger contemporary communities, each illustrated, with occasional features called 'Voices of Experience' presenting more of the oral history testimony gathered for the project. The final section consists of a listing of all of the institutions in London, national and local, that were found during Rozina Visram's research to have material relevant to the 'Peopling of London' theme. Each entry has a brief summary of the kind of material available, and details about the institution. The book ends with an extensive bibliography. This final section, it is hoped, will prove a useful resource in itself and stimulate further research.

## Resource pack

Discussions with advisory teachers and inspectors at an early stage of the project revealed a great deal of enthusiasm for the theme and a clear desire for teaching materials. A resource pack for the exhibition was developed by education department staff in consultation with advisors. It provides basic source materials for use in the classroom, and gives examples of how a visit to the exhibition could be tied into various aspects of the National Curriculum – not only history, but also English, geography, religious education, art, technology, music and mathematics. Four case studies, with illustrative material, are provided. The first concerns Elizabeth Lindsay, a black woman who became a companion and servant of Lady Elizabeth Murray, and lived at Kenwood House in London in the eighteenth century. The second is a study of the building on the corner of Fournier Street and Brick Lane in Spitalfields, which started out as a Huguenot church, was a synagogue for 80 years, and is currently a mosque. The third concerns Haji Mohammad Abdul Rahman, a Bengali sailor who served with the British merchant navy earlier this century and settled in London in 1965, and the fourth outlines the life story of Suzanne Samson, who came to England in 1939 as a child fleeing Nazi persecution because of her Jewish parentage. Her story is accompanied by a cassette. Some of the production costs were offset by sponsorship from Carlton Television.

## The events programme

One of the key elements of the project was to be the programme of public events for adults and family groups. This, it was planned, would animate the static exhibition, attract new audiences, allow for participation, debate and comment, and enable certain issues to be treated in greater depth and with more subtlety than an exhibition permits. In choosing the different elements of the project, the team tried as much as possible to select the appropriate medium for each particular topic. Thus, while an exhibition is an excellent vehicle for a historical overview using objects, images, music and small amounts of text, it is not a good medium for a sensitive treatment of, for example, racism and anti-racism, which may be better served by a film, play or debate (although these issues were raised in outline form in the exhibition).

The public events programme was itself divided into a number of different elements. Alongside several one-off events such as the 'World Music in London' weekend held to mark the opening of the exhibition, poetry readings and drama performances, the principal strands consisted of a series of lectures designed to highlight the themes 'Women in a Multicultural Capital' and 'Images, Myths and Realities', and a series of 'focus weeks' which highlighted particular communities.

The two lecture series were put on by the museum's education department because it was felt that there were certain important themes relating to anti-racist education that warranted serious exposition using a traditional lecture format followed by discussion. The first theme was aimed at highlighting the often neglected experience of women in minority communities, while the second theme examined how stereo-typical views of certain communities had become historically constituted, and how these contrasted with contemporary reality.

The focus weeks formed the core of the public programme. The principle behind these was that community groups were invited to use any or all of the museum's public spaces (entrance hall, galleries, temporary exhibition areas, lecture theatre and corridor, classroom and refectory) to represent, in their own terms, something of the community's historical presence and cultural distinctiveness in London, to other Londoners. The community groups were to have complete editorial control, with museum staff acting as facilitators and providing publicity. No suggestion was turned down unless it was financially or logistically unrealistic.

A total of seven focus weeks were arranged by groups from the Cypriot, Jewish, Chinese, Arab, Irish, African-Caribbean and South Asian Communities. In addition there was a refugee focus week co-ordinated by the Refugee Council, a Spitalfields focus week and a shorter programme examining the Soho area. The different groups organizing the focus weeks put on a huge variety of activities. These included formal lectures, discussion workshops, films, videos, dance, music, exhibitions, poetry readings, food tastings, drama, craft workshops and even a fashion show. Publicity was undertaken both by the museum and by the community groups themselves.

The museum also organized a number of programmes itself, such as the three-month residency of an artist, Timo Lehtonen. He produced works of art in response to the exhibition in a studio adjacent to the display space, which visitors could walk through. At Christmas the museum departed from tradition by, for example, organizing a Caribbean Christmas festivity, and displaying a 'Celebration Tree' which drew on the end-of-year celebrations of various cultures. The museum's season of films, 'Made in London', incorporated films that reflected London's cosmopolitanism.

## The schools programme

The *Peopling of London* gave the museum's eduction department an opportunity to develop a programme for schools which targeted a much wider variety of curriculum areas and involved a broader range of interpretive strategies than had previously been possible.

In consultation with advisory teachers, the department organized a full programme of curricular teaching for ages 5–18, using methods such as exhibition trails, gallery drama presentations and creative art workshops, as well as more formal teaching sessions. The gallery drama sessions were also aimed at families, and included a dramatization of the life of Olaudah Equiano and a play called *The Amazing Arnos*, about a family of Italian settlers. Teachers' courses were held to show how the exhibition and resource pack might be used to cover aspects of various curricula.

The project also enabled education department staff to develop new links with schools, teachers and other educational organizations or projects. One of the most valuable of these links was with the group Artists and Craftspersons in Education (ACE). Museum staff worked with ACE members to develop a project which involved children from two London schools working with artists to produce their own creative responses to the exhibition theme. The project was a new departure for the education department in that it involved the same pupils working for a sustained period (five days) in the museum towards a specific outcome, which was the display of their work in a well-received temporary exhibition in the museum.

With encouragement from the museum a number of London primary schools used the exhibition to generate class research projects into pupils' own families to discover patterns of recent immigration and settlement. Elements of these projects were incorporated into the introductory 'World in a City' part of the exhibition, including video footage of a primary school pupil discussing his own family history, and a montage of photos, creative writing, pictures and transcripts of interviews with their parents by pupils from Lucas Vale School in Lewisham.

More explicitly anti-racist strategies were followed in a wide variety of school activities. For example, in the Refugee Focus Week, which was co-ordinated by the Refugee Council, there were two programmes for schools. One, for primary schools, 'Learning about Refugees', consisted of an interactive puppet show about refugees supported by the Save the Children Fund. Another, for secondary schools, 'Who are Refugees?' consisted of workshops about refugees coming to London, past and present. Both programmes invited pupils to question their attitudes and assumptions about refugee settlers.

## Fundraising

Despite a great deal of effort, it was found to be very difficult to raise commercial sponsorship for the project. This was presumably because of the combined effect of the economic recession and the potentially controversial nature of the subject matter. In the event the only sponsorship forthcoming was £3000 from Carlton Television towards the production of the resource packs.

However, the subject matter was fortunately one that matched the policies of a number of charitable funding bodies. The largest grant to the project came from the Baring Foundation, followed by the City Parochial Fund. Smaller donations from other charitable foundations and City livery companies brought the total raised to around £40,000. It is clear, though, that commercial sponsors are generally not willing to take risks on exhibitions dealing with potentially difficult subjects, whereas charitable and educational foundations may be, although they may not be able to cover all costs.

## Marketing campaign

In attempting to generate a wider audience for the museum, an extensive marketing campaign was essential. The five audiences identified at the beginning of the project (existing audiences; current non-users, especially ethnic minorities; school groups; tourists; and museum professionals), were targeted by a combination of intensifying existing approaches and exploring new avenues.

General publicity coverage was intensified by targeting greater numbers of newspapers and radio stations than ever before. These included building up a press list of 250 contacts catering for minority community interests. Particularly useful was Spectrum Radio, a station entirely devoted to specialist ethnic minority programming. For the first time, interviews were secured with satellite and cable TV stations. The education department sent information about the education pro- gramme and the exhibition to all primary and secondary schools in Greater London. All members of visiting school parties were given vouchers entitling children to come back free if they bought a paying parent with them.

Given the small budget available for marketing, it was decided to target much of the publicity campaign on London Underground poster sites. These were chosen because the tube is used both by a high proportion of Londoners, including those who do not visit museums, and a high proportion of tourists. A series of posters were designed, each targeting one of the three major communities in London today: South Asian, Chinese and African-Caribbean. The posters showed members of these groups dressed in the costume of pearly kings and queens – the traditional cockney Londoners – accompanied by a slogan pointing out the long period of time these communities have actually been in London. These were also sent to community centres in an attempt to target communities directly.

A second, more traditional, poster showing the oil portrait of Olaudah Equiano, was produced to target existing audiences and sent to local libraries and museums. The leaflets summarizing the content of the exhibition, which were made available in nine different languages, were also used as promotional material. Over 36,000 were sent directly to community centres and local libraries. As already mentioned, those communities more closely involved in the project, either in providing oral history interviewees, or organizing focus week activities, also generated their own publicity about the project, which greatly added to the coverage already provided by the museum.

## Evaluation of the project: was it successful?

Measurement of the success or failure of a project is always relatively subjective and dependent on the approach taken. What follows is an attempt to assess some of the qualitative and quantitative information that was gathered as part of the evaluation programme. Quantitative research was undertaken by the museum's marketing department, while the qualitative evaluation was facilitated by the New Ethnicities Unit at the University of East London and carried out by Sara Selwood and Diana Irving for Art and Society. A fuller summary of the evaluation is available in Selwood (1996).

Some of the exhibition aims, such as widening the focus of the museum by presenting different community histories, or challenging views of what it is to be a Londoner, were achieved to a certain extent simply by implementing the project itself. Others, such as attracting and including new audiences, required more detailed assessment.

## The exhibition

Over the course of its six-month run, the exhibition attracted 94,250 people. This compares favourably with the museum's previous exhibition *The Purple, White and Green* on the women's suffrage movement, which attracted 62,547 over a nine-month period. Of visitors to the museum over the duration of the *Peopling of London* exhibition, 64 per cent actually visited the exhibition itself, and 10 per cent said they had come specifically to see it. This also compares favourably with the previous exhibition.

In terms of broadening the museum's audience, the exhibition can be deemed a success. From a pre-exhibition baseline of 4 per cent ethnic minority visitors, market research showed that the proportion of ethnic minority visitors to the museum during the exhibition rose to 20 per cent (but see note 2).

This did at least demonstrate unequivocally that, with extensive community liaison and a relevant theme, it is perfectly possible to attract people who do not normally visit museums. The challenge then becomes to persuade one-off visitors to become regular visitors (see below).

In order to assess the extent to which the exhibition achieved its other aims, it was necessary to undertake a qualitative evaluation exercise using focus groups. Four focus groups took part, including regular museum visitors and first-time visitors from minority communities. Reactions to the exhibition were also gauged from the comment books, from press reviews and from letters received.

From these it was clear that the fundamental aim of the exhibition – to demonstrate London's long heritage of cultural diversity – had been achieved. Typical comments were 'An important reminder that we are all immigrants, and that diversity has been part of life since well before 1950' and 'Made me realize that our history lessons at school were often biased'. Both press and visitors commented on the timeliness of the exhibition with respect to growing public concern about the activities of the British National Party in London (Selwood, 1996).

Within this overall positive response there was a great deal of varied comment. While much was favourable, a significant proportion was critical in some way or other, showing that the exhibition theme provoked debate and raised thoughts about ways in which the theme could have been treated more satisfactorily. As with most such exercises, there was little consensus. For example, some visitors felt that there had been too much text in the exhibition. Others, however, wished there had been more information on their particular area of interest. Others complained that the exhibition was rather cramped or that there was not enough for younger children to do. Some felt that the lower quality of the finishes in the design compared with the main permanent exhibition implied a disparagement of the subject.

In terms of the content of the exhibition, the commonest criticism from the focus groups was that there was not sufficient information on their own particular community. This was particularly acute in instances where, due to the thematic approach, some contemporary communities did not have an explicit section devoted to them, but were subsumed in, for example, a section on 'Living and Working in the Port', as the Chinese were. This highlights the tension between separatist and inclusivist approaches outlined in an earlier section. The strongest criticism, almost inevitably, was voiced concerning the most recent section 'The world in a city', which many group members felt was unfocused and difficult to follow. Again, the decision not to concentrate on specific communities was criticized by community members themselves.

This aspect of the evaluation showed that, in tackling a subject such as the history of immigration and trying to attract a new audience, a museum creates a new constituency of expectation, even if its overall aims are successfully achieved. It is also clear that very broad-brush treatments may be unsatisfactory to those who have a detailed stake in one particular aspect of the broad theme. Nevertheless, the exhibition's aim to bring together the histories of diverse communities in an account of London's population, does seem to have been achieved. There was a noticeably strong call amongst visitors' comments and focus group members for the exhibition to be made a permanent feature of the museum.

## Other elements of the project

The focus weeks, as predicted, were the most successful element of the public programme, and possibly of the whole project. The fact that they were co-ordinated by community groups themselves meant that each community added its own publicity to that of the museum, and brought its own audience. The majority of people coming for many of the focus week events were first-time visitors to the museum. The programme of events had the additional advantage of providing a further impetus to visit the museum, alongside the temporary exhibition. The focus weeks seem generally to have achieved their aim of adding another, deeper dimension to the necessarily relatively superficial treatment of an exhibition. In one instance, though, there was criticism that the museum had marginalized some of the community panel exhibitions brought in for the focus weeks by mounting them in non-prominent areas. In total, 135 activities or events were put on during the six months of the exhibition, generating 8400 visits.

From the museum's point of view the publicity for the exhibition and events was successful. The wider press campaign, coupled with the television and radio coverage, as well as word of mouth, seems to have helped generate a wider audience. The column inches devoted to the exhibition were calculated to be the equivalent of £244,000 worth of advertising. Research showed that 7 per cent of visitors came to the exhibition purely because of the tube poster campaign, while 25 per cent recognized the posters once shown them. The downside of this was that some people felt that the exhibition did not deliver what the posters promised, as they could be read to imply an exhibition mostly concentrating on the Chinese, South Asian and African-Caribbean communities.

The *Peopling of London* book has sold over 3500 copies to date and has been reprinted. The resource pack, however, has sold less than 500, possibly because the (cheaper) book may have been perceived as a competing, rather than a complementary item. At £14.95 it was unusually expensive for museum materials. Despite this, all education programmes and workshops were fully booked by school groups for the duration of the exhibition.

## Conclusion and future prospects

The *Peopling of London* project was a new departure for the Museum of London, and one that was successful in achieving most of its aims. It showed that a museum can tackle supposedly difficult topics of contemporary relevance and place them in long-term historical context in such a way as to interest a new audience. Through the extensive campaign of outreach and consultation, the museum achieved a much higher profile amongst communities with whom it had previously had little or no contact. We also gained practical experience of the different forms that 'community involvement' can take. Given the complexity of the *Peopling of London* project, especially the number of communities represented, it was not practicable to 'hand over control' to a range of communities. In practice, museum staff had to develop the confidence to direct the project themselves and take full responsibility for the content of the project, while *consulting* closely with communities. The museum also learned that this approach is extremely time-consuming and resource-intensive. Altogether almost all of the museum's staff were involved in some aspect of the project, however briefly. An estimate of the amount of staff time spent on the project is around 1000 person weeks. At the same time, we learned that concentrating our resources on a single project comprising a number of different elements was extremely beneficial both because of economies of scale and because of the resulting highly focused and high profile project. As a result, the *Peopling of London* was probably the most prominent project the museum has undertaken. Well over a year after its closure visitors continue to ask if the exhibition is still on, and a steady stream of requests for further information are received.

This in turn results in much higher expectations from London's communities. The task for the museum now is to ensure that those expectations are not dashed in the future. Accordingly, since the exhibition closed, a number of initiatives have been taking place to keep up its momentum. The first of these is the gradual refurbishment of the museum's permanent galleries, which will include explicit recognition of London's diverse communities from earliest times. An important element of this will be a display on post-war London that will be installed in 1996. The museum is also in the process of appointing a Community Access Officer with funding from the London's Docklands Development Corporation, Midland Bank and from Museum of London income. His or her role will be to continue some of the relationships already established with community groups, and work with them on community history projects resulting in exhibitions that will be shown at community venues and the Museum of London. This is part of a plan by the museum to use some of its spaces, such as the entrance hall, for community exhibitions. The Community Access Officer will also help formulate a long-term policy on community access. In the meantime, the museum has been adopting some of the approaches and lessons learned in the 'Peopling of London' project to the rest of its activities. We hope and intend that from now on cultural diversity is no longer something dealt with in separate projects, but at the heart of everything we do.

## Acknowledgements

I would like to thank Valerie Cumming, Max Hebditch, Rory O'Connell, Rozina Visram and Emma Webb for reading and commenting on a draft of this chapter. Any errors or omissions are of course entirely my responsibility.

## Notes

1. Figure taken from a 1993 survey by the Association of London Authorities, quoted in *The Runnymede Bulletin*, No. 266, June 1993, p. 6.
2. It is difficult to be precise about the absolute proportion of ethnic minority visitors to the museum before the 'Peopling of London' exhibition because the sample of visitors surveyed on this question was too small to be entirely reliable. The size of sample was increased during the exhibition.
3. The term 'ethnic minority' is an unsatisfactory one, both because of the difficulties of defining ethnicity and the implied marginalization of the term 'minority'. In the absence of a better alternative, however, the term is used here as a shorthand for non-dominant cultural groups self-defined through their ethnicity and/or religion.
4. Strictly speaking one needs to compare statistics of ethnic minority museum visitors *from London* against statistics of ethnic minorities in London overall. The former figures are unfortunately not available. It was nevertheless clear to museum staff that we were not attracting members of ethnic minority communities in anything like their proportions in London's overall population.
5. The project involved most of the museum's staff at some stage. The initiators of the project were Nick Merriman and Nichola Johnson, with help from Peter Stott. When the latter two moved to new posts, the basic Project Team developing the project consisted of Nick Merriman, Rozina Visram, Rory O'Connell, Sophia Pegers, Andy Topping, Geoffrey Toms, Emma Webb and Russell Clark, with contributions from Suzie Burt and William Tayleur. Other colleagues, too numerous to mention here, were involved at later stages.

## References

Crew, S.R. and Sims, J.E. (1991) Locating authenticity: fragments of a dialogue, in I. Karp and S.D. Lavine (eds), *Exhibiting Cultures. The Poetics and Politics of Museum Display*, pp. 159–175, Smithsonian Institution Press, Washington, DC.

Fraser, P. and Visram, R. (1988) *Black Contribution to History*, CUES Community Division and Geffrye Museum, London.

Merriman, N. (1991) *Beyond the Glass Case. The Past, the Heritage and the Public in Britain*, Leicester University Press, Leicester.

Peirson Jones, J. (1992) The colonial legacy and the community: the Gallery 33 project, in I. Karp, C.M. Kreamer and S.D. Lavine (eds), *Museums and Communities. The Politics of Public Culture*, pp. 221–241, Smithsonian Institution Press, Washington, DC.

Selwood, S. (1996) *The Peopling of London: an Evaluation of the Exhibition*, Museum of London/New Ethnicities Unit, University of East London joint publication, London.

Trevelyan, V. (ed.) (1991) *'Dingy Places with Different Kinds of Bits'. An Attitudes Survey of London Museums amongst Non-visitors*, London Museums Service, London.

Visram, R. (1986) *Ayahs, Lascars and Princes. The Story of Indians in Britain 1700–1947*, Pluto Press, London.

# 8

## Academic and public domains: when is a dagger a sword?

NIMA POOVAYA SMITH

An overwhelming proportion of Bradford Asians are from the Punjab in the Indian subcontinent. Through a circumlocutory process of history, an industrial city in the north of England has replicated in part the composition of the population of the Punjab, which in its post-independence divided state belongs to both Pakistan and India, and has a population consisting of Muslims, Sikhs and Hindus. In addition, Bradford and Punjab have another parallel; both regions have been home to diverse groups of people, producing a cultural mix that has often led to volatile situations.

Today the Asian population of Bradford comprises approximately 70,000 Muslims, Sikhs and Hindus, most of whom are deeply committed to their particular faiths. It is a city that prides itself on its pioneering spirit. It boasted the first Asian Lord Mayor in Britain and the current Vicar of Bradford is a Pakistani Anglican. On the other hand, Bradford has also had one of the largest numbers of race discrimination cases brought against the council and copies of Salman Rushdie's *The Satanic Verses* had their first public burning in this city.

My post as Keeper of Arts was created for politic and political reasons nearly 10 years ago and was, until recently, mainly central government funded. The race riots of 1981 had badly shaken the country and, as a result, a number of posts catering to minority requirements were created within social services, health and education all over Britain. Provision for the arts was viewed as something of a luxury, but Bradford with its high proportion of Asians saw the necessity for the city's cultural diversity to be reflected in its arts policies.

The post, although primarily curatorial, prioritized networking with the communities of Bradford as an important strand of its function. This manifests itself in regular consultation meetings where museum policies, the collections and the exhibitions programme are the principal topics on the agenda. The close interaction with some members of the Asian community, in particular, has led to a series of unique and often creative partnerships between museum and community. For instance, the communities' input into the museum's most public aspect, its exhibitions programme, has resulted in a number of successful displays.

Since 1987 three major exhibitions have been initiated by members of the Asian community; they have also had an increasing degree of involvement with each show which was quite remarkable. The exhibitions directly related to the faiths of the three main groups – Muslims, Hindus and Sikhs: *Islamic Calligraphy* in 1987, *The Ramayana* in 1989 and *Warm and Rich and Fearless*, an exhibition of Sikh art in 1991. (What might appear a rather bizarre title is actually a quotation from Lord Baden Powell's description of the Sikh artists' use of colour.) These cultures, particularly those of the Muslims and Sikhs, have often been represented as violent and uncompromising. While it would be presumptuous to say that the exhibitions were intended to redress this imbalance, the aim was to contribute towards a re-evaluation.

Because of their religious underpinnings, the exhibitions needed careful planning, and community consultations often helped to avert possible disasters. *Islamic Calligraphy* for instance, included a number of rare and beautiful Korans. Representatives of the Muslim community advised us to display them in such a manner that they were elevated above the other more secular objects within the exhibition. The Mullahs were then invited to bless the gallery before it was officially opened to the public.

Similarly, *The Ramayana*, which consisted of exquisite manuscript paintings based on one of Hinduism's major epics, had a devotional dance-recital on the opening night, a dance-drama choreographed around the important episode of the abduction of the heroine Sita and several story-telling session, not only as aids to interpretation, but also to convey something of the auspicious meaning that the epic holds for most Hindus.

This paper will concentrate on the most recent of these three exhibitions – *Warm and Rich and Fearless*, an exhibition of Sikh art, as it illustrates even more comprehensively than the other two the process of transmission of ideas from the curatorial/academic arena to the public domain and the challenges and problems attendant upon it.

That this is not an issue peculiar to museums and galleries alone, was forcibly brought home in two famous instances. David Jenkins, formerly an academic at the University of Leeds, when appointed Bishop of Durham, publicly questioned the veracity of the Virgin Birth and stated that it served as symbol rather than fact. What would have passed with scarcely a murmur in cloister or common-room, was now suddenly propelled into the public domain. Bishop Jenkins was immediately denounced by sections of the public and the clergy for blasphemy. Salman Rushdie wrote a novel that, in the accepted satirical tradition, held what Rushdie contended was a relentless mirror up to modern society. The consequences of an irreverent and direct critique of Islam and the Prophet are now too well known to be gone into here. Jenkins, and to a much greater extent Rushdie, found that, whilst the demythifying process was perfectly acceptable in the academic world, it elicited a far more direct and violent reaction when admitted to the public domain.

By separating the academic from the public domain, I do not wish to imply that the public is universally a lay or an uninformed public. Indeed, conflicts over interpretation and representation arise particularly with a knowledgeable public, especially if the discourse pertains to their own culture or religious traditions. The responses are, however, not always necessarily knee-jerk. There is often a complex body of thought behind the responses, ranging from sectarianism to liberalism; and it is within this broad spectrum that groups are able to work out their own strategies of resistance, compromise and reconciliation when under attack, if given the opportunity.

Since the 1980s, museums, in response to criticism about elitist policies have in practice or intent, opened up to a much wider audience than hitherto thought possible or even desirable. The inevitable result of this greater accessibility is that the movement of ideas from the academic to the public domain is far more rapid. Scholarly interpretations of a faith or a culture are almost always at variance with the interpretations or the perceptions of the people who are adherents of that particular faith or culture. Yet too often, what is described as intellectual freedom is in reality arrogance and what are apparently intellectual truths can be rooted in shallow misconceptions. One cannot, therefore, dismiss these differences in simplistic terms as the conflict between the emotionally held beliefs of a particular public against the intellectually maintained truths of an academic community.

The academic domain is often far removed from the cut and thrust of ordinary life. This gulf is doubly reinforced in a European context when the culture in question is non-Western. The latter has its own reality and operational dynamics of which academic analyses often do not take sufficient cognisance. This refusal or inability to recognize these dynamics perhaps explains the inbuilt obsolescence of most orientalist research.

There have been other developments that have altered the nature of the movement of ideas from the academic to the public domain. By and large, the Asian public in Britain today is increasingly sceptical and suspicious about academic credentials. This is particularly true of orientalism, where up until recently the discourse was dominated by Western orientalists who brought their own prejudices and preconceptions to bear on their work. Edward Said in his influential book *Orientalism* remarks on how:

> A vast number of pages on the Orient exist, and they of course signify a degree and quantity of interaction with the Orient that are quite formidable, but the crucial index of Western strength is that there is no possibility of comparing the movement of Westerners eastwards (since the end of the 18th century) with the movement of Easterners westwards (Said, 1978, p. 204).

Said concludes that the 'Orientalist's presence is enabled by the Orient's effective absence' (Said, 1978, p. 208).

However, today, factors such as immigration, the thrust of cultural diversity policies and a more demanding and articulate minority community have changed the nature of orientalist discourse. The Asian public itself is an important repository of a deep and varied subculture, of knowledge that is atavistic, received or direct. This is a formidable databank of information and seldom tapped. It is usually ignored by the 'orientalist' academic community, unless they choose to make a group itself an object of study.

It is against this background that I shall return to the exhibition already stated as embodying the main theme of the paper, *Warm and Rich and Fearless*. The modern curator faces a number of dilemmas. If belief is the lynchpin of a certain group, the motivating force that shapes and gives their existence meaning, how much of a right does one have to dismantle or deconstruct this belief system as an intellectual exercise? The curator can be faced with conflicting responsibilities – to present a show that has veracity, although truth is always subjective, and/or to build bridges with new communities and new audiences; the two, if badly handled, can be antithetical.

I posit a theory that the stance of confronting issues head-on, of hammering out every detail in public debate, even if well intentioned, may not always be the solution to difficult situations. While being sensitive to minority concerns, to create an issue artificially can be damaging. This form of confrontation, though not without its positive side, often fixes and crystallizes a culture, which if left sympathetically to its own devices, might have resolved conflicts in its own way.

My own favourite role models are the wily merchants of the sub-continent, its true statesmen; they can come from any of the three main religious groups, Hindu, Muslim or Sikh. Through political and religious vicissitudes, their desire to retain customers from all faiths has developed in them finely honed political and survival instincts, from which we can all learn a lesson. My particular favourite is a restaurant owner in Leeds, a neighbouring city of Bradford. On the walls of his little cafe are the icons of all his clients – the Royal Family, film stars, Jesus Christ, the pantheon of Hindu gods and goddesses, Allah's name in Arabic calligraphy and a portrait of the founder of Sikhism – Guru Nanak. Incongruous though they may be, they are an excellent exercise in public relations. Yet the Hindu owner would not happily countenance his own children marrying into other faiths. A number of people would describe his gesture with the portraits as tokenism; I wonder if it is not wisdom.

The general perception of Sikh males as a turbanned, bearded group, and where uncut hair is the norm for men and women, has been superseded by the more recent perception of a disaffected separatist group seeking an independent homeland, Khalistan. It was this perception that the Sikh advisors to the exhibition were anxious to alter and to replace with a more complex discourse that reasserted the individual as well as the group.

The exhibition was intended to trace the salient aspects of Sikh art and through it provide people with an insight into Sikh history and the manner in which its past informs its present. Members of the Sikh community of Bradford who had initiated the idea, generously offered time and expertise to the project. The exhibition consisted mainly of nineteenth-century paintings, costumes, textiles, weaponry and armour. A significant proportion of the material was produced during or just after the reign of Maharaja Ranjit Singh (1770–1839), the premier Sikh king who was the first to forge an independent, powerful Sikh kingdom. Even though this barely survived beyond his lifetime, it was to become the archetype and golden model for subsequent Sikh dreams of an autonomous homeland.

The exhibition also included British depictions of the Punjab, particularly scenes from the three Anglo-Sikh wars, which resulted in British victory over the Sikhs in 1849. Paintings recording this painful period of Sikh history were exclusively by British artists. The vanquished tend not to depict defeat in art, particularly in the sub-continent, where art was usually celebratory.

An attempt was also made (circumscribed by what one could borrow) to display replicas of objects that appeared in the paintings. Thus a peacock feather fan, two resplendent robes and a horse necklace of rubies and turquoises and gold perfume-holders were among some of the objects on display. There were also a number of rare Sikh sacred texts such as the *Janam Sakhi* (stories of the life of Guru Nanak) and the *Dasam Granth*, compiled by the last and most charismatic Sikh Guru, Guru Gobind Singh.

The funding of the exhibition merits some attention, as this materially affected its nature. *Warm and Rich and Fearless* was funded diversely if somewhat curiously. Bradford Art Galleries and Museums and Visiting Arts provided it with base funding. The Museums and Galleries Commission awarded it £10,000 on condition that it toured to two other venues. The Department of Environment granted-aided it up to £15,000 on condition that efforts were made to attract a certain number of visitors from outside Bradford. The rationale behind this condition was based on market research findings that visitors to the district spent a minimum average of £8.00 per person. As this was invested into the local economy it also gave the Department of Environment a return for its investment, so to speak. The Task Force of Bradford, a body set up to increase employment through training in targeted areas, gave the exhibition a grant of £1500. This sum was reserved for training courses on the exhibition in particular and the gallery services in general with the intention that people would come to view the museums services as another area of possible employment. The Sikh community of Bradford decided to make their contribution in kind and provided a sumptuous meal for the exhibition preview. As this involved dinner for nearly 900 guests, it was no mean contribution.

The conditions of grant-aid engendered more work in an area where the workload was already formidable, but it also meant that a much wider public had an opportunity to see the show. It travelled to Walsall, near Birmingham (see Cox and Singh, this volume), and to London. The daunting Department of the Environment condition of attracting notable numbers of outside visitors meant that networking and publicity were in deadly earnest and had to hit various targets.

Some of the networking had already been put in motion a year before the exhibition actually opened. Two introductory lectures on Sikh art and religion were delivered to the Friends of Bradford Art Galleries and Museums by Mohinder Singh Chana, one of the principal Sikh advisors, and myself. Networking, in addition to targeted mailshots of posters and leaflets, also included a number of visits to the various Sikh *Gurudwaras* of West Yorkshire, where Sikhs gather for congregational worship. With characteristic generosity I was allowed to make an announcement after each prayer-meeting, providing people with details about the exhibition and encouraging them to visit it. *The Sikh Messenger*, a monthly magazine with a national Sikh readership, carried an article by Mohinder Singh Chana and myself on the forthcoming exhibition. Word of mouth publicity among the Sikhs and others also proved to be an extremely effective device.

In order to fulfil Task Force requirements, a series of illustrated talks on the exhibition was organized before it was due to open. All the objects selected for the show were presented through slides, consequently those members of the public who attended these well-subscribed lectures developed a familiarity with the exhibits and a sense of involvement with them even before they went on display. The exhibition, therefore, seemed set to reach an extremely wide cross-section of the public; a large proportion were inevitably the Sikhs themselves, who felt a vested interest in the exhibition. Coach-loads of Sikh visitors travelled from London, Manchester, Coventry and Glasgow to view the show.

The evening of the preview gave a clear indication of the manner in which the exhibition would be appropriated by a much wider public. Doctors, engineers and academics jostled shoulders with plumbers and garage mechanics. This meeting ground was characterized by what I call the episode of the whisk, the dagger, the painting and the battle-standard.

The initial publicity blurbs had waxed eloquent about ornamental silver-handled fly-whisks or *chauris* that would go on display. They were not only frequently depicted in Sikh paintings, either being waved over the figure of one of the 10 gurus or a member of Sikh royalty, but also form an indispensable part of contemporary Sikh worship. They are used to gently and rhythmically fan the Sikh sacred text, the *Guru Granth Saheb*, during congregational worship. *Chauris* also figure copiously in Hindu, Buddhist and Jain art, both in sculpture and painting.

The translation of *chauri* into fly-whisk, something that had been accepted unquestioningly and perhaps unthinkingly by me, because of its long and undisputed usage, was immediately singled out as a point of contention by different members of the Sikh community. The *chauri* had, they pointed out, a far more sacred and symbolic function than keeping flies at bay. The *Guru Granth Saheb* was the source of all wisdom to the Sikhs and some actually referred to it as the eleventh Guru. Waving the *chauri* could even be a trance-inducing aid that led to mystic visions.

Whatever its etymology and original function, as far as the Sikhs were concerned its meaning had been transformed since their incorporation of it. Obviously, because of a shared language with their Hindu and Muslim neighbours, there was a common terminology, but a number of words had been imbued with wholly new meanings by them. This was an appropriation of language or sections of a language to suit a newly evolving philosophical and moral framework. Through this they also proclaimed their separateness from other groups and their essential autonomy. I found these arguments hard to refute and duly made the change from fly-whisk to whisk.

The fact that this had evoked instant and separate responses from several Sikhs who could not possibly have communicated with one another before approaching me was also indicative of another development. The Sikhs were obviously very carefully and meticulously reinterpreting many aspects of their religious history and carefully monitoring secular non-Sikh responses to the changes. Philology and semantics obviously came under close scrutiny. Words with sacral associations, but with profane functions had the latter assiduously edited out. What made this continuing process even more fascinating was the fact that this effort was not confined to a small group of Sikh scholars and theologians. It was a re-assessment that had percolated to a surprisingly broad base. What one was witnessing was the further codifying and unifying of a faith already given a remarkably tight structure in the early eighteenth century by its last Guru, Guru Gobind Singh.

This was brought home, even more forcibly, through the episode of the 'dagger'. The Sikhs were formalized into an immediately recognizable group by their tenth and last Guru, Guru Gobind Singh, who had not only declared that the Guruship would come to an end after his death, but also vested sole spiritual authority in the *Guru Granth Saheb*, the Sikh sacred text. In order to inculcate a separate identity and keep the Sikhs as a distinct and cohesive group, Guru Gobind Singh had through an emotionally charged ceremony fused a disparate band of people together by initiating those who volunteered themselves into the rites of the Khalsa or the brotherhood of the pure. The initiates had an exacting code of conduct to follow, and the use of weapons in defence of the faith was sanctioned. Even today some Sikhs describe themselves as 'Defenders of all faiths'. Their distinctness was reinforced by what is popularly referred to as the five Ks, the external symbols (though each with a spiritual meaning) of *Kesh* or uncut hair, *Kanga* or comb, *Kacha* or shorts, *Khada* or steel bracelet and *Kirpan* or 'dagger'.

It was over the last K that I came unstuck. Along with Sikh bridal jewellery and textiles, the five Ks had been duly displayed, with the *Kirpan* described as a 'dagger'. When the exhibition was opened to the public, Sikh response was swift. It was not a 'dagger' I was informed, it was a sword. I was puzzled by this, as to me it had all the appearance of a dagger, but, they informed me, the *Kirpan* was an important and sacred Sikh symbol. It was a badge of honour. The Sikh or Khalsa symbol showed two swords which stood for the balance of Miri and Piri, the secular and the sacred. 'Dagger' in the English language, they said, had pejorative connotations. You tended to stab people in the back with daggers. Swords were used for honourable face-to-face combat. At first, I must admit that I was annoyed by what I considered as an attempt to sanitize all aspects of Sikhism, but their cogently argued case made me concede that they had a point. To them spiritually and symbolically the *Kirpan* was not a dagger, though it may look like a dagger. A word already loaded with shades of calculated treachery, although technically correct, did not convey the spirit. This was a subtle point but an important one. The labels were all duly changed to read 'sword' instead of 'dagger'.

I now turn to the lighter and more humbling episode of the William Carpenter painting. A charming painting in its own way, entitled 'Two Sikhs reading the *Granth Saheb* in front of the Golden Temple', it showed two men poring over a book. I had not thought to question what was essentially the artist's own title, but closer examination by a Sikh revealed that the two men not only had what are popularly known as Hindu caste-marks (albeit faint) on their forehead, but the book they were perusing was not large enough to be the *Guru Granth Saheb*, and the shadow cast by the building behind them was not the right shape or size to be the Golden Temple. A member of the public, by virtue of being a Sikh, instinctively possessed an eye for fine detail when it came to his own culture.

Finally I turn to the debate of the Sikh battle-standards. Loaned to us by a collector/dealer and previously in the collection of Lord Dalhousie, one time Governor General of India, they had been used in the last Anglo-Sikh battle of 1849 and therefore held a particular poignance for the Sikhs as that battle had effectively put an end to an independent Sikh kingdom. They are handsome red silk and gold affairs, and contained within the central blockprinted gold sunburst was the faded but unmistakable figure of the Hindu goddess, Kali Durga, seated on a tiger. In their drive for a distinct identity, some Sikh reinterpretations tend to either eschew any Hindu influence or to view such an influence as a vitiating or debasing force. They do not accept Sikhism as a reformist religion in reaction against Hinduism, but as a revealed religion with a reforming mission. This is by no means a universally held view among Sikhs for like all groups, they have many schools of thought, but it is certainly a majority Sikh view within Britain. The battle-standards, because of the Hindu goddess image, obviously became a talking point among Sikh visitors, who were clearly unconvinced about its Sikh antecedents even after I had catalogued to them the details of its water-tight provenance. They were obviously unhappy about its inclusion in the exhibition and about its implicit challenge of carefully nurtured beliefs of exclusiveness and autonomy.

The psychology in operation was once again fascinating and subtle. This was a potentially major issue for the Sikhs. The separateness of Sikhism from Hinduism is a focal point of the demand from sections of the Sikh community for an independent Sikh state. The banners undermined this argument. They were, as far as a number of Sikhs were concerned, a false representation of history. When I refused to concede to this point of view, the rationalization of one Sikh elder recalled my role model merchants. Ranjit Singh, he pointed out, like the mighty Emperor Akbar before him, was not a religious bigot. He had employed Hindus, Muslims and even Europeans in his highly trained army. Each group had been encouraged to carry on with the practice of their own faith. This was clearly the battle-standard of a Hindu battalion. The Sikh elder had enabled everyone to save face without anyone abandoning any convictions, but what was significant about this episode was that at no time was I asked to take the battle-standards down or alter the information panel and label. In a delicate balancing act between academic and public domains, a major concession had been won.

Here was a group of people, determined to have an involvement in the portrayal of their cultural history, and who had a better right? 'The modern Orient in short, participates in its own Orientalizing', Said (1978, p. 324) has said, but this self-parodying, this conforming to an occidental stereotype, becomes more difficult when the academic and public domains are allowed to, dare I say, merge judicially. There are undoubted pitfalls. The desire to glorify one's history must always be a temptation, particularly for minority groups, but as the episode of the battle-standard reveals, it can be a temptation that is successfully resisted even by a strong and self-willed group, through a system of internal checks and balances. The Sikhs could have attempted to exert their collective will over one lone curator. The fact that they chose not to do so was their ultimate act of triumph, just as the fact that they unquestioningly allowed me, a Hindu, to curate the exhibition was their ultimate act of generosity.

## Reference

Said, E. (1978) *Orientalism*. Routledge and Kegan Paul, London, p. 204.

# 9

## Walsall Museum and Art Gallery and the Sikh community: a case study

ALISON COX WITH AMARJIT SINGH

Ten miles north of Birmingham, the Metropolitan Borough of Walsall covers several towns and is an area of increasing urban deprivation, with low car ownership, poor health records, unemployment higher than the national average and the highest teenage pregnancy rate in Europe. Contrary to popular belief, however, Walsall is *not* the home of the 'anorak wearers' club' as suggested recently in a television comedy show and has an identity rather stronger than its image as a minor suburb of Birmingham would suggest. Walsall Museum and Art Gallery is funded by the local authority and exists primarily to serve a culturally diverse audience of some 270,000 people drawn from across this wide area. According to recent census data, almost one in 10 of this number is of non-white European origin. Seven per cent of the population are of 'Asian' origin, meaning principally Sikh, Hindu and Muslim peoples.

Walsall Museum and Art Gallery comprises a community history gallery, an exhibition space mainly showing contemporary visual arts and an extraordinary art collection given to Walsall by Lady Kathleen Garman, widow of sculptor Sir Jacob Epstein, which includes works by Van Gogh, Pissarro, Constable, Turner and other luminaries of Western European art, as well as art works from Ancient Greece and Rome, China and Africa. The museum's audience is primarily local, with seven out of 10 visitors coming from Walsall and the surrounding borough. There is a very high percentage of repeat visits and most users are under 25 – a surprisingly youthful visitorship compared to many museums.

For many years the museum has been making strenuous efforts to find new ways of involving local people in its programmes, and of challenging the legacy of the Victorian moral and social values which underpinned its creation a century ago. At the opening speech of 1892, the Mayor, Alderman Brownhill declared that:

> If the Art Gallery was successful in its purpose, they would see that the manners of the people would become softer and less uncouth than they were at present, for they could not see pictures and mix with others as they would do in that room without being cheered and instructed and lifted to a higher level.

In keeping with the era, the original aim of Walsall Museum and Art Gallery was in part to help 'improve' its citizens, who were viewed as the passive consumers of a neatly packaged version of the dominant culture.

At Walsall Museum and Art Gallery, as with most museums today, there is still a keen sense of the social and educational value of museums, but the emphasis is now increasingly on active participation, on working *with* people as much as *for* them and on inclusiveness rather than exclusivity. Within the museum world in England, perhaps the best known initiative is 'The People's Show' which began in 1990 and has been repeated several times since with an ever increasing number of participating museums from across the county. In 'The People's Show', local people are invited to display their own collections no matter how grand, small, bizarre or commonplace, challenging assumptions of taste and value, questioning the canons of curatorial control and blurring distinctions between fine art and popular culture. 'The People's Show' has attracted much interest, but perhaps none so gratifying as that of one of its participants, Tom Holmes, a tie collector in his seventies, who presented the museum with a plaque in recognition of the work of the gallery in displaying his collection. Walsall must be one of the first galleries in Britain to be given an award by a member of its audience! Other exhibitions have been planned around the needs of particular audiences in consultation with potential users. 'Start', for example, was an exhibition for three- to five-year-olds based on art works from the collections. Here the needs of the audiences were a primary, rather than a secondary consideration (Walsall Museum and Art Gallery, 1996). History and art collecting and display policies now actively try to represent the diversity of contemporary society. For example, 'The Journey', by black photographer Vanley Burke, traced a personal view of peoples' experiences of migration from the Caribbean to Britain since the 1950s. 'Captives', by Keith Khan and Ali Zaidi, was an installation commissioned as part of the West Midlands South Asian Art Festival of 1994. There is also active collecting around women's history and of art by women artists.

The basic aim behind all of this work is to explore the role of the museum and to discover just what it is that 'access to the arts' means to museums today. It is within this context that the case study outlined below should be seen. The subject of the study is a project undertaken with Walsall's Sikh community in 1991–1992. It describes and analyses the background and history to the project, the strategies used to involve local Sikh people, and the short- and long-term effects on both the museum and the Sikh community. As with most 'community' projects, it raises complex issues for museums today. Most of the information is taken from a final evaluation of the project in 1992 and from a follow-up discussion between the authors prior to writing this article.

In Spring 1992 Walsall Museum and Art Gallery hosted 'Warm and Rich and Fearless – an Exhibition of Sikh Art'. This major exhibition, the first of its kind in Britain, was initiated by Bradford Art Galleries and Museums in consultation with the Sikh community in Bradford (see Poovaya Smith, this volume). Largely historical in content, it aimed to celebrate Sikh history, culture and religion through stunning displays of miniature paintings, prints, costume, textiles, rare manuscripts, precious metalwork, jewellery, arms and weaponry. Objects were drawn from various collections including the Royal Collection, the Victoria and Albert Museum and the India Office Library. Although many pieces had not been on public display before and were unknown until this exhibition, the tone was intentionally celebratory rather than critical.

'Warm and Rich and Fearless' presented an important and rare opportunity to celebrate the cultural traditions of a particular community at a time when the glorious moments of a European tradition are more usually celebrated. Sikh peoples have had a significant part in British society for many years and yet much of this history is rarely acknowledged. In Walsall the Sikh population is the largest within the 'Asian' population and, although it would have been naive and patronizing to assume that an exhibition of Sikh 'heritage' would necessarily appeal to local Sikhs, the positive experience in Bradford suggested that there would be reasonable interest. These reasons informed the selection of the exhibition for Walsall as part of its national tour.

From the outset there was an awareness among staff that new kinds of encouragement would be needed in order to engage people with the exhibition. As the contents of *Warm and Rich and Fearless* were a 'given', it was felt that the most appropriate way of making active links with people was through a wide-ranging education programme. This would involve an intensive period of consultation and planning which was beyond the scope and, much more importantly, beyond the knowledge and experience of museum staff. Following a successful funding application to the Regional Arts Board (West Midlands Arts), a temporary post of Community Events Co-ordinator was advertised.

The brief, developed with support from Walsall's experienced Community Arts Team, was to develop and implement a lively programme of events and activities, open to all, but stemming initially from the needs and interests of local Sikh people. In essence, the museum was looking for a good communicator with experience of arts development work and a track record of translating ideas into action. At this stage it was not considered essential that the post holder be Sikh or have experience of working with Sikh communities. It was also understood at the outset that this project involved risk. What if there was no interest in it? Whatever the outcome, however, the museum stood to learn more about how – or how not – to make links with one part of its community.

The post went to Amarjit Singh, a young, energetic and local Sikh arts worker who teaches part time at Walsall College of Arts and Technology in the Special Needs Department. Although not a strict, orthodox Sikh, Amarjit was passionately interested in Sikh culture, was proficient in Punjabi and already had a wide network of contacts within the community including links with the *Gurudwaras* (Sikh temples) which, being both social centres and places of worship, form a focal point for many Sikhs. The importance of his knowledge and experience became increasingly apparent to museum staff as the project progressed. Firstly, as a Sikh, Amarjit had a subtle understanding of the customs, beliefs and values of the community. A non-Sikh would have had to gain this understanding or find an equivalent to Amarjit within the community, thereby extending the chain of communication and adding another layer of complexity to the project. Secondly, as a Punjabi speaker, communication was greatly improved, making it much easier to build a trusting relationship with people and to negotiate from an equal basis. The importance of this became apparent from the outset of the consultative period when certain community representatives – particularly in the *Gurudwaras* – appeared to view the project with some suspicion.

It was a relief to Amarjit that the post carried a high degree of autonomy, and that he was not intended simply to act as a messenger service between *Gurudwara* and museum – something he had feared at first and an issue that is often raised in projects which are initiated by an external agency. He was also relieved that he was not expected to deliver a programme that had already been decided by the museum. At the same time it was important to him that the post was well supported at all stages by a team of museum staff committed to the project and to improving their understanding of Sikh culture and religion. From the beginning of the consultation period Amarjit made it clear that he was offering members of the Sikh community an opportunity for active involvement, not simply delivering a service. People needed to own the project in order for it to be a success. He was also keen to cater for a broad range of interests and to use the exhibition as a springboard for addressing key issues and concerns within the Sikh community. Initially the consultation period got off to a slow start.

As a mark of respect and in acknowledgement of the central role of the two *Gurudwaras* in Sikh affairs in Walsall, it was important to seek their advice and help. At first support was lukewarm. Amarjit has suggested various reasons for this. As a young liberal-minded Sikh it may have been considered that he did not have sufficient knowledge and understanding of the religious and cultural background to be working on a project of this nature. There was also some concern that Amarjit would be a puppet for the museum and hence for the local authority and that the exhibition and project would be a tokenistic gesture. What, it was felt by others, could this project contribute to the Sikh community which it couldn't provide for itself? Amarjit believes that these concerns may stem from previous local authority initiatives imperfectly planned and acquitted. As the project progressed and gained in momentum, however, it gained the confidence of representatives within the *Gurudwaras* and they became tremendously supportive, later providing essential assistance with the opening celebrations, for example, and arranging many visits by young people to the exhibition.

For Amarjit, the fact that he was not an orthodox Sikh was a positive advantage to the project. Like him, many Sikh people share a passionate interest in their culture, even if they are not orthodox and do not regularly worship at the *Gurudwaras*. His liberalism gave him opportunities to consult widely and hence to cater for other needs than may otherwise have been possible. It also meant that he could balance these needs with the organizational and practical needs of the museum. For example, it was felt by some elders at the *Gurudwaras* that there should be compulsory removal of shoes and covering of heads when entering the exhibition, particularly as the *Dasam Granth* (the holy book) was on display. Amarjit did not feel compromised by explaining that in the context of the exhibition this would not be appropriate for everyone, although all visitors would have the opportunity to make this mark of respect.

Following discussions at the *Gurudwaras*, an informal advisory group grew up around the project, consisting of a number of young, forward-thinking and active members of the Sikh community, including a local youth worker, a careers advisor interested in women's issues, a sports development worker, a solicitor and other highly committed individuals, some of whom had close links to the *Gurudwaras* and could therefore act as negotiators on behalf of the project. This group was instrumental in various ways throughout the project, suggesting some events, organizing and leading others, networking, and generally helping to publicize the exhibition and related activities. Some of these people were already known to Amarjit either socially or professionally, and others were introduced to him. Amarjit felt it essential to enlist the support of individuals 'out there' and not to rely solely on people who could be contacted through official channels – officers within the local authority, for example – or others in a representative role. Staff at the museum attended the first meetings of the Advisory Group, but thereafter their main role was to support Amarjit and to help with the administration of the programme.

The response to the consultation around *Warm and Rich and Fearless* was energetic, with much support completely unforeseen. For example, a group of local women made and embroidered a canopy for the holy book, the *Dasam Granth*, when it was realized that this essential item was not provided by the initiating venue and, later on, elders from the Sikh community worked with school groups in the exhibition to explain some of the principles behind the Sikh faith. The consultative period resulted in a wide range of events and activities, some large-scale, some small, and catering for a wide range of interests; some of these are outlined below. They show how the exhibition was used as a catalyst for various kinds of involvement.

The traditional exhibition preview was replaced by opening celebrations which were attended by over 400 people. Following opening prayers by a priest from one of the *Gurudwaras*, a spectacular entertainment took place at the nearby Garage Arts and Media Centre (now sadly closed), which included musical performances and a stunning display of *gatka* – a Sikh martial art form. Men contacted via the *Gurudwaras* acted as voluntary stewards for the event, and free food was generously provided by members of the Sikh community. This event helped to generate excitement and support for the project and was attended by whole family groups, an unusual occurrence in a community in which men tend to socialize separately from women and children. A similar evening took place some weeks later and was equally well attended. This second event include *bhangra* (Punjabi folk dance), which was excluded from the opening celebrations because of concern within the Sikh community that it is seen as a Sikh art form when in fact it is part of a more general Punjabi culture. With confidence in the project running high, Amarjit felt it appropriate to introduce this important aspect of youth culture into the programme.

Other activities organized around *Warm and Rich and Fearless* had quite different aims. One member of the advisory group felt that the exhibition had a masculine bias with its emphasis on war in displays of armour and battle scenes, and that the exhibition could usefully be used to explore issues of sexual equality within Sikh society. Young men and women at Walsall College of Arts and Technology initially responded favourably to the opportunity to discuss this issue. However a women-

only session was, disappointingly, poorly attended. Various reasons
were given for this, including fear of parental disapproval, despite the
confidentiality of the discussions, and the belief that change for women
was impossible. A mixed session was dominated by young men who, it
was felt by group leaders, were shockingly reactionary. At the final
evaluation of the project the advisory group agreed that the exhibition
project had helped to identify pressing issues that needed to be
addressed from within the Sikh community itself. Some months later, at
a Sikh Summer School, there were opportunities to discuss sexual
equality and Amarjit has suggested that this may have been partly
influenced by the exhibition project.

The public programme of talks and discussions included an evening
seminar entitled 'Sikh Heritage and Culture Under Threat?' which was
stimulated by concerns about widespread ignorance within the Sikh
community about the current situation in the Punjab. Amongst the
speakers was a lawyer currently working in the Punjab and a
representative from Amnesty International. The organization and
administration of this event was wholly carried out by members of the
advisory group. A talk on the history of Sikh art by the exhibition
organizer was well attended by a mixed audience of Sikhs and non-
Sikhs and had particular resonance for one participant, a local
orthodox Sikh art student, who had never realized that such art
existed. Stimulated by the talk into writing a college essay on Sikh art,
he realized that, as much of it is unauthored, it would be difficult to fit
it into the traditional Western European framework for writing essays
on 'the great artists'.

Among other activities were *kabbadi* workshops (a popular game
with similarities to rugby but involving no ball), and *gatka* workshops
which resulted in petitions to the local authority sports department for
further provision. Art workshops included silk painting with contemporary artist Sarbjit Natt, whose work was represented in the
exhibition and storytelling sessions held in both Punjabi and English,
which pleased many adults whose children had not heard these stories
before because of a limited understanding of Punjabi. Although the
events were open to all, some, particularly the storytelling sessions,
were mainly attended by Sikh people, which was perhaps disappointing
but not surprising.

Following the close of the exhibition, staff at the museum met with
the advisory group to evaluate the project. Several key points were
raised. The exhibition was seen as a catalyst for positive involvement in
the local authority services by Sikh people. It had helped to create new
awareness of Sikh heritage and culture, particularly among young
people, many of whom had had little opportunity to see such evidence
of their material culture. The strategy of developing contacts and

enlisting support beyond the *Gurudwaras* had been important in this, as many young people feel alienated from them. The project had also shown the creative potential of the Sikh community itself. It may have been *initiated* by the museum, but it was the energy from within the Sikh community that got things done and to extremely high standards. On a practical level, it had helped identify useful resources and contacts which could be used by the Sikh community in the future. There was general agreement from the advisory group that it was now up to the community to start actively representing itself, with the initiative coming from within and not from outside. Following the *Warm and Rich and Fearless* project, some members of the advisory group continue to meet. One of the group met with representatives from the Victoria & Albert Museum in London shortly after the project to discuss ways in which access to their collections could be gained.

For the museum in the short term, the *Warm and Rich and Fearless* project helped to attract a new audience and to form refreshing new working partnerships. It also brought new knowledge and understanding of a particular culture and religion into the institution. For the long term it raised a pressing issue. How was this momentum to be maintained in the long term given that exhibition projects of this type could not be planned on a regular basis? The advisory group felt that the museum needed to be realistic about maintaining very high levels of interest among Sikh people, given that many came to the exhibition because of its very direct relevance. This was not necessarily seen by the group as a negative thing. Recent visitor surveys show that the percentage of 'Asian' visitors to the museum is proportionately greater than figures revealed in general census statistics for Walsall Borough, although it is difficult to tell how many of these are Sikhs, and no formal evaluation has taken place. Of course, it is not only through exhibitions that communities are represented. If internal structures and policies are not changed, many projects run the risk of being tokenistic. Although the advisory group did not feel that this was the case with the *Warm and Rich and Fearless* project, some immediate opportunities for making longer-term links with the Sikh community were lost. For example, the post of Community History Officer was vacant at the time and so the opportunity to explore an enlightened collecting policy was not pursued. This imbalance is now being addressed and the museum continues to have contact with both Amarjit and other representatives of the Advisory Group.

This project took place over a period of eight months and involved an exhibition that had been organized elsewhere and collections which not only belonged elsewhere, but which are rarely seen in public. Although important for Walsall, it was clearly just a beginning and it raises huge issues not only for Walsall Museum and Art Gallery, but for museums nationally regarding the representation of cultural diversity. Who decides what is collected and seen and how it is interpreted? How can meaningful change take place when staff are unrepresentative of the diversity of local communities? Amarjit's work in Walsall was incredibly important, but it was temporary and relied on funding extra to that provided by the museum itself. How can museums dominated by culturally unrepresentative art and history collections begin to represent diversity without appearing tokenistic? And what is cultural diversity anyway? The *Warm and Rich and Fearless* exhibition had a very specific cultural and religious focus. The Sikh community in Walsall has very strong social and religious networks. These factors were the root of its success – at least for those Sikh people who chose to take part. Not every perceived 'community' has this network or this shared interest. Most people probably belong to any number of communities based on almost anything – age, origin, locality, interest and so on. Perhaps if there is not an awareness of this, muscums run the risk of patronizing the people they hope to involve and represent.

## Reference

Walsall Museum and Art Gallery (1996) 'Just like drawing in your dinner ...'; the story behind START – the first interactive art gallery experience designed for three- to five-year-olds, Walsall Museum and Art Gallery, Walsall.

# 10

# Audience participation: working with local people at the Geffrye Museum, London

## STEVE HEMMING

### Introduction

The Geffrye Museum is located in Hackney, close to the border with Tower Hamlets, two of the poorest and most culturally diverse boroughs in Britain. The museum was opened by the London County Council in 1914 as a museum of furniture for local apprentices, at a time when furniture-making was the most important trade in the area. In the 1930s the displays were rearranged to create a series of period room sets and the museum now displays middle-class English domestic interiors from 1600 to the 1950s.

The museum was administered by the Inner London Education Authority (ILEA) until 1990, when the ILEA was abolished and the museum became an independent charitable trust, grant-aided by the Department of National Heritage. Because of its administration by an education authority, the museum has had a long tradition of education work. Organized educational work with schoolchildren began in the 1950s, and by the end of the 1980s the education department employed five full-time members of staff, one-fifth of the museum's workforce, and had a large budget for freelance staff.

The political aspirations of the ILEA towards extending equality of opportunity and cultural democracy (Kelly, 1984; Henry, 1993) have also been important to the museum. In 1988 the museum commissioned a report entitled *Black Contribution to History*. Written by Peter Fraser and Rozina Visram, two eminent black historians, the document examined ways in which the museum's collection could give due reference to the role black history had played in the development of English interiors, and the ways in which the museum's Eurocentric displays could be made more accessible to a non-Western audience. A year later the museum developed a community education post to look at ways of developing community involvement in the museum.

Consultation with the public over the content of two special exhibitions took place in the late 1980s: *Furnishing the World*, which looked at the history of the furniture trade within the area, and *Putting on the Style: Setting up Home in the 1950s*. Both these exhibitions focused museum staff on the relevance of the museum and its collections to the locality and looked at ways of involving local people in developing the exhibitions. Part of the exhibition *Putting on the Style* involved the construction of a London bedsit of the kind lived in by Afro-Caribbean people recently arrived in London from the Caribbean.

Both Hackney and Tower Hamlets have a long tradition of cultural diversity. Due to their close proximity to the Thames and the low cost of housing, they have been the first port of call for many people arriving in London, from Huguenots, Jews and Afro-Caribbeans to Bengalis, Somalis and now Chinese. Hackney at present has nine official languages, while the Asian community in Tower Hamlets is expected to become the majority cultural group in the borough by the year 2000. While this diversity has often brought racial tension to the area, it has also brought a cultural variety and richness that is unique in Britain.

The cultural diversity of the area and the educational and political tradition of the museum has, in many ways, influenced the way that education work has been approached at the Geffrye. This article will focus on two different educational projects that have involved working with groups and individuals from diverse cultural backgrounds. The first half of the chapter will look at the community education work that led to the museum's exhibition *Chinese Homes: Chinese Traditions in English Homes*. The second part will look at courses that have been run by the museum and targeted specifically at people who could be described as 'non-museum visitors', the most notable of which is an historic crafts course for local women.

## Developing links with the Chinese community in Hackney

The exhibition *Chinese Homes: Chinese Traditions in English Homes* ran for three months in 1992 following many months of preparation. The exhibition took a tripartite approach: it used the museum's permanent collection as a way of tracing the influence of Chinese culture on English style and domestic life over the last 400 years, a second section of the exhibition looked at the history of the Chinese community in London and a third looked at how Chinese people living in East London today celebrate Chinese New Year in their homes.

There was no particular reason for singling out the Chinese

community as one to work with on an exhibition and, in fact, during the initial period of contact there was no intention that the work would lead to such an involvement. In retrospect, the potential of the subject for an exhibition at the Geffrye seems obvious. One can see the strong influence Chinese culture has had on English life and how this had led to a large Chinese population arriving in this country. One can also see how the barriers of language and cultural difference have led to a lack of awareness of this influence. However, the original intention was merely to work with a very marginalized group and explore their cultural links with Britain.

The Chinese community has existed in East London since seamen, employed by the East India company, settled in Limehouse at the end of the nineteenth century. Since then the Chinese population in London has increased from a few hundred to over 100,000 today. The end of the World War II saw a large influx of people from the Far East, the Nationality Act of 1948 having granted citizenship to residents of Britain's colonies and former colonies.

In recent years the majority of immigrants have come to Britain as a result of conflict. In 1977, suspicious of China's relations with the US, Vietnam deliberately alienated its ethnic Chinese population. Chinese schools were closed and work permits and ration cards were withdrawn, making it virtually impossible for Chinese people to earn a living in Vietnam and many left as refugees. Britain has accepted around 20,000 refugees from Vietnam, of whom around 75 per cent are ethnic Chines. While they have been dispersed throughout the country, a large number of them, around 2,000, have settled in Hackney.

These recent arrivals face numerous difficulties. Many suffered severe trauma during the Vietnam War and subsequently from the difficult and dangerous passage, often on crowded boats, from Vietnam to refugee holding camps in Hong Kong. These factors, as well as language and cultural barriers, make integration into English society difficult. The working patterns of the community have contributed to the problem of integration, as a large number of the refugees work in catering. The long working hours and the need for restaurants to be broadly dispersed has made it harder to preserve a sense of community and identity. The establishment of community centres that are able to assist in the process of integration has been a vital development. They employ professional social workers who help with interpretation, advice and support as well as organizing social functions.

It was through the Chinese Community Centre in Hackney that the museum did most of its work with the community, nearly all of whom were Chinese refugees who had fled from Vietnam. The first work the museum did with the community was a series of simple visits that were seen as an opportunity for the groups that came to the museum to see some aspects of English history and the links that could be made with their own. It was as a follow-up to these visits that a joint decision was made to develop an educational project which focused on the difficult transition from East to West. The project ran over several weeks and used both art and oral history to put together a small booklet that looked at each member of the group's history in Vietnam, the story of how they arrived here and what they felt was both good and bad about being in Britain.

Doing this educational project was key to developing what ultimately became an exhibition. It illustrated the richness of the subject matter, which played a crucial part in developing an interest amongst museum staff and persuading colleagues in other departments that an exhibition could be a dynamic and successful proposition. The education project also started to develop a sense of trust between the community group and the museum. The participants felt that the project had been useful to them. They gained a real sense of achievement at having completed it, and one could suggest that it acted as a stepping stone towards greater involvement.

The museum initiated further discussions with the community and the staff at the centre about the possibility of putting on some sort of exhibition. The discussion focused on what elements they thought that they, as a community, would like to display. This discussion was difficult, mainly because the concept of an exhibition was something that most of the group was not familiar with. It took a long time, and a lot of patient translating, to explain what the museum was suggesting. The discussion highlighted many of the issues that the community felt strongly about. These included issues such as access to health care, the poll tax and racist attacks. This presented difficulties, for while these issues were obviously of great importance, they did not link in with the museum's purpose. By explaining this problem, the discussion moved on to other issues that the group felt were important. A major area of concern for them was the lack of understanding of their culture in England, and particularly their celebrations, the most important of which was Chinese New Year.

This celebration seemed to be the most appropriate starting point. In order to gather information on Chinese New Year, other oral history projects were developed with the community to try and gather views on the different aspects of the festival. These projects took two angles. First, an overview project, which gathered a wide range of information from many different people in the community. By doing this it was apparent which elements of the festival were the most common, which elements varied according to age, which part of the Far East people had come from originally, which class they were from and what kind of religious fervour they celebrated the festival with.

A secondary stage took a more in-depth look and was able to gather more detailed information from a number of people who offered a broad range of views and experiences. This stage of the overall project took several months to complete, not only in gathering the information on audio tape using an interpreter, but then collating the information and returning to do secondary interviews to fill in the gaps and iron out inconsistencies. It was also important that the individuals who had given the information had it read back to them so that we could ensure that the original translation had been accurate.

A continuous feature of the work was the need to gather recollections and views that would, in the end, contribute to the exhibition. This work was done in small bites so that it didn't become a chore for those taking part. Each interview session was made into an occasion, with cakes and tea providing stimulus and comfortable chairs providing an informal setting. Like any qualitative interview, interviewees are likely to give more if they are in a relaxed atmosphere and are questioned in a series of short interviews rather than in a gruelling long session that is more convenient to the interviewer. Working in this way enabled a stronger relationship and familiarity to build up. It also allowed thoughts on the part of the interviewer and the interviewee to develop over time.

All these interview sessions were carried out at the Chinese Community Centre at a time when the people who were being interviewed were going to be there anyway. This said, the interviews did have their drawbacks. This stage of the project took a long time, and there were perhaps two dozen visits to the centre over a few months, which took up a lot of staff time. Some people, particularly the elderly, didn't want to talk about their lives, often because they felt nervous about their family's reaction here, despite assurances. This was a factor more common amongst the women at the centre. Perhaps the biggest frustration was the gulf in communication which, despite help from translators, could never quite be bridged.

Translation was a constant issue throughout the initial educational work, the oral history projects and then the final exhibition. Despite the fact that virtually all the participants had fled Vietnam, they originated from a wide range of places. This meant that there was a range of dialects to overcome as well as the difficulty of some individuals speaking Cantonese and others speaking Mandarin. The museum was fortunate in that the Chinese Liaison Officer with whom we worked, Gill Tan, was so versatile and perceptive in her own use of the language and was able, by asking people in a variety of ways, to ascertain what it was that they were really trying to say.

Translation, it could be said, is rather a simplistic term for the job that Gill Tan, and the other translators who took part, had to do. It involved trying to bridge a vast cultural gap, and required not only the knowledge of the language, but an empathy for the different perspectives of both cultures. This had to be accompanied by the skill to open people up conversationally, and get them to feel at ease and talk freely about their experience. Without this skill and expertise, it would have been impossible for the exhibition to develop in the way it did in terms of its community involvement.

The other elements of the exhibition were developed after the part that was chosen by the community, but were important in making sense of the exhibition as a whole. The element that looked at the historic nature of the Chinese community in Britain helped put a context behind the part of the exhibition that looked at Chinese New Year. It showed how the development of trade had led to Chinese people first coming to London. By using oral history transcripts gathered at other Chinese community centres in London, this part of the exhibition also showed the side of the story of Chinese immigrants who arrived in London in the 1940s.

Another section of the exhibition looked at the influence of Chinese culture on the museum's period rooms. While the museum needed to borrow some objects from other museums in order to do this, it was, on the whole, able to rely on its own collection and highlight the objects in each of the rooms that had been influenced by contact with China by using a small red dragon motif, which was then explained on an accompanying panel. Doing this tied the whole exhibition to the museum's permanent collection, and enabled the design history to be linked to its social consequences.

The element of the exhibition that looked at Chinese New Year also consisted of room sets. Two rooms were decorated to represent Chinese New Year's Eve in the home of a Chinese family living in Britain (Figure 10.1). The objects and decoration used in the rooms were chosen for it by a group from the Chinese Community Centre. They accompanied museum staff on trips to West End shops to choose objects that the museum then borrowed to put in the rooms. They also came to the museum to put the objects into the rooms and decorate them. Many smaller objects were loaned to the museum by Chinese people at the Hackney Centre, and also other Chinese community centres in London. Involving the community in this way was crucial to the ethos of the exhibition. Working with room sets inevitably results in the construction of a social and cultural context. Involving the Chinese community meant that this construction was, broadly speaking, representative of the community's wishes. It also meant that they had been involved in the exhibition from start to finish.

The project team responsible for planning the exhibition needed to be diverse to enable community involvement. Most of the planning was

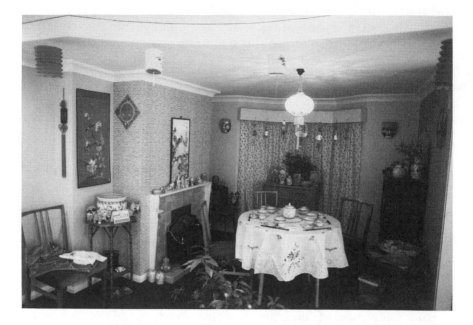

**Figure 10.1** *Period room interior decorated by the Chinese community in Hackney for the Geffrye Museum's exhibition* **Chinese Homes: Chinese Traditions in English Homes.** *The room shows Chinese New Year being celebrated by a family recently arrived in East London. Photo Steve Hemming, with kind permission of Geffrye Museum Trust.*

done by the Director of the museum, the Community Education Officer, the exhibition designer and a member of the curatorial department. While it wasn't possible for the Chinese Liaison Officer and members of the community to be present at all meetings, they were involved at all key meetings, with the exhibition content and design being shown to them before being finally agreed. This helped ensure that the information being used was as accurate as possible, and that any comments that could be misinterpreted were corrected early in the process.

The panels, exhibition catalogue and publicity were all translated into Cantonese. This helped make the exhibition more accessible, but also maintained an interest in developing the exhibition from the Chinese people taking part, as it demonstrated, more than anything else, the museum's commitment to the group, and enabled them to understand how the exhibition was developing. The use of bilingual information is essential if a museum intends to seriously involve community groups from different cultural backgrounds. Similarly, the designing of images for the poster and publicity material was done in consultation with the group and the results were dramatically different from the general publicity material that the museum uses, appealing more to the aesthetic values of the community.

The group also helped in developing the education programme that accompanied the exhibition. Because of the links that had grown, it was easy to choose a range of events and activities that reflected the cultural values of the community and also find artists who were able to do them. The fact that the exhibition had been initiated by the education department and that there was involvement of education staff on the exhibition planning team meant that there was a greater linkage between the content of the exhibition and the education programme. This programme included projects for schools, events for the general public and also events which were targeted at the Chinese community. The aim of this was to provide as wide a range of educational activities as possible in order to provide a greater understanding of the diversity of Chinese culture. General events included different musical performances as well as a lion dance and talks to further explain the exhibition, while activities for children included storytelling, making Chinese kites and calligraphy.

Additional educational initiatives took place during the period. One of these was a project with a local college that involved school leavers working on a six-week art and design project based on a Chinese screen. The activities specifically for Chinese people involved workshops that were led in Cantonese and numerous visits arranged in conjunction with both the community centre and a local school which had weekend classes for Chinese children. The latter was seen as very important by many of the Chinese community workers who are aware of a growing divide in many families between the parents, who speak Cantonese, and their children, who are being taught in English schools and who now have English as their mother tongue and have very little knowledge of Chinese culture or the history of why they are in England.

It is worth pointing out that, while from Western eyes the exhibition represented a point of interest and perhaps provided an insight into the lives of a group of immigrants, for the majority of the Chinese people themselves, the portrayal of a room in which there was an altar and numerous other religious artefacts was a very sensitive issue. Similarly, the lion dance may be an entertaining diversion for non-Chinese people, but for many of the people we worked with it was a powerful reminder of their emigration, and its significance as a cultural, social and religious occasion was obviously much stronger for the Chinese community than for a Western audience.

There have been numerous learning points to emerge from the

exhibition. The combination of education and curatorial staff on the planning team, along with community involvement, meant that there was a breadth of experience and a variety of angles from which issues could be viewed. It brought a freshness to the exhibition that comes with critical debate from differing viewpoints. Bringing a wide range of experiences to a planning team means that problems can often be solved very quickly. It also means that there is a greater awareness within the institution as a whole of what is happening with the development of the exhibition, because there are people involved from different departments. This has a knock-on effect in that secondary planning, such as marketing, publicity and education events, can develop at an advanced stage.

There are, however, drawbacks to working on this kind of exhibition. First, it involves a strong commitment from the institution in terms of the budget. Translation into a second language incurs costs in terms of the hiring of translators, but it also requires twice as much published material in terms of the explanatory panels, the exhibition catalogue and the publicity. This has the effect of taking up more of the designer's time. Second, working with the community, securing their trust and developing ideas with them is a time-consuming process. It requires numerous skills that most museums don't possess, and thus involves networking with people who do possess them, again a time-consuming process.

Involving a community in making decisions does take time, but also the will to make it happen. However, if the museum had tried to impose its own narrative on the exhibition without the consultation process, the results would have been disastrous. The chances are that the exhibition would have alienated the Chinese community and been a rather shallow attempt to portray their culture.

The two parts of the exhibition that looked at Chinese New Year and the development of the Chinese community in London are still being used. After the exhibition closed, this part was redeveloped so that it was sturdy enough to travel, and so that it could be varied in size and still make sense. It has since travelled to a number of community-based venues in London, several libraries, Hackney Museum and the Ragged School Museum.

The Geffrye learnt a great deal from the *Chinese Homes* exhibition. Learning ways of communicating with a minority group that had virtually no experience of a museum was an edifying experience for many of the staff. Reinterpreting the collection from the perspective of a different culture was also important, but perhaps the key development of the exhibition was the fact that it stemmed out of a community education initiative and that the community involvement was maintained all the way through.

In this sense, *Chinese Homes* has provided the museum with a different format for approaching exhibitions of this kind in the future. It is important to stress that this would not be appropriate to every kind of exhibition that will be held at the Geffrye, but represents another way for exhibition planners, whether they are curators, educators or interpreters, to plan exhibitions of a specific nature that may involve issues that need to be handled sensitively or working with people who aren't used to a museum environment.

The wider implications of the exhibition on the Chinese community in Hackney are harder to gauge. In the short term, it was apparent that the group taking part in the exhibition felt an enormous sense of achievement when it was finally complete and many of them brought their friends to the museum to see it. It gave the group a chance to share experiences and bring into focus ideas about their arrival here and the effect that living in Britain has had on their way of life. One also hopes that the exhibition went some way towards increasing awareness in those who saw it, of the great impact China has had on English life.

In the long term, it is harder to evaluate the exhibition's impact. While it has provided an example of good practice for a specific type of exhibition planning, it would be wrong to suggest that it has radically changed the scale of museum-visiting by either the Chinese community in Hackney to museums in general, or by the wider Chinese community to the Geffrye. It would also be unrealistic for the museum to expect this to happen through one exhibition.

While the Chinese Community Centre gained many skills in presenting issues of concern to them, the effect of an exhibition in helping the integration and acceptance of a cultural minority into the English way of life is a small one. Yet one hopes that initiatives such as this will lead to the development of other similar projects, not just within the Chinese community, but within society at large, helping to being about a greater understanding of, and empathy for, cultural difference.

## Developing new audiences through community education

Since the introduction of the post of Community Education Officer in 1989, the museum has developed several courses which have specifically targeted different groups of people within the local community. For the majority of participants on these courses, visiting a museum was a new experience for them. In a similar vein to the *Chinese Homes* exhibition, a major reason for the success of these courses has been the consultation with participants to develop the content and structure of each course. One such course was English for speakers of other languages, where the museum is used as a resource for developing knowledge of English language and history amongst students, many of whom are refugees. Another short course looked to give young adults with learning difficulties the basic skills that they needed in order to decorate their own homes, while another has looked at developing fabric design skills amongst young Asian women, using the museum's collection as a starting point. However, the most significant course the museum has developed has been the accredited course, 'Historic Crafts for Women'.

Accreditation means that the participants are awarded credits through the London Open College Federation, a central body that moderates selected courses, and awards the participants on those courses credits. To be a part of the scheme, the museum had to fulfil a rigorous selection process that closely examined the aims and objectives of the course, the curriculum that was on offer to the students, how the students were involved in the moderation process, how the museum was going to ensure that there was equality of opportunity and what support facilities there were for the students. What accreditation means for the students involved is that they can use credits to progress onto other courses in further, and ultimately, higher education. In reality, it has very much been the case that, although accreditation allows the student to do this, it is the body of work, together with the confidence that they build up over the duration of the course, that enables them to move on.

The course is run jointly with Hackney Community College, which is the main provider of both vocational and non-vocational adult education in the area (Figure 10.2). Being a large organization, they are able to provide a wide range of expertise and support in many areas. The course has crèche facilities and a language support tutor, both provided by the college. They also help promote the course to students and assist financially with the cost of the accreditation process. The museum provides the craft tutor, the workshop space and the main bulk of the administrative work. While a partnership of this kind has obvious benefits in increasing what can be offered to students and pooling resources and expertise, it has its frustrations too. Communication may become more difficult and, ultimately, the different organizations have different goals and different priorities to consider.

The course was set up in 1990 after discussions with local community workers identified a need for skill-based projects of this kind for local women. Shoreditch, where the museum is based, has one of the highest unemployment rates in inner London, especially amongst women. The original purpose was to provide local women with a recreational course that introduced them to the museum. This was intended to be a short-term venture. The course was targeted at women who attended two local community centres, and was scheduled for a

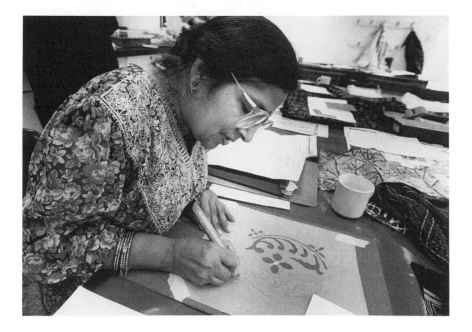

Figure 10.2 *Ranjan Dasani, a participant in the Geffrye Museum's course 'Historic Crafts for Women', cuts a stencil for use in fabric printing. Photo Julian Anderson, with kind permission of Geffrye Museum Trust.*

time that was convenient to both the participants and the community centres.

As with *Chinese Homes* there was a great deal of discussion at this early stage about what the course would offer the women. As with the exhibition, this took the form of a negotiation, where it was important to establish the limitations within which the museum could work. The selection of staff to work on the project was crucial. There are numerous characteristics that are vital to community development with people who are from diverse cultural backgrounds who have often been left with a very negative impression of education from their school experience. Tutors need to be non-threatening, empathetic with the individuals' circumstances and able to introduce the subject, whether it is language support or a particular craft, in a very straightforward and clear way. Without these skills, building the participants' confidence would be extremely difficult, and encouraging them to visit the museum even more so.

The students who attend the course come from a wide range of cultural backgrounds. The role of the language support tutor is an important one. A key aim of the course is for the students to improve their English. Writing is an important element of design, but it is also necessary for the students to improve their writing skills if they want to apply for courses and express to other people what it is they are trying to achieve. The breadth of cultural background is a tremendous strength for the course. Students are very keen to share information about their background and culture. Festivals, such as Eid, Diwali and Hanukkah, are always a cause for celebration. This confidence about cultural expression also finds its way into the students' work. While the museum is used as a resource for fabric or furniture design, the students' work is usually also an expression of their own cultural background. This is no doubt helped by the fact that many of the craft techniques that are used, such as indigo dyeing or papier mâché, are common in a wide range of cultures.

Each year around 14 women take part in the course. There are selection criteria that each participant has to fulfil so that the museum can ensure that the accreditation process will be made use of. The criteria ensure that the women come from within a specific geographical area and that they aren't over-qualified. The course also has a two-year limit for each participant, which ensures that there is a regular flow of new students and prevents the course from becoming a craft club.

The course is divided into three 10-week terms, a demanding schedule for new students who are just coming back into education, but each term is structured so that the work can be taken on in small bites. The actual content of the course is kept relatively loose so that students can develop their own work. They have a general requirement for each of the three terms that the course runs. In the first term they have to produce a fabric, in the second an object for the home and in the third an object of their choice. Each student is also given a criterion for the assessment for each term. This means that they are aware of how the course is moderated. More importantly, they have to contribute to the assessment by talking with the tutors about their achievements over the term. Students are awarded credits at three different levels that basically reflect the amount of work they are able to do independently, the amount they contribute to the rest of the group and their ability to follow the design process. The students are aware of their progress throughout the year and are able to discuss this with the external moderator who attends the course twice-yearly. This takes the form of a final-year show, which is done more in a spirit of achievement and pride than in anxiety.

The course is now in its fourth year of accreditation. During that time some 60 local women have completed the course and gained credits. For most of them, doing the course has been a starting point that has given them educational and employment opportunities. Several of the women have gone on to college to gain other qualifications, notably one student who went on to do a foundation year and then a fine art degree and another who went on to do a course in teaching adult education. Others have gone on to get jobs in nurseries or crèches and are still using the art skills they gained at the museum. Most of the students still come back to the museum occasionally and many now go regularly to other museums and galleries.

What this shows is the degree to which the sense of ownership of the museum by the participants changes during their stay. While most of the women who attend the course live locally, and some of them have done so for all of their lives, few had been to the museum before. The fact that a course is able to get them to attend a museum that they hadn't thought twice about, and get them to come back every week for a year, is illustrative of its impact. It would appear to show that a lot of non-visitors to museums don't necessarily refuse to come out of choice, often they stay away because they either don't understand what the museum is about or feel it isn't relevant to them. Given the right approach and the warm welcome, you may never get them out again!

## Developments and learning points that have arisen from the projects

Numerous learning points arose from these two projects. It is worth pointing out that neither one followed a recognized format. They both involved a lot of 'feeling your way along', which meant that the projects were often slow to progress and took patience to build up. While this meant that there were inevitable weaknesses, it meant too that there was a flexibility about the work and that the projects were open to change according to the needs of the group. Flexibility, and the need for the work to be, as much as possible, 'client-led', is a key ingredient if the project is to succeed and have a meaningful level of input from the community. By working in this way a dialogue is created, and there is the potential for the museum to learn as much from the process as the participants themselves.

Similarly, when working with other agencies that aren't familiar with a museum as an organization, it takes time for an understanding to develop. However, in the Geffrye's case, the time invested has paid enormous dividends. It is very healthy for a museum to be able to generate a sense of ownership within its community, as it creates a dynamic relationship which the organization thrives on.

Both the projects in this chapter have dealt with two main issues: increasing accessibility to the museum and its resources, and promoting cultural awareness. They have been, and will continue to be, important issues for the Geffrye to address, given its location, but they are pertinent to all museums. Britain is becoming increasingly diverse in its cultural make-up. Museums have an important role to play in making sense of this. By providing the access for different cultural groups to explore, understand and express historical and cultural concerns that are important to them, they can provide an awareness that will help enrich us all.

# References

Fraser, P. and Visram R. (1988) *Black Contribution to History*, Geffrye Museum, London.

Henry, I. (1993) *The Politics of Leisure Policy*, Macmillan, London.

Kelly, O. (1984) *Community, Art and the State*, Comedian, London.

# 11

---

# Developing new audiences at the National Portrait Gallery, London

ROGER HARGREAVES

Museums and galleries are by their very nature unique and fiercely individual places. Any case study must inevitably be deeply rooted within the context of the individual institution. It is my intention in this chapter to relate my experiences of implementing a programme for new audiences from within the education department of the National Portrait Gallery (NPG). As a department we have attempted to address a particular set of aims and objectives, many of which are likely to be of relevance across the wider museums and galleries sector. Our experiences of implementing a programme will I hope offer some valuable pointers for those planning similar initiatives and at the very least prove useful as a comparative study to set against others who have already taken an established lead in the field.

I want to start by setting out the context against which the initiative for new audiences must be set. I want to consider the NPG firstly as an institution, explain its collection and examine its structure. Within this I will need to place the education department, defining its function and relating its perception of audience. I will need to clarify the audience for the gallery as a whole and sketch out an audit of precisely who that audience was at the time the initiative was conceived, but to begin with I would like to consider the context that is almost a pre-requisite for the successful implementation of any new initiative, and that is the context of a heathy climate for change.

When I joined the NPG in January 1993 to take up the half-time post of education officer for new audiences I was presented with a set of very new agendas. This was my first job within the museum and gallery sector. The post was a new one within the education department. In addition it occurred within a period of great change for the gallery itself, coinciding with the completion of a major phase of redevelopment and the retirement of the outgoing director, the appointment of a new director and the subsequent restructuring of the gallery's management and curatorial staff.

The NPG is delightfully and almost perversely unique, driven by its split personality, made up of being on the one hand a gallery of art and on the other a museum of history. Founded in 1856 to assemble the likenesses of famous British men and women, its collection spans five centuries of portraiture, boasting a primary collection of over 9000 works and supported by an immense archive. It has been variously described as a pantheon of the great and the good, a national family album and the museological equivalent of *Hello!* magazine. While the subject may be narrow, the selection of medium is wide-ranging, incorporating oil painting, watercolours, drawings, miniatures, sculpture, caricatures, silhouettes and, since 1970, photographs. While the gallery's collection policy is to acquire the best available portraits of its sitters, it is the drive to acquire a representation of the sitter that is the primary motive. As a result great works of art rub shoulders with more pedestrian efforts selected by virtue of being the only known likenesses. The gallery houses a permanent collection organized chronologically by century and the subject of constant rehangs and temporary displays. This is complemented by a programme of biographical, historical and artist-centred temporary exhibitions ranging from small displays in a single case to large international blockbuster exhibitions arranged across several galleries.

Compared with other national institutions the NPG is relatively small. However, it is of a size that affords the full range of gallery functions including curation, conservation, education, research, publication, development, publicity and press. The gallery employs a staff of around 120, of whom 60 fulfil the functions mentioned.

There is generally good communication throughout the structure, people tend to know one another, there is a high level of co-operation and dialogue between departments, and the low staff turnover may be one indicator of high degree of job satisfaction. This prevailing mood of well-being has permeated through to visitors, who find the atmosphere in the building welcoming, relaxed and friendly.

There is one last important context in which to understand the development of a programme for new audiences and my role as an education officer in implementing that programme, and that is as a complement to the existing provision of the gallery's education department. The education department has a highly regarded and well established programme of activities serving the needs of primary, secondary and tertiary education. The department also maintains the interest and involvement of frequent visitors through leisure-based activities and its policy states that:

> it is our policy to direct a higher proportion of resources to providing activities during people's leisure time. This should ensure a more widespread and cost effective use of the new education centre. (National Portrait Gallery, 1994)

The full complement of department staff is three full-time and two part-time staff. These are a head of department, one full-time officer responsible for primary education, one part-time officer responsible for secondary and adult art education, a second part-time officer for new audiences and a full-time departmental administrator whose principal task if the booking and programming of group visits. These permanent staff are supported by a wide-ranging team of freelances. The policy of the department is to focus energies on providing a taught, face-to-face service for visitors, rather than mediating education experiences through the production of resource material. One direct benefit of the policy is that education work has a high public profile within the gallery and on any day a visitor is likely to encounter groups and individuals working in front of the pictures, engaged in activities such as drawing, performance or discussion, while more formal lectures, film and video screenings, and practical art sessions occur in the studio and lecture rooms. As well as pro-actively devising initiatives to encourage and support visitors, the department responds to a heavy demand for sessions in support of school syllabuses ranging from A level to the National Curriculum. The heaviest demand comes from teachers following the National Curriculum for history, for which we provide a range of both basic discussion sessions and more specialized activities on Tudor, Stuart and Victorian themes.

The audience for the NPG has been consistent with the popular notion of traditional gallery-visiting audiences. A recent visitor's survey of museums and galleries (including the NPG) conducted by the National Audit Office (NAO) produced a clear picture of the character of that audience (National Audit Office, 1993). The profile of attenders for the NPG was broadly in line with other institutions, particularly those housing fine art collections: the majority of visitors (52%) were from higher income groups, 54% of visitors were female and 29% were aged 55 or over.

The NAO research also found that the NPG visitor is more likely to come to the gallery alone rather than with friends or as part of a group and is likely to be a relatively frequent visitor. The most recent analysis of visitors to the NPG characterized the frequent visitors as envisioning the NPG as a place of refuge and quoted one respondent as saying 'the

NPG is like a nice local church ... pop in and leave your troubles behind' (National Portrait Gallery, 1995).

The achievements of the outgoing management team were to have brought about a substantial upgrading of the gallery infrastructure and with it a new capacity for expanding and broadening the gallery's audience. A new site had been acquired adjacent to the main gallery and this provided for the relocation of the library and archive from a site in South London, the provision of a new conservation department and space for offices decanted from the main gallery building. This freeing up of the main building provided greatly expanded permanent and temporary gallery space, improved access and an expanded education facility. The new education centre provided office space, a purpose-built teaching studio, a teaching darkroom, a material store and a new basement studio gallery.

The job to which I was appointed was as an education officer with a specific brief to develop work with new audiences, principally through practical photography education. At the time of my appointment the education department was housed in temporary offices and the new facilities were still in the planning stages, six months away from completion. It was presented to me that I should approach the job through a series of phases. The phases were research, planning and then finally implementation, coinciding with the opening of the new facilities. The major task in the run-up to implementation was taking responsibility for equipping the studio and darkroom for practical photography work. It was agreed that the best approach to this planning phase was to produce a series of internal discussion papers. The first was 'Defining new audiences' (Hargreaves, 1993a). This comprised a literature review based on recent surveys of the NPG's audience profile and an analysis of other papers relevant to the notion of new audiences plus a systematic definition of particular audience types. Following discussion of this paper I produced a second document 'A strategy for new audiences' (Hargreaves, 1993b), which attempted to identify how best my limited time and available resources could be targeted at a number of key audience groups and how these groups may best be developed over a three-year period. The final document was a draft programme for audiences for the first year (Hargreaves, 1993c).

It is within this wider context of the department within the institution that I want to now map out the detail of devising and implementing a programme for new audiences. To begin with I want to re-examine the research that informed the planning. I have identified the profile of the audience as it existed in 1993 and highlighted the development of the gallery's infrastructure in preparation for expansion and change. The questions that immediately followed were who visits galleries?, why? and how different audiences enjoy and benefit from gallery visits. The principal piece of research I turned to was undertaken in Toledo, Ohio, in 1980–1981 (Hood, 1983). The Toledo study considered patterns of attendance and audience attitudes to gallery visits. The findings offer some valuable insights into the categories of gallery visitors and the underlying reasons that inform their choice of leisure-time activities. The report suggested that, rather than thinking of two audience segments, participants and non-participants, there are in reality three distinct audience segments in the current and potential museum clientele. These are *frequent participants, occasional participants* and *non-participants*. The research further examined the kinds of factors which inform people's decisions about visiting museums. It argues that six main attributes underlay adults' choice in their use of leisure time in general. The attributes are (in alphabetical order):

- being with people, or social interaction;
- doing something worthwhile;
- feeling comfortable and at ease in one's surroundings;
- having a challenge or new experiences;
- having an opportunity to learn;
- participating actively.

For each of the three audience segments the relative weighting and choice of those attributes is different. The *frequent visitors* – those who go to museums at least three times a year (and some as often as 40 times a year) highly value all of the six leisure attributes and perceive all of them to be present in museums. The attributes they value most highly are having an opportunity to learn, having the challenge of a new experience and doing something worthwhile in leisure time.

The research suggests that the assumption that museum visitors, regardless of frequency of attendance, share many common interests and characteristics, is ill-founded. The *occasional visitors* (people who attend museums and galleries less than twice a year) are distinctly different from the *frequent visitors* in their socialization patterns and leisure values. In fact they more closely resemble the *non-participants*. For this group, leisure is equated with relaxation. The attributes of greatest significance in informing their leisure choice were socializing, feeling comfortable in one's surrounding and participating actively.

*Non-participants* tend to be influenced by similar leisure choices, seeking activities that emphasize active participation, casual surroundings and interacting socially with other people.

The report concludes that museum and gallery providers can:

> solve many of our audience development problems if we recognise that occasional participants and non-participants are looking for experiences

and rewards different from those they now find in museums. If we want them to love museums, we must offer them some of the values that are important to them, in programmes that meet some of their needs, while we continue to provide what the frequent visitors already find satisfying and rewarding. (Hood, 1983)

The report dates from the early 1980s, and it is possible that many of the changes proposed are already being implemented in the museum and gallery sector. In addition the audiences surveyed are American, exhibiting some differences in patterns of leisure choice and socialization. However, the findings and conclusions of the survey arguably provide an important key to understanding both why there is a need to develop new areas of provision to attract new audiences, and how this might be achieved.

Fundamental to the approach is an understanding that we are able to identify attendance patterns by leisure values and to realize that leisure choices, although they may be correlated with demographics, are not *determined* by demographics. It is particularly useful to have a broad and generalized understanding of what motivates people to visit a gallery and, once there, how they engage with the material they find there. An understanding of these points underpinned many of my recommendations in developing first a strategy and then a programme for new audiences. Against this broader canvas we can consider the particular concerns of specific segments of the audience.

Before beginning the process of selecting, matching and giving priority to finite resources I attempted to identify a range of audience segments that were under-represented within the wider audience for the NPG. The primary groups I gave particular consideration to were people with disabilities, young people, and black and ethnic minority people. To this was added a secondary list, including family groups, adult peer groups, adult learners, elderly people and women, with further consideration given to the possibility of targeting geographic areas.

I would like to now consider in some detail the issues relevant to those three main groups in relation to gallery and museum-visiting, beginning with people with disabilities (Figures 11.1 and 11.2). It is impossible to underestimate the importance of addressing the needs of people with disabilities as part of mainstream gallery provision. In the UK, 14 per cent of the population has a disability of some kind; 6.2 million are adults. If one takes into account the families, friends and carers of disabled people, a large section of the population is likely to be affected by issues of access and provision.

Carolyn Keen, Disability Advisor to the Museums and Galleries Commission has written that:

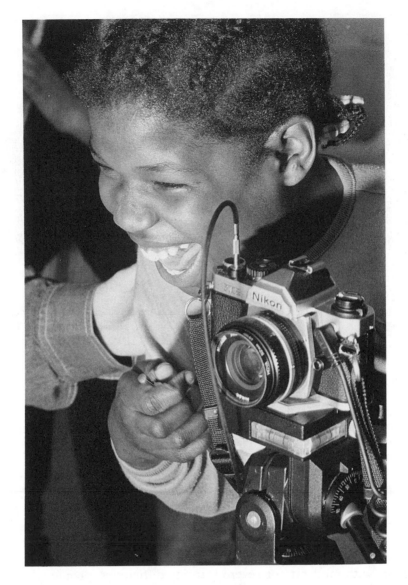

Figure 11.1 *Photography workshop for deaf children at the National Portrait Gallery, London, June 1994.* © *National Portrait Gallery.*

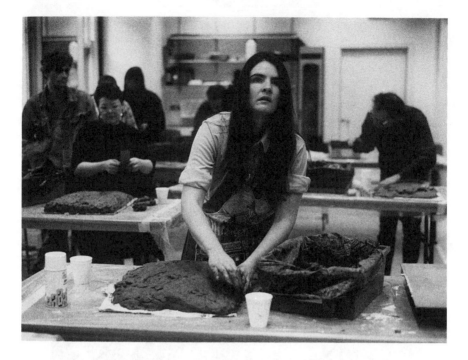

Figure 11.2 *Sculpture workshop for blind and partially-sighted people at the National Portrait Gallery, London, March 1995.* © *National Portrait Gallery.*

> Demographic changes (for example, by the year 2000, 25% of the population will be over retirement age, and the incidence of disability is closely linked to aging), increased leisure time, the requirements of funders and an articulate and more discerning public are just a few of the reasons why disability issues have to be addressed in a coherent and comprehensive way. (Keen, 1991)

It is further important to stress the diversity of disabilities. These include people who are physically impaired (wheelchair users account for just 2 per cent of all people with disabilities), people who are totally or partially blind or deaf, people with speech impairment, as well as people with moderate or severe learning difficulties, people who have suffered mental illness and people who have hidden disabilities resulting from conditions such as epilepsy.

As part of the redevelopment of the public gallery spaces the NPG placed particular emphasis on improved independent access for disabled visitors. This principally involved ramp access, new lifts and disabled toilets and was supplemented by improved signage and specialist interpretive materials. The proposed changes engendered a degree of enthusiasm across the gallery's staff. However in hindsight there was little direct consultation between the staff and disabled people themselves. The consultation that did take place happened between secondary parties of consultants, architects and designers. Consequently the early momentum of enthusiastic change has mellowed a little. This is not to detract from the early positive achievements and very real success in improving access and creating a welcoming environment fuelled by good intentions. However it is worth remembering the point raised by Anne Pearson, then Education Officer at the British Museum, who noted in a recent survey of initiatives in museum education that, 'arrangements made on behalf of disabled people but without their involvement are invariably inappropriate and under-used. This in turn can lead to disillusionment on the part of the museum and even a reluctance to make further improvements' (Pearson, 1985).

In developing services for audiences with disabilities there are two broad approaches. One is to provide specialist activities exclusively for groups of disabled visitors, tailoring work to meet their needs and catering for medium-sized groups, endeavouring to establish then build a niche audience. The second approach is to ensure accessibility for a range of disabilities to mainstream educational provision. For example providing induction loop facilities, sign language interpretation and wheelchair facilities at talks, tours and workshops. At the planning stage we were keen to pursue both lines of approach.

Young people, aged 13–23, were clearly under-represented as a sector of the wider audience and the education department was keen to address this through the targeting of relevant workshops and activities.

According to the Arts Attitude Survey carried out by the Greater London Arts in 1989, white respondents are nearly 50 per cent more likely to visit museums than Asian respondents and more than 100 per cent more likely to visit museums than Afro-Caribbeans. The 1991 survey of London museums amongst non-visitors, commissioned by the London Museums Consultative Committee, 'Dingy places with different kinds of bits', suggests that:

> Afro-Caribbean respondents saw museums as being almost totally devoted to white culture and wanted more of an ethnic focus. Lack of attention to ethnic culture made museums seem of limited relevance to these respondents. (Trevelyan, 1991)

The black and ethnic minority population are a significant new audience amongst whom there is a high incidence of non-attendance to all museums and galleries, not just the NPG. To redress this trend is likely to be a long-term goal, best achieved through targeting the next generation among children and young people. There is practical scope to offer educational services through youth work, particularly by

targeting geographic area and through adult education provision in the
form of workshops and lectures relating to photography. However,
such initiatives are limited and the fundamental issue is not one of
interpretation or access but of the gallery's content. To quote from the
'Dingy places . . .' survey:

> Afro-Caribbean and Asian respondents felt strongly that museums
> should cover ethnic cultures. Not only did they want this for reasons of
> personal identification, but it was felt that it would give white people the
> chance to learn about and understand other cultures.
>
> It was also felt particularly by Afro-Caribbean respondents that the
> role of black people in British history should be recognized. This would
> enable white people to appreciate the contribution made by cultures
> other than their own. (Trevelyan, 1991)

If people of black and ethnic minority origin are to be addressed as a
significant new audience then the lead must come from the gallery's
acquisitions, commissions and exhibitions policy. One of the strengths
of the gallery is in providing a social and historical context for
portraiture across the ages.

Clearly, for a programme to be developed on the back of a part-time
job, this potentially endless shopping list of possibilities would need to
be reduced to a manageable and coherent strategy. The proposition was
to target just three groups around which to develop the core of the
programme and then to select up to six secondary groups for whom
one-off initiatives could be devised within the first two years, with a
view to expanding and developing those initiatives over subsequent
years. These taster projects would prove a valuable exercise for the
gallery with expectations for their immediate success being limited and
a greater emphasis placed on observation, monitoring and evaluation.

The core programme then was to be targeted at three broad
groupings made up of people with disabilities, young people aged 13–23
and adults, particularly those returning to learning. It was decided in
the first instance not to provide exclusively for discrete groups of black
and ethnic minority participants, but rather to encourage and develop
participation through the three core groupings. It was envisaged that
this could be best achieved through outreach, targeting and sensitive
marketing. This strategy should then be backed up by a commitment to
broadening of the gallery's acquisitions and exhibition policy sensitive
to the needs and interests of ethnic minority audiences.

Having identified and considered the wider notion of new audiences,
having developed a strategy and designed a programme, I now want to
consider implementation and its corollary, evaluation. In outlining the
delivery of a programme designed to attract and encourage new
audiences, there are a number of salient points that are important to

highlight. These are the design and costs of the service, the targeting and reaching of the audience, the experience and perceived value of the activity as determined by evaluation, and finally an assessment of how the experiences might inform subsequent services.

The first grouping I wish to focus on is young people. This is partly because this is more of a coherent and easily identifiable grouping, and partly because this has generated the most successful audience response and has followed the most linear development. The rationale for the proposed programme was to encourage a diverse mix of young people, the majority of whom were non-visitors to galleries.

On offer would be practical art and photography-based workshops rooted in and inspired by the galleries' permanent and temporary exhibitions. The workshops would be given a profile in the gallery with displays mounted as a way of promoting the place of education to the wider gallery audience and of encouraging back the workshop participants. The intention over time would be to foster the gallery-going experience amongst young people, to create a programme of activities that would emphasize the educational and the challenging, but would encompass socializing, pleasure and entertainment, and finally, by establishing a reputation amongst teachers, youth workers, parents, but most importantly young people themselves, would create an expectation of the NPG as being a place of interest, relevance and on the circuit. The activities would be free with running tutor time and equipment costs met from the department budget and materials met from a mix of the department budget, sponsorship and donations, and cross-subsidy from charges levied on adult workshops.

The gallery had previously run activities for the 13–23 age group, but had recruited its audience through mailing lists built up from interested gallery visitors. As a result, when activities were programmed the available spaces were filled by the sons and daughters of frequent visitors; young people who were tuned in to events listings and whose social lives existed on a circuit of diversions and organized activities of which galleries and museums were just one point of reference. There was also a high level of parental encouragement, which can occasionally be a mixed blessing, as young people who are increasingly flexing their independence may be more receptive to engaging with an activity which they have been more active in choosing. The first activities planned under the new programme were specifically targeted at groups contacted through youth services. I had written an introductory letter promoting our services and welcoming collaborations with existing youth groups in inner London. I had also encouraged youth workers to promote the activities to interested individuals.

The first workshop was photography-based, exploring studio

photography and self-portraiture. Spaces were filled and each session made up of two or three groupings of young people from different youth centres. The format would be a visit to the exhibition space and a group discussion as a prelude to the practical activities. We would then introduce equipment, cameras, film type and lighting. The group would begin to explore and experiment and then apply their skills in working to a brief in small groups and increasingly independently. The focus for the work was to address the language and conventions of more formal portraiture, particularly introducing the notion of theatre with backdrops, staging, props and artificially replicated light. This is, of course, highly relevant to our collection of both the painted and the photographed portrait, to our historical photography collection and to the work of contemporary practitioners. Theatre is a product of team work and the approach is especially appropriate for workshops, since it affords a range of designated roles which can be rotated amongst the group, allowing everyone to be actively engaged and offering a complete and rounded perspective on the full experience. Consequently the larger group was subdivided into smaller groups and roles allocated for a photographer, assistant, lighting operator, art director and sitter. Having created the illusionary performance space we would encourage the participants to then act up within that space, to pose, gesture and project themselves. The work is challenging as it demands a range of new skills and disciplines. There is scope for self-expression and creativity coupled with problem-solving technique and the discipline of health and safety. In the first six months I ran a series of 10 photography activities lasting for between one and three days and with an average attendance of 12 from a maximum of 15 places.

In the summer months the NPG hosts the BP (British Petroleum) portrait award exhibition, an event designed to highlight contemporary portrait painting and to encourage the work of younger artists. The department has traditionally provided practical art workshops, supported by the sponsorship, to coincide with the event. In the first year of the new audience programme the activities were extended to include 10 half-day painting workshops for young people together with two, two-day photography workshops, again for young people. The photography workshops filled up, while the painting workshops remained relatively poorly subscribed.

In informal staff discussions a suggestion was made to include a flyer in the next annual school mailing, a comprehensive listing including all secondary schools and colleges in London and the South East. The flyer was targeted at art teachers to present to students, inviting names to be put forward for a mailing list through which to advertise future photography and art activities. The production and inclusion of the flyer was of negligible additional cost to the scheduled mail-out. The approach was both basic and simple. However, the results it generated were unexpectedly positive and offer a useful insight into how galleries might market themselves to young people and how in turn young people may respond favourably to the experiences galleries have to offer. In the first instance young people themselves made the choice to put their names forward for inclusion on the list. By the end of October we had received over 400 responses, with some schools returning as many as 20 names and addressees and others two or three. When we came to advertise a new programme of activities in the autumn we mailed directly to those individuals who had expressed an initial interest. This way people were receiving information first-hand rather than through a teacher or parent and were then making the individual choice to respond and book themselves a place. The response was again impressive, with a cartoon and caricature workshop and three photography workshops becoming oversubscribed within two weeks of being advertised. As the activities were free and there was no penalty for non-attendance I was initially concerned that there would be a high drop-out rate, with places booked but people not turning up to take their places. In the event non-take-up of places was almost negligible. We did subsequently experience a higher degree of non-attendance for a workshop series I had organized with the longer lead time of 10 weeks between advertising and the event occurring, as opposed to the usual five weeks. Inevitably there was more time for initial enthusiasm to wane and for competing attractions to appear in people's diaries. It's a mistake I've since been careful to avoid, and I now ensure that there is never more than five weeks between advertising an event and the event taking place.

The most satisfying surprise from using self-subscribing mailing lists was the mix of the groups who appeared at the workshops. The common link between everyone was an enthusiasm for art, photography and design, coupled to the fact that few had visited a gallery since primary school and almost no one would have though of making an independent visit. At the start of one workshop I asked the 15 people there who had ever visited the NPG. Only one person had and she confessed to having 'taken one look inside the place and immediately run out'. The young people came from all parts of London and the South-east, 70 per cent were girls and around 40 per cent were black and Asian young people. The response from young black and Asian people was particularly impressive and seemed to compare favourably with responses to initiatives more specifically targeted at ethnic groups run by other galleries. By promoting ourselves to as wide a group of young people as possible on the back of a comprehensive mailing list and by offering places on practical activity-based programmes through a process of self-selection, we had stumbled upon an appropriate method of marketing that was generating a diverse and enthusiastic audience of first-time visitors.

Two years into the programme we are now becoming increasingly confident of the quality of the work on offer and more ambitious in the projects we are undertaking. The major temporary exhibition of 1995 was a retrospective of the work of the American photographer Richard Avedon. His stylistic hallmark is to place his subjects in front of a white paper background, so isolating them, creating a stage and almost inviting a performance for his camera. The pictures are lit by soft northerly natural light brightened with white reflectors. They are made on large-format plate cameras of the type where the photographer disappears under a black cloth to focus and compose their image on the ground glass before loading the film and taking the picture.

I organized a lecture and film series to accompany the show and devised a programme of weekend workshops for adults, targeted through City and Guilds courses, deaf people, run by a deaf photographer using sign language, and young people contacted through our mailing list. Two photographers, Steve Pyke and Nick Sinclair ran the courses, which followed a similar format regardless of the client group. Between the side of the gallery building and the road is a high-walled drop from the pavement level to the basement and an eight-foot-wide north-facing empty moat accessible through the rear of a store room. This proved the ideal setting for an Avedon project.

Over the course of a weekend the photographers would visit the exhibition with the group and then introduce them to large-format photography. Pictures were made using Polaroid 5 × 4″ film, of a type which gives an instant proof and a black and white negative that can be washed and printed from. We were fortunate in persuading Polaroid to supply copious amounts of the material, thus reducing our material costs to a minimum. The participants were encouraged to persuade visitors to the exhibition to then come and pose for portraits based on the exhibition. The moat was overlooked by the main street above and small crowds gathered to look down on the scene of white backdrops being unrolled, people placed in front of them, hooded photographers and countless others holding bounce cards, washing negatives and loading film.

In the gallery foyer I had mounted a framed exhibition of the education work that coincided with the Avedon exhibition (Figures 11.3–11.5). This included a large wall-mounted display case and every week following on from each workshop I would print up a selection of the pictures and change the display. The workshop series succeeded in working at a number of levels. It provided a challenging experience for the people enrolled on the course. It involved several hundred other gallery visitors in a direct experience of our education work and it was

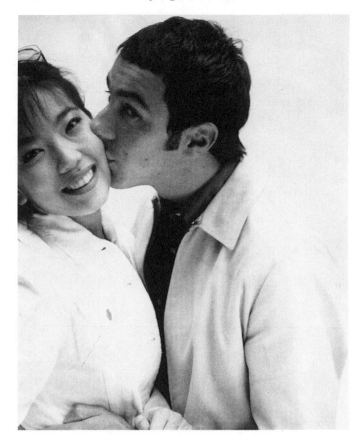

Figures 11.3–11.5 *Photographs made by participants at the Richard Avedon Workshops, National Portrait Gallery, London, Summer 1995.* © *National Portrait Gallery.*

seen by thousands of others overlooking the activities from the street. The foyer exhibition attracted back many of those involved to view the changing display and raised awareness of the event amongst the general visitors. The pictures were of an exceptionally good quality. As a final footnote, one of the contributing photographers, Nick Sinclair, stayed on to make his own white background pictures of the gallery's warding staff, which were published in the *Evening Standard* magazine.

I would now like to consider the place of people with disabilities in the programme for new audiences. As I have already noted, people with disabilities represent a potentially significant section of the overall gallery audience, with 14 per cent of the population having a disability of some kind. While some of the most basic issues concerning disability, such as physical access, access to exhibits through specialist

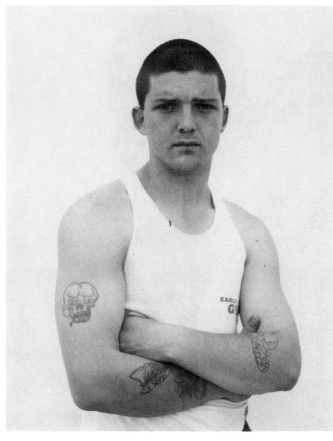

Figure 11.4

interpretation and the attitudes and training of gallery staff, are of concern to all visitors with disability, the specific needs of individual visitors are as diverse as disability itself. The point we are learning through experience is that initiatives targeted at specific sectors of the disabled audience, for example blind or partially sighted people or deaf people, will only ever generate a relatively small audience, but that over time that audience will become established, will want to come back and will become pro-actively involved with the gallery in promoting and further improving access.

The groupings we have addressed through the first two years of the programme are people with special learning needs, people with physical disabilities, people who are blind or partially sighted and people who are deaf or who have partial hearing. We have run workshops and talk programmes and provided sign language interpretation for a selection of our mainstream lecture programme. Activities have been targeted at

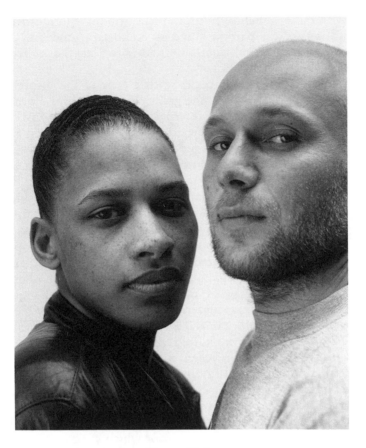

**Figure 11.5**

self-selecting individuals and at establishing groups, often reached through local authority adult education centres.

I would like to concentrate on one particular initiative as an example of the wider programme and concentrate on the planning, marketing and delivery of the service. We are soon to be running the fifth in a series of two-day sculpture workshops for blind and partially sighted people.

An important aspect of the improvements made to the new twentieth-century galleries was the inclusion of a touch trail for visually impaired people. This involved the selection and placement of 10 sculpted portraits chosen for their range of material and of technique and, in the best tradition of the gallery, for their range of sitter. While this is a facility promoted as being for touching, this may only be done while wearing cotton or latex gloves. The trail is supplemented by 12 paintings selected for their scale and graphic boldness and with access

aided by Braille labelling, large print guide, thermoform relief
representations of the paintings and an audio-tape guide, all of which
are available at the information desks sited at the gallery's two
entrances.

The sculpture workshops began with a tour of the displays which
introduced the participants to the gallery's collection and provided us
with useful feedback on the interpretive tools. The gloves proved
irritating and inevitably detracted from the real enjoyment of touch,
while responses to the various aides was mixed. There was no clear
favourite and one person would find the thermoforms extremely useful
while someone else found them totally distracting preferring the audio
guide instead. We were extremely fortunate to find a skilled and
enthusiastic sculpture tutor, Andie Scott, who was experienced in
working with partially sighted people and teamed her with a partially
sighted artist, Terry Hands, to co-plan and run the workshops.

The first event was organized in partnership with Waltham Forest
Adult Education Service, who contacted the participants and helped co-
ordinate transport. The two days proved extremely challenging, with
people exploring unfamiliar materials and working on new techniques.
Waltham Forest in turn organized an exhibition of the pieces made in
the workshop together with photographs of the workshops in progress
supplied by the gallery. This meant a gallery activity was feeding back
into a local community and finding a wider, secondary audience.

We were encouraged by the enthusiasm for the project to expand the
programme and offer future events to a self-selecting audience reached
through targeted advertising. We promoted events through the
disability press and arts listings, many of which are available in Braille
or on audio tape. However, I also persuaded three local radio stations
to broadcast details of the workshops during daytime and evening
broadcasts. Radio is the obvious mainstream media service for reaching
blind and partially sighted people. A significant number of respondents
were reached through the radio station plugs, a service which cost the
gallery little more than a few phone calls and a handful of faxes. In
addition, it emerged that the radio respondents were people who were
unaware of disability arts listings and who were initially most reluctant
to visit a gallery.

In reviewing the first two full years of this programme for new
audiences I am struck by how many of the initial objectives have been
achieved and yet how far we still have to go. There is still scope for
further broadening the audience profile, developing programmes for
family groups and older people, fostering outreach and targeting
specific geographic areas. However, these ambitions are tempered with
the realization that the momentum of change for expanding the
audience of young people and the foothold established amongst people

with disabilities could so easily evaporate if we were to focus our energies and resources elsewhere. So before considering where and by what means the programme may go in the future I want to review the most important lessons learned from the first two years.

Before embarking on education work designed to encourage new audiences it is essential to articulate your intentions across the wider institution and to gain at least the tacit support of colleagues. Argue, persuade and cajole for the need for change. Where possible, research similar initiatives undertaken elsewhere and present the evidence of positive developments. Emphasize the benefits of potential fundraising opportunities, enhanced marketing and increased publicity that such initiatives may generate. Then comes the absolutely essential enshrining of your intentions as written policy. From policy comes planning, from planning comes programming in turn leading on to the nirvana of implementation. Before embarking on the programme consider and identify the audiences you are targeting. Devise appropriate and structured events and resources that are true to the collection of your individual gallery or museum. Consider your marketing, make it as cheap and effective as possible and target it carefully at the audiences you are hoping to reach. Finally, when things do begin to happen, document, promote, monitor and evaluate wherever possible.

We are nearing the completion of a three-year cycle of activity for the programme for new audiences at the NPG. Thankfully the post of education officer for new audiences has been expanded from a half-time to a full-time post. Before embarking upon the next phase of development it is important to review the work that has been undertaken and revise the strategy document that will inform future programming.

At this stage the outline plan is to consolidate the work with young people and with people with disabilities. I hope to concentrate on increasing the number and range of activities for each group and to then focus on further raising the profile of the work with the wider staff and audience of the gallery. By creating a secondary audience for education work through displays and publicity the intention is to both extend the involvement of the original participants and to help create a wider public perception of the programme. This in turn may help to build a reputation for the gallery as a centre where groups are welcome and are encouraged and an expectation amongst future potential visitors that if they become involved in our programmes they will find it a fulfilling and satisfactory experience. My initial plans for diversifying the programme focus on three areas of categories of audience. I am planning a new initiative aimed at family groups through eduction work and an exhibition of family albums. I would want to increase workshops, talk programmes and study days for adults returning to learning. Finally I am actively exploring a new initiative to work with a diverse range of groups in Tower Hamlets, targeting a specific geographic area.

The desire to encourage new audiences is rooted in a belief that galleries and museums at their best are places of stimulation, enquiry and engagement. They should be places with a buzz of excitement where people meet and socialize and shop and eat, even when they are not visiting exhibitions. Museums and galleries are some of the last free public resources; they should extend their role as being centre-pieces of communities and should concentrate on addressing and serving as wide a public as possible. I hope that the education work targeted at new audiences at the NPG is just one part of a wider effort across the whole gallery to embrace this ethos and create a better, more responsive and lively institution.

# References

Hargreaves, R. (1993a) Defining new audiences, unpublished paper, National Portrait Gallery, London.

Hargreaves, R. (1993b) A strategy for new audiences, unpublished paper, National Portrait Gallery, London.

Hargreaves, R. (1993c) A programme for new audiences, unpublished paper, National Portrait Gallery, London.

Hood, M. (1983) Staying away: why people choose not to visit museums, *Museum News* 61(4), 50–57.

Keen, C. (1991) Provision for disabled people, in T. Ambrose and S. Runyard (eds), *Forward Planning*, Routledge, London.

National Audit Office (1993) *Museums and Galleries – Quality of Service to the Public*, Department of National Heritage, London.

National Portrait Gallery (1994) Education policy, unpublished document, National Portrait Gallery, London.

National Portrait Gallery (1995) *Visitors and their Responses*, SRU.

Pearson, A. (1985) *Arts for Everyone: Guidance on Provision for Disabled People*, Carnegie United Kingdom Trust and Centre for Environment for the Handicapped.

Trevelyan, V. (ed.) (1991) *'Dingy Places with Different Kinds of Bits' – an Attitude Survey of London Museums amongst Non-visitors*, London Museums Service, London.

# 12

## Meaning and truth in multicultural museum education

### VIVIEN GOLDING

Race prejudice in fact obeys a flawless logic. A country that lives, draws it substance from the exploitation of other peoples, makes those peoples inferior. Race prejudice applied to those peoples is normal. Racism is therefore not a constant of the human spirit. (Fanon, 1970, p. 50)

This chapter is intended to provide a starting point for a much wider inquiry into the enormous potential for multicultural museum education, utilizing a variety of collections. I will present an account of two practical projects carried out at the Horniman Museum, London, with one class of six-year-old children who attend an inner London school. The first project utilizes a collection of ethnographic musical instruments and the second project a natural history collection. These projects will be explored within a theoretical perspective which privileges feminism and illuminates the concepts of meaning and truth in multicultural museum education. Feminist ideas from hermeneutic philosophy, psychoanalysis and literary theory will be discussed briefly at the beginning of the first section before the museum work with musical instruments. I will then return to a feminist reading of psychoanalysis following the second project on the use of narrative with natural history objects.[1]

These underpinnings to methodology are offered so that people from various disciplines with a range of viewpoints may consider techniques in which the multicultural museum curriculum can become a vital part of a general strategy for antiracism. In the 1990s, the resurgence of an increasingly fascist Europe has surrounded our individual work on multiculturalism with a sense of urgency to present a more forceful opposition to racism in Britain today. An effective challenge to racism can be made by sharing ideas and developing programmes both inside and outside the museum world.

A number of museums are becoming more aware of the need to counteract their historical view of the 'Other,' as exotic curiosity, as feared or noble savage.[2] The inferior status implied by this lens of Western capitalist perceptions has of course justified exploitation of what was necessarily regarded as the underbelly of a divisive society. Women everywhere, the white working classes and black colonial subjects share this history of oppression. Feminist discourse suggests that it is from the silence of shared experiences painfully achieving speech that we may all glimpse alternatives, possibilities of working together to break out of the limiting mould imposed upon us. Women and oppressed peoples writing 'in the margins' will understand that at times it may be necessary to 'turn the proper upside down' in order to achieve this speech (Cixous, 1987, p. 95). The views expressed here will reflect my position as a 'dissident' (Kristeva, 1989a, pp. 292–293).

In order for the marginalized to find a voice my prime concern as a museum educator is for multiculturalism to take up a seat at the very centre of our curriculum. Multicultural museum education aims to increase knowledge and understanding of world cultures through a study of actual cultural products and the wider world from which they came. This involves encouraging teachers to proceed from their enthusiasms about our collections to find ways to instil in their students a sense of moral and social responsibility, a form of education whereby care and respect for others is paramount. Education is understood in its widest sense, which emphasizes a common humanity, the similarities between peoples, while acknowledging and respecting differences. It builds upon strengths and achievements gained from working with museum objects. In short, I believe there are creative methods in which real objects can be a stimulus to an imaginative engagement with the minds of peoples the world over (Gilroy, 1994).

The objectives of the multicultural curriculum then are far wider than the reduction to a general wariness about politically correct language which too often results in deeper silence, fear of misrecognition/misunderstandings. I desire instead a veritable cacophony, a babble of sound from combined voices which may lead to our writing, 'with white ink' if possible (Cixous, 1987, p. 94). Then we may at last all emerge strengthened from the nets of those whose use of words is intended as a disparagement, a barrier to true intercultural understanding. Cooperation and working together is vital here. Pooling ideas has been achieved at the Horniman Museum through networking, which is also a useful tool to ensure projects possess a certain depth and breadth of approach. Networking has led to ongoing in-service training for teachers (INSET) and input from individuals working within external organizations has provided safeguard against shallow interpretation to an extent. This is not to suggest that there is ever a final correct or true way of looking, which brings us to the question of truth and meaning with regard to the knowledge which objects hold and the relationship of this question with racism.

Racism is the supreme discourse of hierarchy and oppression. It attempts to fix people in an immovable past. I want to argue that racism is always and everywhere wrong, but I recognize that my judgements are not value-free. I struggle for words within these master/slave relationships. The museum with its collection of historical objects, ripped from the site of original meaning and context, is ideally placed to speak on these issues. All understanding which takes place at the museum cases is partial, temporary, incomplete. Feminist thought is at home here. The voices of women have always occurred in the blank spaces between words since the experience of women cannot easily be reflected according to the law of the father in patriarchy. Ways and means of subverting, 'doing violence to the text', or 'introducing disorder' have necessarily been devised to account for our thoughts and feelings and this is a stance we can profitably take with museum objects (Cixous, 1987, p. 96).

A major contention of this chapter then is that while museum objects may have been collected and displayed to demonstrate the power of a male white middle-class, for the 'male gaze', through a subversive rereading they can nevertheless lead us all to access certain fundamental truths, to a greater knowledge of ourselves as human beings (Mulvey, 1989, pp. 14–26). Through the self-knowledge gained during the course of work within the multicultural curriculum we may proceed to place ourselves in wider circumstances, that allow us all, men, women and children, to lead richer fuller lives. This is not to justify every shallow piece of interpretation or misinterpretation, but to encourage everyone in making a beginning and to point in the direction of ever increasing knowledge of ourselves in the world. Feminist hermeneutics elucidate these ideas as according to an 'I–Thou' relationship before objects which we will continuously return to (Henderson, 1993, p. 260).

It has been suggested that white people should begin to make a stronger justification of this project choice, to develop a multicultural curriculum, to look in depth at black and other ethnic cultures before proceeding. How can we answer Barbara Smith's (1993, p. 172) warning against 'cultural imperialism'? How can we attempt to understand a world-view which stems from the experience of someone whose racial makeup is different from our own? Is this work based within a framework so different from ours that to attempt a reading of it will be tantamount to engaging in an impossible enterprise? We appear to be stuck with an unresolved problem which, viewed from Wittgenstein's (1974, paras 96 and 560–596) 'game' theory of language makes any form of dialogue across such radically different 'worlds' impossible.

Felly Nkweto Simmonds offers a way out of this seeming impasse by focusing attention on the similarities or 'points of contact' between peoples. In her view we are misguided if we attempt to prioritize within areas of race, class, gender or disability, for outrage and resistance against oppression should proceed on all fronts that are threatened by the political establishment of the day.[3] Similar and indeed stronger positions have been stated by a number of black feminist writers who feel that alternative readings of difference should be encouraged. Mae Gwendolyn Henderson cites Barbara Christian's observation of Audre Lorde's poetry, as leading us all to a positive 'means of conducting creative dialogue' in this context (1993, p. 260). Henderson makes a spirited case for discourse and hopefully for a movement towards understanding. Henderson expresses her understanding of this issue from a hermeneutical framework by recourse to the concept of 'speaking in tongues'. I quote:

> Like Janie, black women must speak in a plurality of voices as well as in a multiplicity of discourses. This discursive diversity, or simultaneity of discourses, I call 'speaking in tongues' . . . This literature speaks as much to the notion of commonality and universalism as it does to the sense of difference and diversity. (Henderson, 1993, pp. 262–264)

These arguments help us to approach the basic 'lack' which Barbara Smith has further suggested lies in the approach of white feminist readers. A detailed study of the art, crafts and natural history in museum collections helps to bridge the experience and knowledge gap, to illuminate that which lies 'beneath consideration, invisible, unknown', to which Smith alludes and the outline of work in the Horniman Museum will illustrate this (Smith, 1993, p. 168). Furthermore, it is my contention that if access to and understanding of the wider world of arts and crafts from around the world is increased, then this will benefit all our communities in multicultural Britain today. The multicultural curriculum is not set in place simply to raise the self-esteem of ethnic communities, although it would appear to serve an important purpose in this regard as the musical instruments project demonstrates.

The value of multicultural museum education lies rather in the striking similarities it bears with feminist women's writing. In brief, it is multifaceted and non-linear in form. It has found existence in the gaps and spaces between the words of discourse. It can allow for multiple readings which will serve to disrupt our comfortable notions of ourselves and our world (Showalter, 1993, pp. 125–143). This perspective is far removed from 'theoretical tourism' and indulgence in a 'poetics of the exotic' by virtue of an essentially self-reflective stance in all participants (Lippard, 1992, p. 164). I will further elucidate this open questioning position which is vital to multicultural museum projects by summarizing aspects of hermeneutic practice.

I am employing Hans Georg Gadamer's 'dialectical model of conversation' for use with museum objects and appealing to his analysis of meaning as ultimately residing in a position which is personal yet already involves an exterior world of language which must be common. Gadamer argued forcefully for various claims to truth at a time when the products of artists were deemed to be 'senseless' by the British logical positivist philosophers and only a practice which approximated that of science could furnish true belief. This is important here as my second piece of practice involves natural history objects and the value of creative work with them. Gadamer located the 'knowledge in art' to the 'experience of art' as containing 'a claim to truth which is certainly different from that of science but equally certain is not inferior to it' (Gadamer, 1981, p. 87). Artistic truth is understood by Gadamer as part of an intimate human relationship with a work of art, an object made by one person and viewed by another, possibly in another time and place.

The concept of the hermeneutic 'circle' provides clarification here. This is not simply a methodological circle whereby we are called upon to understand the parts in terms of the whole and the whole in terms of the parts, but a much wider concept which 'describes an ontological structural element in understanding' (Gadamer, 1981, p. 261). This circle of understanding addresses the question, how can I know anything? In order to know anything we must already have formed some conception of it, otherwise the formation of the question seems to be an impossibility. Knowledge then appears to be a reworking of something already known to some extent. It is this vicious circle which constitutes human knowing. Knowing is always a deepening process, we can never know anything exhaustively and the best approach to knowledge would seem to be a questioning one. We are guided in these questioning efforts towards understanding by the object itself. The production and reception of works of art and artefacts then is seen in hermeneutics as a vital human activity and essential if people are to live full, rich lives.

I am now in a position to begin a discussion of actual practice. The Horniman Museum Education Centre is involved at primary level with a Section 11 project[4] in the London borough of Lambeth, entitled English Language Support Project, (ELSP). The Education Centre is able to provide opportunities for direct visual and tactile experiences in learning which are so important to the development of study skills for all children in the primary age group. A study of objects from the different cultural traditions which we have begun to speak of can develop receptive and positive attitudes to education in general as well as increasing children's awareness and appreciation of other people's art forms and culture. The language specialists in Lambeth who are working with the education team on these issues see this as an important way of challenging bias. We believe that students may come to a gradual recognition that other people have minds and feelings like our own through handling objects.

The focus of discussion in this paper will be on the collaborative ELSP work with Stockwell Infants School in South London where the project co-ordinator is Karen Mears. She is also one of the Horniman Museum freelance Art and Craft Workshop leaders. The ELSP in Lambeth has as a broad aim the development of children's oral and written communication skills in English alongside their English-speaking peers. Bilingual children who are learning to speak English are supported in their school groups to give them access to the whole school curriculum, and in this way the whole class benefits from the efforts of the ELSP teachers. In addition English as a second language speakers are not excluded and thereby made to feel isolated from the group. The cross-curricular work which the language teams initiate to enhance the use of language by all class members is often based on multicultural themes. The multicultural curriculum is of benefit to all children and not just those whose particular culture is being studied, although these students certainly gain in confidence through their active participation and contribution to the pool of knowledge.

The Horniman Museum Education Centre is regarded as an essential starting point and a vital component for much of the ELSP multicultural project work. Regular meetings are organized with group leaders to discuss the most appropriate ways of utilizing the collections to increase general group knowledge and appreciation as well as boost individual confidence in home cultures and counteract the low self-esteem from which some children suffer. Towards this end INSET is negotiated and jointly planned with teachers and the local education advisors. The theme for 1994–1995 short course INSET was early years education with a focus on storytelling, art design and technology. An extended INSET course, entitled Multicultural Musical Traditions, fulfils part of a need to begin more in-depth study. This structured music course essentially provided teachers with an opportunity for developing their own looking, listening and appraising, composing and performing skills.

A number of parallels are drawn between societies, their musical forms and structures at the extended music INSET sessions. For example work on drones, time cycles and notations is included so that a mutual respect for the complexity of diverse cultures can be fostered by the teachers of school groups. Further learning is achieved through the direct practical experience of creating musical performances around these themes in small groups with the handling collection. The problems of racism which can arise if these aspects of diversity are ignored or inappropriately tackled are thereby confronted directly and strategies for dealing with racism shared. These hands-on interactive methods act as the first stimulus to initiating detailed programmes of study across the curriculum that may later transfer knowledge and understanding to the students.

The Multicultural Musical Traditions INSET and work with booked school groups takes place in the centre music room. Further information about the displays of more than 1500 instruments can be accessed from the 16 touch-activated computer screens positioned at regular intervals around the room. The computers permit students to see video clips of players and hear original sound recordings taken in the field. Our handling collection of original musical instruments and sound recordings from all over the world complements these displays. Working directly from the handling collection is a multisensory experience that enables everyone to participate whatever their ability level, nursery or INSET groups.

In 1994 the intensive pre-visit preparation which includes INSET was singled out for a special part of a Channel 4 programme for schools, *Using Museums*. In this way the requirements for a successful museum visit as a partnership between the individual needs of school and the purpose of the museum were emphasized so that other teachers might feel enabled to make an educational visit. Stockwell Infants was selected by the director of the programme from our long-term link-up schools as representative of an inner city multiethnic school. Incorporating a successful museum visit into the multicultural curriculum is dependent to a large extent on good working relationships between educators inside and outside of the museum, although the onus is still on the teacher to carry out the preparatory work with the group so that the detailed plans discussed for the museum input can be carried out.

At school Karen discussed with the children in Gill Campbell's class what would happen when they came to the museum. It had been decided that a concentration on the skills of makers with different materials and technologies could be used as a focal point and a tool with which to challenge bias and counter prejudice. The children were told they would get a chance to see what materials makers had used in different parts of the world to make and decorate their work. Students were familiarized with the qualities of materials such as wood, metal, string, skin, etc., as examples of those they would see at the museum.

They were also made aware that they would be able to see how musical instruments work by using techniques of vibrating string, columns of air, naturally sonorous materials or membranes. In addition the relationship of size with musical qualities such as high and low, long and short, loud and soft sounds would be demonstrated by the museum work with real objects.

The children spent some school time looking at how sound is made and conducting some practical experiments to reinforce their learning, which is so important for children of this age. The Education Centre also supported the parents who were visiting the museum for the television programme by providing a detailed guide to the New Music Room with concise notes on the most relevant displays. On the music visit the parents were previously well briefed by Karen and Gill. Parents and guardians visit the museum as part of the school group for two reasons. One reason is to accompany their family and to make up the required numbers of adult carers legally required for educational trips. A second reason is to further their own interests and enthusiasms. Thus the life-long learning of parents and guardians is often supported at the museum alongside the children in school groups.

On the day of the visit it was decided to place an emphasis on percussion work and concentrate especially on the drums in the museum. The children were told they needed to gather visual information by drawing details from the collections which they would later incorporate into their drum designs from recycled materials back at school. The museum talk and handling session made extensive use of the percussion instruments in the handling collection so that everyone could participate at their own ability level. The museum-led session was followed on this occasion by a music-making workshop conducted by Nana Appiah, a Ghanaian drummer (Figure 12.1). In addition he has more than 10 years' experience of working with mixed ability school and community groups in this country. The children first listened to and then performed a rhythm accompaniment with the professional musicians. The previous school work on rhythm and the causes of varying pitch made an essential contribution to the success of this workshop practice. Nana quickly established a rapport with the students and his workshop made a lively finale to the Horniman Museum section of the video.

Nana was accompanied by a drummer called Kwame Addo in the workshops. A ripple of recognition ran through the children when he was introduced, making it obvious that they were pleasantly familiar with the Ghanaian name for a boy child born on Saturday. There are moments when museum educators working face to face with students can respond to the feeling of the group dynamics and, with due reference to the teachers' greater knowledge of the individual children,

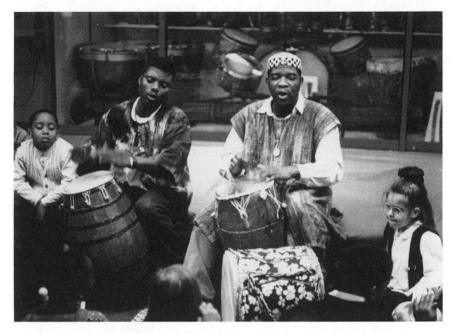

Figure 12.1 *Nana Appiah and Kwame Addo work with children from Stockwell Infants School at the Horniman Museum.* © *Channel 4.*

build on the group potential which has newly opened to learning. Gill, the teacher on this occasion, indicated that Kwame from this group would be proud to participate. This cannot be assumed as many children do not relish standing up and speaking out, although our aim is to encourage the confidence that makes this possible. If individuals are enabled to stand alone and apart from the group stating their opinions and describing their experiences, we may truly tackle discrimination in the long term. This work for me is the emotional equivalent to what is described as the setting up of an intellectual scaffolding so that the child may reach a higher 'zone of proximal development', a fundamental idea of Vygotsky's which has been further elucidated by Bruner (Vygotsky, 1986, p. 187; Bruner, 1986, pp. 71–78). If multicultural museum educators can provide a structure for the young ego this demonstrates to the individual psyche a potential, the possibility of developing sufficient strength to withstand the fear of attack for being different.

When Nana began to drum a basic rhythm with which the children had become familiar thanks to the excellence of Gill's earlier instruction, a previously silent child made his way forward and joined Nana and Kwame on the stage. He used no verbal language, but he slowly started to participate in the music-making, encouraged all the while by the professional musicians. This child was actually a refugee finding a means of expressing himself again for the first time after being severely traumatized by dreadful experiences in his home country. He had simply wandered the school in an understandable daze since his recent arrival in England. Nana and Kwame were sensitive to the special needs of the boy and responded to these through their art. When they learned the details of the therapy afforded to this child after the session, the artists simply spoke of the tremendous power of the objects they played to move, to transform or to effect lasting change. On this occasion it seems to be the special contextualizing, the drum object brought to life by professional use which largely constituted the healing process.

This dramatic example speaks from the heart of working directly with ethnographic objects. Children can use their hands and eyes in conjunction with speech to enhance and build upon the undoubted pleasure derived from looking (Bruner, 1986, p. 122). It may be described as differentiated learning, a fundamental root of museum education. The needs of individuals within a school group vary enormously. In the group we have been discussing, eight children were deemed to require extra help with learning and are still continuing the stages of assessment for Special Educational Needs in accordance with the criteria established by Warnock.[5] In addition to these students, at the start of the school year, a number of the bilingual children were only just beginning to speak English, 16 out of the class of 31. Eleven different first languages were spoken by the group. The first languages of the children were Ibo, Ashanti, Yoruba, Portuguese, Bengali, Vietnamese, Wolof, French/ Lingala, Spanish, Nyanja and Urdu/Punjabi. Three children were newly arrived in this country. One other child arrived as a severely traumatized refugee. Ten children are the first generation to be born in England. Three members of the group are ethnic English.

Table 12.1 illustrates the progress in English language competency of the bilingual children. Column four shows the language level at the start of the multicultural museum education programme in 1994 and the level attained at the end of the school year in column five. On the chart, 1 represents the beginning level of competency in English and 3 represents the highest level. According to this system, which is used in Lambeth, it is not possible to enter a higher stage, 2 or 3, unless the child is able to demonstrate similar ability in reading and written work. The nine children who have surpassed their entry grade have made astounding leaps in levels of literacy. The seven children who appear to have remained at the beginning stages of English have nevertheless all gained quite considerable levels of oral competency during the year according to their teachers and Pat Pinsent (1992) has shown this to be a prerequisite for literacy.

Table 12.1 *Progress in English language competency of six-year-old bilingual children at Stockwell Infants School, London.*

| Name | Country | Language | Stage '94 | Stage '95 |
|------|---------|----------|-----------|-----------|
| D.M. | Nigeria | Ibo | 1 | 1 |
| L.B. | Ghana | Ashanti | 2 | 3? |
| K.P. | Nigeria | Yoruba | 1 | 2 |
| U.P.E. | Portugal | Portuguese | 1 | 1 |
| N.M.Q. | Vietnam | Vietnamese | 1 | 2 |
| I.N. | Bangladesh | Bengali | 1 | 1 |
| F.P. | Nigeria | Yoruba | 1 | 2? |
| M.I. | Bangladesh | Bengali | 1 | 2? |
| N.T. | Portugal | Portuguese | 1 | 1 |
| K.D. | Gambia | Wolof | 1 | 2? |
| C.C. | Zambia | French/Lingala | 1 | 1 |
| L.Q.S. | Peru | Spanish | 1 | 1 |
| N.P. | Nigeria | Ibo | 1 | 2 |
| R.I.I. | Vietnam | Vietnamese | 1 | 2? |
| F.P. | Zambia | Nyanji | 1 | 1 left |
| B.S. | Pakistan | Urdu/Punjabi | 2 | 3? |

English Language Support Project (ELSP) co-ordinator Karen Mears. Teacher Gill Cambell. This table illustrates the degree of English language competency on entering Gill Cambell's class in 1994 and the level attained at the end of the school year in 1995. The stages 1, 2 and 3 refer to the second language development of the individual children with 1 representing the beginning stage and 3 the highest level. According to this system used in Lambeth it is not possible to enter a higher stage unless the child has demonstrated similar ability in reading and written work. The seven children who appear to have remained at stage 1 have all gained considerable levels of oral competency during the multicultural museum project work according to the teachers and this is considered to be a prerequisite for literacy (Pinsent, 1992). The names have been changed for reasons of confidentiality.

We might now ask how it is that this enormous progress has been possible. Is it the case that the language teachers are simply brilliant specialist teachers? I would argue that this is in large part responsible for such impressive results. If teachers can work from their individual strengths and genuine enthusiasms this is truly inspiring for the students, who are naturally carried along with the project work. In the case of the particular teachers at Stockwell Infants it was also their deep appreciation of the diverse cultures represented in their classroom which lay at the centre of the project work and this is where the Museum Education Centre was able to contribute. The objects jointly chosen were scrutinized for different ways into speech. Silence on racism, prejudice, blackness, discrimination, issues of vital importance to all our children, can be broken through attending closely to the pertinent features of objects, comparing, contrasting and bringing this attention to detail creatively into coherent thought and word. Multicultural museum education at the Horniman Museum is regarded as uniquely valuable by Stockwell Infants for establishing a unique sensory threshold from which further learning across a range of curriculum areas can be achieved, most notably for Gill's group in language development.

We turn now to speak more precisely of what is understood by knowledge, truth and multiculturalism in the wider context of museum objects. How can objects which are not works of art or craft but have been displayed for our gaze be incorporated into the multicultural curriculum? What are the points of contact that we can build upon with objects that do not speak directly within a framework of ethnographic significance? We have arrived at a position where these questions may be usefully addressed with reference to the oral tradition and the development of a storytelling programme for our youngest visitors based around traditional tales at the Horniman Museum. This project would not have been possible without the co-operation and guidance of Joan Anim-Addo and Jan Blake from the Caribbean Centre at Goldsmiths College. In their training programme I have been able to develop skills and expertise to aid the process of museum inquiry in our smallest visitors. The storytelling project further demonstrates the importance of networking with external agencies.

This project is not analogous to a rationalist inquiry which might seek to objectively record physical features, truths of the external world, although such work does enter the project. Bruno Bettelheim has emphasized that traditional tales importantly enable children to contemplate their inner lives, their feelings and fears (Bettelheim, 1991, p. 117). The truth of tales is that of an imaginative engagement with, not a realist description of, the world. To employ Wittgenstein's (1974, p. 172) terminology, they properly belong to different 'forms of life'. Traditional tales operate according to the rules of the 'game' of storytelling and are correctly appreciated if they embody the particular set of values within the world of the tale. Bettelheim forcefully expresses the importance of telling rather than reading tales. Unfortunately the oral tradition has been devalued and marginalized by the primacy afforded to the written word in our literate Western culture. It seems likely that the absence of a written language system in many cultures displayed in the museum has contributed to the attribution of an intellectual lack onto those peoples, which is in turn used as a justification for oppression.

Bettelheim emphasizes that it is the telling of tales which most powerfully captures the imagination as well as providing a stimulus to writing. For many of the children at Stockwell Infants the oral tradition is considerably stronger in their home culture than in present day

English society and for these children learning can be enhanced through a familiar mode. Multicultural museum education also publicly validates individual experiences by making special what are familiar everyday objects for a number of children as part of the storytelling programme. Memories of ongoing traditions can profitably be awakened, and shown to be highly valued by the museum setting. The children can then actively participate in this sense of worth which is transferred to them through acknowledgement of their home culture. It is possible for example that the traumatized boy I referred to earlier was helped by being able to recall happier experiences of village music-making through the drumming workshop.

In this paper I will relate these different areas of truth in the arts to a particular West African story which uses objects from the Natural History Gallery. This collection was displayed in the Horniman Museum at the turn of the century according to a certain scientific understanding of the natural world. Animal classification, animal defences and animal movement are included in the themes displayed. The level of interpretation on the information panels is estimated to be appropriate for sixth-form or first-year science degree students but nursery, infant and art teachers regularly bring their students to these cases with a different agenda. Such a critical attitude, one which seeks some expression of radical unorthodox viewpoints, is perhaps part of any creative interaction with the world and artists from many disciplines seem to share this desire to resist with us as women the status quo. James Joyce for example is referred to by Kristeva in this context (Kristeva, 1989a, p. 122). The fascination of children and enthusiasm of teachers gradually influenced our co-operative, sub-versive re-presentations of objects such as these from our handling collection, in re-displays that would promote imaginative work on language.

The importance of these points may be clarified if we listen to 'Squirrel and Hedgehog', a West African dilemma tale (Figure 12.2). Dilemma tales actively involve all the participants in completing the story. Listeners debate the conflicts and make the ending. There is no one correct answer in this approach, which is child-centred and allows children to develop their imaginative capacities, their aesthetic awareness and their moral sensibilities for making complex decisions. Our first concern is with increasing the child's mastery of language simply by engaging in 'talk'. This is a feat in itself as Beryl Gilroy notes; children quickly come to feel that only right answers are acceptable and we must bring them to an understanding that, 'talking for its own sake is important' (Gilroy, 1994, p. 162). Through talking children become individuals capable of independent decision-making. The talk here is quite different from the often banal exchanges which pertain to a

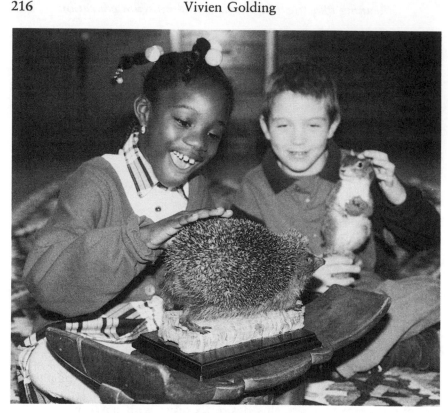

**Figure 12.2** *Children from Stockwell Infants School handle Squirrel and Hedgehog as part of a storytelling workshop at the Horniman Museum.* © *Stockwell Infants School and Horniman Museum.*

simple relation with everyday life. The storyteller, teacher and children co-operate to enable real and meaningful discussion over wide subject areas.

It is also the shared context of this talk, which is partly based on an imagined world, that gives it an entirely different quality. This creative sharing in the world of the imagination resonates positively within the child, who sees that using creative faculties is an important grown-up activity. This tale is retold here from the oral and written comments of two classes of year one children accompanied by their teachers from Stockwell Infants School. The reward educators derive from children's spontaneous remarks is direct information about our practice. Listening to our students we come to a better understanding of our effectiveness. The two sessions were recorded onto audio tape.

> Vivien came to our school and told us a story. The story that came to our school first came from Africa. Viv's friend Jan told her the story and Jan's mum told her the story when she was little in Grenada. Stories can

travel about like that. It's a bit like travelling when we hear them and think of different places. We don't know if its a true story or not, but if its not true Vivien, Jan and Stockwell Infants didn't make it up in the first place!

One day it rained and rained and rained. The water made big puddles and bigger and bigger puddles. The water got higher and higher. Squirrel was happy she had made a nest high up in a tree. Then she saw her friend Hedgehog. Hedgehog couldn't swim so squirrel helped him. She let him go into her house. It was hard work for Hedgehog to climb into Squirrel's high nest. The friends were very tired that night and they soon went to sleep together.

Hedgehog rolled into a ball because they like to sleep like that. He slept very well but he prickled Squirrel! She tried to wake him but she couldn't because Hedgehog has such a good armour. In the morning Hedgehog said, 'I had a good sleep.' Squirrel said, 'Lucky you, I didn't. You prickled me and you snore.' Hedgehog was very sorry and said he would be more careful.

The next night Hedgehog tried to sleep on one side of the nest. Squirrel tried to sleep on the other side of the nest. When Hedgehog fell asleep he rolled over and prickled Squirrel again! Squirrel tried to wake Hedgehog but she couldn't. If only they had a blanket they could put between them but they didn't. The next morning Hedgehog was very very sorry he kept Squirrel awake again. Hedgehog said he would have to be even more careful.

On the third night Hedgehog tried to sleep even closer to the edge of the nest. Squirrel tried to sleep even closer to the other side of the nest. When Hedgehog fell asleep he rolled over and prickled Squirrel again! If only they had some hard bricks they could put a wall in the middle of the nest but they didn't have any.

Squirrel was very cross because she hadn't slept well for three nights. She said, 'You must leave my home. We can't sleep together. Your prickles hurt me.' Hedgehog said, 'I'm really sorry but it's still raining. I can't swim and I'll die if I leave.' They decided to build a bigger nest together. They did it with their hands and used some twigs from the top of the tree.

This story was followed by careful handling of Squirrel and Hedgehog from our handling collection, literally brought to life from the words of the story. They proved a potent source of fascination and wonder. Handling these creatures, physical features of survival, protection and shelter is made obvious. Some everyday craft objects from West Africa were also made available. A Yoruba gourd bowl with carved decoration of combs and goats, a cassava resist-printed shirt, a musical instrument called an mbira or thumb piano. By looking closely at these goods children can perceive something of the breadth of human thought and creativity. Present day items such as medicine were also handled so that historical artefacts were not fixing peoples into an immovable past, but the ever developing nature of culture could be emphasized. Children can also come to understand some of the reasons behind differences between peoples, their clothing, food and customs, through conversation. If we look at the determining factors such as land and climatic effects on natural resources, which in turn impinge on the different ways people live their lives, differences first seen as odd can be reviewed as an imminently sensible interaction with the world. Culture sharing and cross-cultural influences so readily come to the fore when we work from narrative. Subjects are easily introduced through the framework of discussion and comparison which has been established. Our own favourite animals, their best foods and ours, are perennially popular themes!

Aesthetics, dealing with ideas of the beautiful within culture, is another important area of thought to be addressed in the multicultural museum curriculum. Daily life for some children can severely limit the capacity for being touched by beauty, but through creative work on narrative with objects imaginations can soar. Related questions of worth and value are also shown in our prized museum possessions which are not inordinately expensive. Furthermore we can demonstrate our trust in the children to treat the special objects with care. In addition, Squirrel and Hedgehog here personify moral arguments about justice, right and wrong, fairplay, not hurting others, intentional cruelty, pain and death, personal property and ownership, friendship and hospitality. The creatures in the story were utilized to express human sentiments and were discussed in familiar language which aided the understanding of such difficult concepts.

Motivating with real objects is always a comparatively easy task and so the objects were essentially used as aids to deeper reflection on many aspects of experience. It was essential that imaginations be released for this work, for underlying causes of actions to be determined. Imagination is also valued for its capacity to transcend the limits of what is possible from day to day. In short we use narrative and objects primarily to stimulate the imagination of children to consider a range of different possibilities. The importance of this work is to expand the parameters of thought, for when thinking is confined to stereotypes, the lynchpins of racism may be resorted to. We might usefully quote Beryl Gilroy here:

> I turned to art and drama to help them towards a new awareness of alternatives and set new boundaries in their thinking ... All this helped to give the children the chance to form new percepts, opinions and judgments about situations, incidents and people. (Gilroy, 1994, p. 97)

The creatures also provided a stimulus and inspiration for close observational drawing as well as more imaginative art and their ideas were further drawn out by these means. Drawing can provide another channel of communication and introduce different patterns of thought. Real objects seem to provide a powerful, multisensory springboard of interest, out of which the formation of concepts arises. Tactile experiences can greatly assist and stimulate this process of attaining different forms of speech through creative storytelling, writing and drawing activities. Children gain a different perceptual experience from observing the objects close up and from all angles. An overwhelming desire to communicate then arises from these efforts directed towards looking, encouraging touching and feeling with clarity and purpose. All this work leads students to become more sensitive viewers and critics, by helping children to order their ideas, and by building up experiences which can be called upon in the future. Through handling we can provide some instant success, an exhilarating, immediate experiencing of new shapes and sizes in space, stroking new textures, comparing and contrasting with our own bodies. The pleasure this brings to all children, perhaps especially those who often appear to fail, may in turn result in a certain assurance about an individual's abilities and the positive direction for their energies.

We might profitably return here to the concepts of truth and meaning which we have viewed within a circular hermeneutical framework to a final positioning within feminist psychoanalytical theory. A Lacanian or mentalist reading of Freud's work emphasizes the importance of dynamics and the interpretation of desire. This view stresses psychoanalysis as primarily concerned with the acquisition of ideas, the ideas that people hold and live by in culture. It looks at the order of society, providing us with a description of, not a recommendation for, patriarchy. Finally I believe it empowers us by providing the possibility of rule outside the 'law'. Juliet Mitchell has argued that the Freudian discourse can only properly be understood within the framework of the 'two fundamental theories', of the unconscious and sexuality (Mitchell, 1987, p. 5). I will single out the concept of the unconscious as of paramount importance here.

Briefly, unconscious ideas enjoy certain freedoms from those of consciousness. Most notably they are exempt from contradiction, with love and hate for instance happily co-existing. Neither are they temporally structured or altered by the passing of time, indeed it is often wishes from earliest childhood that are seen to persist most forcefully. Finally, they seem quite impervious to contrary evidence from the experiences of reality. Nevertheless they do obey a certain order articulated in the theory of 'primary processes'. Freud remarked that 'the governing purpose obeyed by these primary processes is easy to recognise; it is described as the pleasure–unpleasure principle, or more shortly the pleasure principle' (Freud, 1984, p. 36). To summarize here we can say that the avowal of certain ideas would cause pain to the conscious agent and so they are relegated to the unconscious by the forces of repression. However, they remain active and as disguised representations they seek to be released at every occasion when conscious control is relaxed, for example in the case of dreams and neurotic symptoms (Freud, 1980, p. 4). The root of these ideas is found through analysis to be connected with an unfulfilled wish which is of a sexual nature and which stems from earliest childhood. We are now in a better position to see if the theory of the unconscious can aid us in the interpretation of the story, Squirrel and Hedgehog.

It is the imaginary world of story, of artistic production, which weakens the repressive censor and allows the unconscious material to emerge and be dealt with in the safe narrative space. A full consideration of the unconscious elements which have been observed rising to the fore in the telling of this tale is impossible in this short chapter. I will therefore exclusively address the issue of conflict in the story. Conflict here, as in so many traditional tales results from 'intentions gone awry', as Bettelheim points out. The idea of conflict is a conscious aspect of the tale and also belongs firmly in the realms of psychoanalysis which is not a theory of conformity and adaption, although it has been criticized as such (Mitchell, 1987, p. 338). One of the most important features of Freud's thought is the conflict which lies at the heart of the theory of the unconscious, the persistent battle between life-affirming Eros, and Thanatos, the urge towards death. Our story importantly permits this conflict to escape the forces of repression through the images of Squirrel and Hedgehog and through the narrative structure.

Structure here is distinct from the more familiar moral fables of Europe such as Little Red Hen, which seek to punish the lazy creatures under the constant sway of the pleasure principle. In Little Red Hen the superego is all powerful and asserts the law. In contrast, the essential structure of the West African tale lies in the completion of the dilemma by the child. In the dilemma tale the audience must decide the fate of the creatures and material banished to the realms of the unconscious 'returns'. This element of freedom to choose gives full rein to imaginative faculties and the solutions which have been suggested to finish the story are ingenious in content and range from kindly to vindictive in scope. 'He should go', 'But he will die', 'Cut off his prickles', 'Try to make the nest bigger', 'Make another nest together'. The young psyche is given time and space in the tale to search for a just solution to the eternal problem of conflict as it is exteriorized and projected onto creatures in the nest (Figure 12.3).

Squirrel and Hedgehog are both viewed as aspects of life which are to be valued by small people who are always incredulous that the

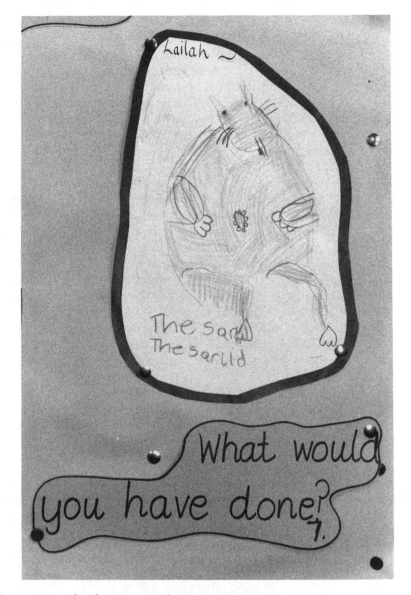

**Figure 12.3** *After listening to the West African dilemma tale about Squirrel and Hedgehog, children are encouraged to draw and discuss possible endings for the story.* © *Stockwell Infants School and Horniman Museum.*

creatures are 'real' but 'dead' and that someone long ago, not the storyteller, may have 'killed' them. The museum animals are potent agents of the unconscious. We bring them to 'real' life in the museum from the imagined world of the story. They are live representation and dead reality, speaking of our desire to escape the transience of existence. The different features of the animals also point to different aspects of ourselves, some of which lie dormant but not defeated. We are Squirrel and we are Hedgehog, we are ego and we are id, we are not yet nor are we ever entirely rational beings. In short, the demands of the individual libido seeking expression must remain unsatisfied for the sake of society that must seek to contain them. Conflict remains though, between the primitive desires of human nature which are relinquished, though not entirely, for the sake of a life within culture. (Gabriel, 1983, p. 30)

Bruno Bettelheim reminds us of an important point to all traditional tales. Through the telling of tales, small children whose very existence is reliant on the care of others are given an opportunity of transcendence from the fears inherent in this attachment, loss and abandonment. One way in which they might achieve transcendence lies in pondering the problem of conflict in the tale, using their imaginative faculties. For Bettelheim the unconscious wish at the heart of the story would seem to be for integration of the disparate aspects of the personality, ego, id and super ego, to be realized (Bettelheim, 1991, p. 146). He appears to share Anna Freud's idea of supporting and strengthening the child's ego so that the child is allowed glimpses of alternative possibilities and can thereby be made to feel confident and secure in their developing cognitive abilities.

This concludes a brief account of some deeper structures, or 'deep play', within narrative from a feminist psychoanalytic perspective (Geertz, 1993, pp. 412–453). Together with the hermeneutical philosophy outlined in the first section of this paper we have the beginnings of a framework which can assist us towards a greater understanding of objects, others and ourselves as part of a multicultural museum education programme. The special root of learning from artefacts lies somewhere in the dialogue whereby we are able to provide a safe space, a return to the maternal chora for Kristeva, in order for the object to speak and in finding speech, in breaking the silence of the work, to bestow a greater ability on the one who engages in the dialogue (Kristeva, 1989b, pp. 124–147). Kristeva borrows the term 'chora' from Plato's 'Timaeus', where it seems to allude to the world of the forms, from whence all life originates and to which it returns (Plato, 1977, pp. 51–52, 70–72; Plato, 1976, pp. 514–521, 227–235). In short, Kristeva appears to argue for access to the maternal chora, the time and space of symbiosis with the mother, as the source of all imagination and creativity. The ability to keep these lines of choric movement open is essentially one of widening horizons and of understanding, self-understanding which increases every time we return to those works which first moved us and which begins with a questioning position.

To question, the question and answer method beloved of the Greeks is the philosophers' path to knowledge and truth when the questions prompt us to profound meditation. We are familiar with museum questions. There are questions which rely on developing perceptual abilities. What is it made from? There are questions which rely on extending our knowledge of social structures. Who might have used this work, how, why? There are questions which rely on encouraging political thought. How did this work arrive here in this space? Were the makers the ones who placed it thus and so? Should the works be here? Why? There are questions which rely on developing aesthetic sensibilities. What are the formal qualities, the perfect marriage of line and colour here which make the beauty of the work resonate within us? Finally and most importantly for multicultural museum education, we must all ask our own questions of these works. Educators can encourage these personal responses to objects in children by generating and interest in authentic museum objects.

In conclusion, multicultural museum education is centrally concerned with objects, and the different ideas which we have attached to them. To handle real things and ask questions about them leads us to different pictures of our place in the world and alternative possibilities of being. It is in this way that objects can be said to expand the mind and widen our 'horizons' (Gadamer, 1981).

## Notes

1. I refer to women writers in the group 'Psych et Po' who utilize Lacanian psychoanalysis and philosophy. For a readable introduction to this body of thought two books are recommended. Firstly, Marks and de Courtivron (1991), and secondly, Kristeva (1989a). Hermeneutics refers to Hermes, the messenger of the gods, who transmitted the word of the gods to the people. It has been used as a theory of interpretation for biblical exegesis and interpretive work in the law as well as the field of art. A readable overview of Hans Georg Gadamer's work on how we come to understand art objects is provided in Gadamer (1977).
2. Two relevant exhibitions are *Yoruba* at Horniman Museum, 1992, curated by Keith Nicklin, and *Fetishism* at Brighton Museum, 1995, curated by Anthony Shelton. These are excellent models.
3. F. Nkweto Simmonds, (1992), from the keynote speech delivered at the Women's Studies Network Conference held in Camden, London.
4. 'Section 11' was originally part of the 1966 Local Government Act which made specialist provision, under a Home Office edict, for New Commonwealth children whose language and customs were different from the majority community. In 1993 Neil Gerrard introduced an amendment that would provide for all children including refugees from countries other than the New Commonwealth. Section 11 now provides 50 per cent

matched funding towards the teaching of English and raising achievement projects for every schoolchild.

5. The Warnock stages of assessment were established in 1994 as part of the Special Educational Needs (S.E.N.) code of practice and relate to children who are perceived to have various difficulties in learning. They require schools to list children and their different learning needs alongside specific plans to address the difficulty over a period of time. The national average of children awaiting assessment is 20 per cent at stage 1 and 2–3 per cent at stage 5 when a statement, a legal document, is issued outlining the child's needs and the provision which will be made.

## Acknowledgements

I would especially like to thank the following people for their insightful comments, co-operation and support with this project: Joan Anim-Addo of the Caribbean Centre, Karen Mears of Lambeth ELSP, and students and staff of Stockwell Infants School.

## References

Bettelheim, B. (1991) *The Uses of Enchantment*, Penguin, Harmondsworth.
Bruner, J. (1986) *Actual Minds, Possible Worlds*, Harvard Press, Cambridge, MA.
Cixous, H. (1987) *Newly Born Woman*, Manchester University Press, Manchester.
Fanon, F. (1970) *Towards the African Revolution*, Pelican, Harmondsworth.
Freud, S. (1980) *The Interpretation of Dreams*, Pelican Freud Library, Harmondsworth (first published 1900).
Freud, S. (1984) Formulations on the two principles of mental functioning, in *On Metapsychology: the Theory of Psychoanalysis*, Pelican Freud Library, Harmondsworth (first published 1911).
Gabriel, Y. (1983) *Freud and Society*, Routledge and Kegan Paul, London.
Gadamer, H.G. (1977) *Philosophical Hermeneutics*, trans. and ed. D.E. Linge, University of California Press, California.
Gadamer, H.G. (1981) *Truth and Method*. Sheed and Ward, London.
Geertz, C. (1993) *The Interpretation of Cultures*, Fontana, London.
Gilroy, B. (1994) *Black Teacher*, Bogle-L'Overture Press, London.
Henderson, M.G. (1993) Speaking in tongues, in P. Williams and L. Chrisman (eds), *Colonial Discourses and Post-colonial Theory*, pp. 257–267, Harvester Wheatsheaf, Hemel Hempstead.
Kristeva, J. (1989a) in T. Moi (ed.), *The Kristeva Reader*, Blackwell, Oxford.
Kristeva, J. (1989b) From one identity to another, in *Desire in Language*, pp. 124–147, Blackwell, Oxford.
Lippard, L. (1992) Mapping, in F. Frascina and J. Harris (eds), *Art and Modern Culture. An Anthology of Critical Texts*, pp. 160–169, Phaidon in association with Oxford University Press, London.

Marks, E. and de Courtivron, I. (1991) *New French Feminisms*, Harvester Wheatsheaf, Hemel Hempstead.

Mitchell, J. (1987) *Psychoanalysis and Feminism*, Penguin, Harmondsworth.

Mulvey, L. (1989) Visual and other pleasures, in *Visual Pleasure and Narrative Cinema*, pp. 14–26, Macmillan, London.

Plato (1977) *Timaeus*, trans. D. Lee, Penguin, Harmondsworth.

Plato (1976) *Republic*, trans. F.M. Cornford, Oxford University Press, New York.

Pinsent, P. (ed.) (1992) *Language, Literature and Young Children*, David Fulton, London.

Smith, B. (1993) Towards a black feminist criticism, in E. Showalter (ed.) *The New Feminist Criticism*, pp. 168–185, Virago, London.

Showalter, E. (ed.) (1993) *The New Feminist Criticism*, Virago, London.

Vygotsky, L.S. (1986) *Thought and Language*, 3rd edn, MIT Press, Cambridge, MA.

Wittgenstein, L. (1974) *Philosophical Investigations*, Blackwell, Oxford.

# Index

Abdul Rahman, Haji Mohammad 138
Addo, Kwame 210, 211, 212
aesthetics 218
Africa: perceptions of 17, 35, 36–8; role played
    in world development 35–6, 40; women 26;
    see also blacks
African collections 20–1
African People's Historical Monument
    Foundation 45–6
African Reparations Movement (ARM) 58–9,
    62
Agyeman, Julian 84, 93, 94
American museums: representation of gender
    26–7
Appiah, Nana 210, 211, 212
Ardener, Edwin 110
artefacts 42, 92; generic use of 9, 127; and
    multicultural museum education 205, 214,
    217–18, 219, 222
Artists and Craftspersons in Education (ACE)
    140–1
Arts Attitude Survey (1989) 191
Asians 2, 152; in Bradford 149–50; bullying 69;
    and countryside 82–3; differing priorities to
    blacks 60; interaction with museums 150;
    population in Britain 60; stereotypes 57; in
    Tower Hamlets 169; see also Merali,
    Shaheen
audiences, museum 1–3; annual attendances 6;
    development of new at National Portrait
    Gallery see NPG; development of new
    through community education 177–81;
    diversity of 103; Toledo report 187–8;
    visitor profiles 1–2, 185–6
Avedon, Richard 196–7

Bailey, David A. 90, 91
Barley, Dr Nigel 35
batik 73

Benin bronzes 56, 57
Bernal, M. 20
Bettelheim, Bruno 214, 219, 222
'Beyond Landscape' photography festival
    (Derby) 90, 91
Bhabha, Homi 102
Birmingham Museum: Gallery 33; project 130
'black art' 92
Black Contribution to History report 124, 168
Black Cultural Archives 59
black cultural museums 4, 32–48; aim to show
    contribution of blacks to society 38, 43, 44,
    47; formation of African People's
    Historical Monument Foundation 45–6;
    lack of 33–4; objectives 47, 48; reasons for
    needing 34–5, 38; and eradication of racism
    36, 43
'black photography' 89–91
blacks 2; attitude to own history 40; audience
    targeting 191–2; and British heritage 38–42;
    contribution from 1930s 44–5; countryside
    experience 86–9, 93–4; devaluing/
    invisibility of contribution 34, 35, 36, 43–4,
    45, 56–7; differing priorities to Asians 60;
    and immigration legislation 53–4;
    perceptions of 36–8; population in Britain
    59–60 [presence in British museums 50–63:
    and ARM 58–9, 62; initiatives 57–60; need
    for black involvement in decision-making
    63; problems faced in 1990s 62; and
    racialized hostility 51–2, 53–7, 59, 61; and
    'Transatlantic Slavery' gallery at
    Merseyside Maritime Museum 50–1, 55–6];
    representation of history 34–6, 92;
    stereotypical image 36, 40–1, 43, 48, 55, 57,
    88; see also racism
blind: sculpture workshops for 199–200
Bolton Initiative 93, 94
botany 27–8

BP (British Petroleum) portrait award
exhibition 194
Bradford: Asian population 149–50; Keeper of
Arts post 149–50; *Warm and Rich Fearless*
exhibition 150, 152–8, 161–7
British Museum 10, 18; Egyptian collections
20; photography 90; visitor profile 1; *see
also Peopling of London* project
Browder, Anthony 43
Brownhill, Alderman 160
Burke, Vanley 160

Carpenter, William 157
China 17, 18
Chinese 170
*Chinese Homes: Chinese Traditions in English
Houses* 8, 169–77; Chinese New Year
section 171–2, 173, 174f; community
involvement 173–5, 176; drawbacks to
working on 176; education programme
175; elements 169, 173; impact on Chinese
community 177; interview sessions 172;
learning points 175–6; origins 171; room
settings 173, 174f; translation 172–3
Christian missions 21
Christopher Columbus quincentenary
exhibition 103
Clark, Carl 73
colonialism 10, 40, 41, 61
Community Education Officer: post of 177
Consortium of Black Organizations (CBO) 51
Cook, Captain 22, 26
Countryside Commission 93
countryside: visiting by ethnic minorities 82–3,
84, 86–9, 93–4
Crew, Spencer and Sims, James 127
*Cultural Trends* 6

Dabydeen, David 87, 89
Davidson, Basil 41
Defoe, Daniel: 'The True Born Englishman'
38–9
dilemma tale 215, 219
disabled people: targeting of needs by NPG
188–91, 197–200
D-Max and Autograph 89–90
Doughty, R. 84
Drummond, Dwight Lowell 112

education, multicultural museum 42–4, 203–
24; and aesthetics 218; aims and objectives
204; and artefacts 205, 214, 217–18, 219,
222; difficulties faced 205–6; and English
Language Support Project 208, 212–13; and
feminism 204, 205, 206–7; and

hermeneutics 207, 221; and 'Musical
Traditions' course 208–12; self-knowledge
gained through 205; storytelling 214–18;
value of 206–7
Egypt 20, 29, 43
Elveden: clash with Sikh community 85–6
English Language Support Project (ELSP)
207–8, 212–13
Environ 83
environment: conflict between rural and urban
83; ethnic minorities and micro- 85–6,
89–92, 94; ethnic minorities and
countryside 82–3, 84, 86–9, 93–4; and
multiculturalism 81–2
'environment-speak' 83–4
ethnic minorities: absence from museums 2, 3,
120; audience targeting 191–2; and
countryside 82–3, 84, 86–9, 93–4; and
micro-environments 85–6, 89–92, 94;
population 10; *see also* Asians; blacks
Europe 17; division within 23–5
European culture 15–16, 19, 29

female: nudity 25, 27; Otherness of 25–8
feminism 203, 204, 205, 206–7
Fenton, J. 83
Freud, Sigmund 219, 221
Fryer, Peter 38

Gadamer, Hans Georg 207
Garman, Lady Kathleen 159
Garvey, Marcus 46
Geertz, Clifford 103
Geffrye Museum 7, 168–72; *Black
Contribution to History* report 124, 168;
*Chinese Homes* exhibition 8, 169–77;
community involvement in 1980s
exhibitions 169; development of new
audiences through courses 177–81;
education department 168; 'Historic Crafts
for Women' course 178–81
gender: representation of 25–8
Gilroy, Beryl 215, 218
Grant, Bernie 58, 59
Greece 20, 24
Guru Gobind Singh 156

Hackney 168, 169; Chinese community links
with Geffrye Museum 169–77
Hackney Community College 178
Hall, Stuart 102
Hands, Terry 200
Hattersley, Roy 53–4
Hayward, L. 91
Hegel 19

Henderson, Mae Gwendolyn 206
heritage: black British 38–42; conflicts 85–6
hermeneutics 207, 221
Hindus 150
'Historic Crafts for Women' course 178–81
Holmes, Tom 160
*Homo sapiens* 28, 35
Horniman Museum 203, 206, 207; and English
    Language Support Project (ELSP) 207–8,
    212–13; networking 204–5; 'Multicultural
    Musical Traditions' course 208–12; natural
    history collection 215; storytelling
    programme 214–22

ILEA (Inner London Education Authority) 168
immigration 53–4, 121
*Independent on Sunday* 83, 84
Indian sculpture 18–19
INIVA (Institute of New International Visual
    Arts) 90
INSET 204, 208, 209
institutional voice 107–10, 112
*Into the Heart of Africa* exhibition 99
*Islamic Calligraphy* exhibition 150

Jeans, D. 81, 82
Jenkins, David 150–1
Jews 25, 46
Jones, Sir William 18–19
Joyce, James 215

Keen, Carolyn 188, 190
King, Sam 44
Kircher, Athanasius 20
*Kirpan* 156–7
Knole 89
Kristeva, J. 222

language 5, 86; differing interpretation of
    100–1, 102; texts written for *Transatlantic
    Slavery* exhibition 103–14
Lehtonen, Timo 140
Levantine empires 17, 18, 26, 29
Lindsay, Elizabeth 138
Linnaeus, C. 27
'Little Red Hen' 219
London: ethnic population 10, 119; *see also
    Peopling of London* project
London Missionary Society 19
London Museums Consultative Committee
    191
London Museums Service: survey 120
London Open College Federation 178
Long, Edward 37
Lowe, P. 83

mailing lists 194–5
Malik, S. 82, 93
*mammalia* 28
Mandela, Nelson 102
Mears, Karen 208
media: black portrayal 38, 55, 61
Merali, Shaheen 4, 67–80; and batik 73–4;
    bullying of 69; *Channels, Echoes and
    Empty Chairs* exhibition 78, 79; creating
    links with the audience 76–7; education
    68–9; first experiences of Britain and
    artistic response 67–8, 70–1; 'Going Native'
    installation 77; 'In Health and Sickness'
    installation 76, 77; 'It Pays to Buy Good
    Tea' installation 74–6, 77; at Newport
    College 71; and photography 78; and
    Rastafarianism 72–3; relationships with
    Turkish-Cypriots 70; trip to India and
    effect of 71–3
Merriman, Nick 85, 94, 125, 137
Merseyside: visitor profiles of museums 1–2
Merseyside African Council (MAC) 51, 56
Merseyside Maritime Museum: *Transatlantic
    Slavery* exhibition 50–1, 55–6, 103–14
microenvironments: and ethnic minorities
    85–6, 89–92, 94
Middle East 17, 18, 25
Mitchell, Juliet 221
Modernism 3, 10, 15, 18, 21, 22, 23, 29
Moores, Peter 50, 51, 56
Morris, Bill 44
Morris, Olive 44–5
Moses Gate Country Park 93
multicultural museum education *see* education
*Museum in Docklands* project 123, 132
Museum of London: appointment of
    Community Access Officer 146;
    concentration on pre-1945 period 120;
    initiatives after *Peopling of London* project
    146; low ethnic participation rate 94; *see
    also Peopling of London* project
museums 33–4; cultural diversity 42, 52, 167,
    182; emphasis on active participation 160;
    goal of 60–1; greater accessibility to 151;
    reasons for non-visiting 181; recent changes
    1; role played in perpetuation of problems
    for blacks 61
'Musical Traditions' course (Horniman
    Museum) 208–12
Muslims 150

National Audit Office (NAO) 185
National Museums and Galleries on
    Merseyside *see* NMGM
National Portrait Gallery see NPG

National Report of Museum Education 5–6
Natt, Sarbjit 165
natural history museums 27
nature 29; gendering of 26–8
networking 214; at Horniman Museum 204–5
Nicholson, B. 83
Niemann, D. 84
NMGM (National Museums and Galleries on Merseyside) 50–1, 55–6
NPG (National Portrait Gallery) 7, 183–202; BP portrait award exhibition 194; collection policy 184; development of infrastructure 183–4, 186; education department within 184–5, 186; evaluation of new audience programme 200–1; future new audience initiatives 201–2; mailing lists 194–5; new audience programme implementation 192–3; photography workshops 193–4, 196; Richard Avedon exhibition and workshops 196–7; sculpture workshops for blind/partially 199–200; targeting of disabled people 188–91, 197–200; targeting of young people 191, 193–6; visitor profile 185–6

O'Connell, Rory 125, 134
orientalism 25–6, 152
Orwell, George 43–4
Other(s): awareness of need to counteract 204; and female 25–8; key traits of 17–20; perceptions 101–2; and 'Us' dichotomy 3–4, 15, 16–17; within Europe 23–5

Pearson, Anne 191
'People's Show, The' 160
*Peopling of London* project 7, 9, 85, 99–100, 101, 119–46; aims and objectives 121–2, 122–3, 128, 131, 143; background 119–22; chronological sections 129; collecting programme 126–8, 132, 134–5, 137; community involvement 123, 124–5, 130, 131, 142, 145–6; criticisms of 144, 145; elements 123–4; evaluation 142–5; exhibition 125–6, 128–31, 136–7; focus weeks 139–40, 144–5; formulation 122–4; fundraising 141; marketing campaign 141–2, 145; 'Museum on the Move' 132–3, 134; number of visitors 143; oral histories 125, 132, 134, 135; post-war section 129–31, 134, 135; public events programme 139–40; publication 137–8, 145; research phase 124–8; resource pack 138–9, 140, 145; schools programme 140–1; success 143, 144, 145, 146; targeted audiences 122, 141–2

Peter Moores Foundation 50, 51, 56
photography: 'black' 89–90; 'Beyond Landscape' festival 90, 91; institutional spaces of 90–1; workshops at NPG 193–4, 196
Pierson Jones, Jane 130
plants: gendering of 27–8; racist attitude towards alien 83–4, 85
Pollard, Ingrid 84, 87–9, 90, 91
Polynesian islands 17, 21–3, 26
Powell, Adam Clayton 46–7
psychoanalysis 219, 221
'Punitive Expedition' 56

race: as a concept 95n
Race Relations Act (1965) 33
racialized hostility 51–2, 53–, 59, 61
racism 33, 60, 121; and alien plants 83–4, 85; eradication of in black cultural museums 36, 43; and multicultural museum education 203, 205, 209, 218
*Ramayana, The* (exhibition) 150
Ramsay, Bishop Malachi 44
Redman, John 136
reparations 58, 62
Royal Ontario Museum (ROM) 99
Rushdie, Salman 151

Said, Edward 101, 152, 158
Samson, Suzanne 138–9
Schiebinger, L. 27
Schildkrout, E. 99
Schomburg Centre (New York) 47
schools 6; 'Musical Traditions' course 208–12; stereotypical images of blacks in 43; storytelling programme 214–22
Schoon, N. 83
Scott, Andie 200
sculpture: Indian 18–19; workshops for the blind 199–200
Severus, Septimus 39
Shoemaker, Nancy 26–7
Sikhs 6; and *chauri* 155; clash with villagers of Elveden 85–6; and five Ks 156; and *Kirpan* 156–7; perception of 153; separateness of Sikhism and Hinduism 157–8; and *Warm and Rich and Fearless* exhibition 150, 152–8, 161–7
Simmonds, Felly Nkweto 206
Simpson, Moira 103
Sinclair, Nick 197
Singh Chana, Mohinder 154
Singh, Amarjit 8, 162–3, 164, 167
Singh, Harbinder 85, 86
slavery 39, 40, 41, 45, 46, 47; *see also Transatlantic Slavery* exhibition

Smith, Barbara 206
Smithsonian Institution's National Museum 27
'Squirrel and Hedgehog' 215, 216–17, 218, 219–21, 221–2
staffing 8–9
stately homes: black experience of 89–90, 92
Stockwell Infants School 208, 210, 213, 214–15, 216–17
storytelling: Horniman Museum programme 214–22
surveys 120, 185, 191, 192

Tan, Gill 172
*Ten.8* 90
text, exhibition 100–14; choice of appropriate language 107; differing interpretation 102–3; importance of words included/omitted 100, 105, 106, 107; institutional voice 107–10; need for awareness of audiences by writers 103; and *Peopling of London* exhibition 137; *Transatlantic Slavery* exhibition writing process 103–14; use of 'Other' 101–2
Thatcher, Margaret 39–40, 68
Toledo study 187–8
Topping, Andy 123
Tower Hamlets 168, 169
Toynbee, Arnold 36
*Transatlantic Slavery* exhibition 50–1, 55–6; dilemma over subject of numbers 110–13; exhibition briefs 104–5; placing people in context of own history 105–7; problems 104; use of institutional voice 107–10, 112; writing text process 103–14
*Trophies of Empire* exhibition 77

unconscious 221, 222

United States 92; adoption of African-American name 46; representation of gender in museums 26–7
*Using Museums* (TV programme) 209

Victoria & Albert Museum 19, 27, 166
visitor profiles 1–2, 185–6
Visram, Rozina 124, 125, 134, 168
Volosinov, Valentin 102

Walsall 159
Walsall Museum and Art Gallery 7; exhibitions 160; original aim 160; *see also* *Warm and Rich and Fearless* exhibition
Waltham Forest Adult Education Service 200
*Warm and Rich Fearless* exhibition 150, 152–8, 161–7; Amarjit Singh as Community Events Co-ordinator 162–3, 164, 167; battle-standards debate 157–8; contention over *Chauri* translation 155; dagger episode 156–7; education programme 161–2; evaluation 165–6; funding 154, 161; networking 154; opening celebrations 164; public events 165; publicity 154–5; sexual equality issue 164–5; Sikh involvement/consultation 153, 155–6, 158, 161–4; successes 165–6; William Carpenter painting 157
West Midlands South Asian Art Festival 160
Wilkins, Sir Charles 19
Williams, Chancellor 41
Wittgenstein, L. 205, 214
women: as 'Other' 25–8, 29
Woodson, Carter G. 48
World War II: black contribution 44
Wright, P. 83